ALSO FROM MODERN LIBRARY: THE MOVIES

Agee on Film, by James Agee

The Art of the Moving Picture, by Vachel Lindsay

Memo from David O. Selznick, selected by Rudy Behlmer

THE MAKING OF
2001:
A SPACE ODYSSEY

THE MAKING OF 2001: A SPACE ODYSSEY

Selected by *Stephanie Schwam*

MARTIN SCORSESE

SERIES EDITOR

Introduction by Jay Cocks

THE MODERN LIBRARY

NEW YORK

The editors would like to thank Robert Haller of Anthology Film Archives in New York City for his assistance in researching this book.

LIBRARY OF CONGRESS CATALOGING-IN-PUBLICATION DATA

The making of 2001, a space odyssey/[selected by Stephanie Schwam for] The
Modern Library.
p. cm.—(Modern Library the movies)
Chiefly a collection of previously published articles, essays, and interviews.
Includes a Stanley Kubrick filmography.
ISBN 0-375-75528-4
1. 2001, a space odyssey (Motion picture) I. Schwam, Stephanie.
II. Modern Library (Firm) III. Series.

PN1997.T86 M35 2000
791.43'72—dc21 99-055776

Modern Library website address: www.modernlibrary.com

Printed in the United States of America

Introduction to Modern Library: The Movies

Martin Scorsese

When as a small boy I first fell in love with the movies, I discovered a book by Deems Taylor entitled *A Pictorial History of the Movies* at our local branch of the New York Public Library. It was the only film book that I knew about, and I borrowed it time and time again. *A Pictorial History* was just that, a chronological collection of movie stills accompanied by brief descriptions of the movies from the silent-film era to 1949. It was the first course in my film education. Its beautiful black-and-white images re-created the visions and emotions of the movies I'd already seen, and allowed me to dream about the others.

It wasn't until some thirty years later that I was able to own a copy of the book (it had gone out of print and was difficult to find). The late Roddy McDowall also grew up with the Deems Taylor book. As a child actor, he would take it on the set and get the cast and crew to sign the stills of the movies on which they had worked. The *How Green Was My Valley* page, for instance, was eventually signed by John Ford, Maureen O'Hara, and Walter Pidgeon. This treasured book awoke in me the desire to collect as many film books as possible. There are now one thousand or so books in my library, covering the past one hundred years of movie history, which I use constantly for information and inspiration.

In the Modern Library: The Movies series, we are publishing some of the classics in the field: personal accounts from movie artists as well as works by film historians and critics in a variety of literary forms. Since the Cave Age there has been a constant battle about the supremacy of the word over the image. Although film is primarily a visual medium, it combines elements from all the arts—literature, music, painting, and dance. For my first list of books, I have chosen two that reflect the felicitous merger of words and images: one by a literary journalist and the other by a poet. I have also chosen two books written in different forms: a collection of memos and a firsthand testimony on the making of a movie classic.

The movies discussed in these books range from early silent films to one of the most modern and innovative films ever made, from obscure lost films to Hollywood extravaganzas. By happenstance, this first list focuses on American movies; foreign films will be included in later seasons. It is my hope that these books will appeal to movie lovers and film professionals alike, and that they'll re-create some of the movie magic I felt as a child with that first book borrowed from the library.

CONTENTS

THE LAST WORD

SK

Jay Cocks

MGM is turning to real-estate parcels all around us, and that night I am facing Stanley Kubrick across the hood of a rented car in Culver City, and he is smiling at me, a little anxiously and still very proudly, and he is saying, "Yes, but did you *like* it?"

He means *2001.* We have just seen it for the first time, he and I and perhaps a dozen others, in the cavernous studio screening room. Stanley's wife, Christiane, is with us. His attorney; the president of Cinerama; the film's editor, Ray Lovejoy; and a few others are also at the screening, but I am the only pair of fresh, disinterested eyes there. I am also, by at least two decades, the youngest member of the audience, an unelected representative of a generation that will eventually rescue this great film from critical infamy and claim it for its own. I am twenty-three years old, very lucky to be here, knowing it, sensing I have just seen something seismic whose full measure I can't take, reaching for something to say that will encompass all this, as well as my startled excitement at the wit and majesty of the movie. I am also trying to say something deeper and more memorable than "Wow."

I start to talk to Stanley and Christiane about the early days of silents, when movies were shown on rooftops, and audiences, watching a train on the screen come straight at them, ducked and screamed at the newness of the experience and, without knowing it, at intimations of the future. The experience of *2001* was, for me, just like that.

"Yeah," said Stanley, still smiling at my excitement, "but did you *really like it?*"

I told him it was one of the greatest things I'd ever seen, and he laughed, and we all drove to dinner.

I had never been to California, never been to a studio, never met a movie director, an author of dreams I seized for my own. I had a new close friend in New York who was working at being a director, was cutting a first feature, and who had seen more movies than I and loved them, if possible, even more than I. His name was Marty Scorsese, and I gave him continued updates on my time with Stanley and awed reflections on *2001.* Kubrick was the kind of maverick who gave us, along with his exhilaratingly risky movies, some personal hope: He was from New York, like us, and, as Marty was doing even then, had risen through the ranks of independent production to finally make his mark. Stanley's background and history made him familiar to us, accessible in a way that most film directors, at that time, were not, even as his work—we particularly loved *Lolita* and James Mason's Humbert—remained daunting, even forbidding.

Stanley turned out to be, in person, not at all forbidding. He was congenial, accessible, bemused, sardonic, a big-city boho who found himself awash on the smoggy provincial shores of Culver City, occupying a corner office that had once belonged to Irving Thalberg. Stanley was one of the few working directors on a lot that was as still as a ghost town, finishing a long-delayed, expensive, and, as it turned out, dangerously unorthodox film on which, as anxious studio PR people frequently told me, the future of MGM, already precarious, teetered like a dime balanced on a rubber band that had already been stretched far past breaking.

He knew the odds well enough, but they didn't seem to weigh on him, and in the studio parking lot that night, with the movie just ended and a hot breeze blowing in from mountains far beyond the silent soundstages and the empty streets of the vast back lot, all that seemed to matter to him was that I liked the movie. I was thrilled. Aside from doting parents, and a few close friends, I don't think there had ever been a time when what I said or thought had mattered to anyone so much.

I'd been with Stanley little more than a week, and he already read me well.

"How was your trip?" he asked me on my first morning as he walked back behind his carrier-deck desk, the legacy of some hapless executive lately deposed as MGM struggled for breath. "Where are you staying? Room okay? Need anything? Want a girl?"

It was a test question, I knew, and I said no, getting him to smile and, I hoped, displaying some seriousness of purpose. I wasn't some junketeer on a fat magazine expense account. I was there to lay the groundwork for what might be a huge publicity break for the film, a cover story for *Time,* where I worked as a reporter and occasional third-string critic.

The magazine didn't have enough room for movie reporting at that time, so I was flagrantly underutilized, and the editors must have been relieved to get me out of the office and off on something that might look like work. *2001* was, in the early winter of 1968, a matter of some mystery and speculation. Coverage of show business, and the movie business in particular, had not yet reached the all-devouring proportions of today, and film production enjoyed a sort of sheltered, regulated anonymity. You could actually work on, and finish, a film without each step being reported in print and on TV as if each stage were a lap in an Olympic relay. It had been something like a half-decade since *Dr. Strangelove,* in which Stanley had set a very high standard of audacity, and the only public Kubrick news of the new film had been a fine *New Yorker* profile, by a writer who specialized in science, and a multipage ad in the Sunday *New York Times Magazine,* which made *2001* seem a rather intrepid exercise in scientific education, like a multimedia planetarium display.

Stanley had the thorough shrewdness and reserve of a master gamesman. He controlled all the publicity for the film, and within minutes of that first meeting, he controlled me, too. I knew it, and became his gleeful accomplice. What was the good of journalistic objectivity when you were in the presence of a great filmmaker who offered you a plunge into his creative process and entertainment in your hotel room besides?

He set the ground rules immediately. There was only one hard stricture: no questions about the movie until I'd seen it. It would be ready in a week's time, and I'd be seeing it completed, first frame to last, when Stanley himself did. Until then, we chatted about the Bronx, and seeing movies at the Museum of Modern Art, and favorite directors, a topic Stanley evaded rather successfully. "I get that question a lot," he said, "and I never know what to say, to tell you the truth. Max Ophuls and David Lean. How's that?" That was fine, and set me off on a windy question about tracking shots. Stanley looked amused while I was speaking, and rather quickly changed the subject after I'd finished.

I walked him to the dubbing stage one very warm morning, and out of the open door came the unmistakable sounds of Strauss. "Is 'The Blue Danube' part of the movie?" I asked, and he grimaced. "You see," he replied, "there's one surprise ruined for you already," and he shooed me off on another bicycle tour of the soon-to-be-sold back lot while he finished the mix.

On other days, to keep me from asking more questions, he had me work up an admonition to the audience to appear at the very beginning of the film, asking anyone who thought there were technical problems in the theater to immediately seek out the manager and projectionist. It was an early version of the sort of technical heads-up that now regularly appears from the THX techies, and Stanley actually shot it (after considerable line editing) and attached it to the film, where it lasted for one screening and was then removed after consultation with a lawyer who feared such a statement might be unduly provocative. Despite its fate, I was thrilled to have done it—my first film collaboration, and with Stanley Kubrick! Or, as he referred to himself in the initialed editorial comments that peppered my two dozen simple drafts, "SK."

After ten days at the studio, and after that first screening of *2001*, when the might of a great imagination scalded me, there was no need for any more busy work. I had witnessed something great, been there at the completion of the creation, and now I was about to take an aisle seat in what, I was sure, would be one of those rare events that change movies and shape history. I told the *Time* editors in New York as much. They sounded skeptical. I resolved to tell Stanley in a more coherent form than my blurtings in the parking lot.

We had dinner at La Scala in Beverly Hills, sunk in a red velvet banquette. I went into my speech, Stanley listening attentively until a low theatrical voice from across the room interrupted us, calling out his name like a gunfighter challenging a rival.

"Stanley Koo-brick..." Stanley looked up. "This town isn't big enough for both of us."

"Oh," Stanley said after a measured beat. "Hi, Leslie." Then he turned away from Leslie Nielsen, star of MGM's only previous large-scale sci-fi excursion, *Forbidden Planet*, with a look that said quietly to me that encounters like this were why he'd chosen to live far outside movie town. "What was that again?"

I launched into the rest of my wishful projections of glory: *Time* was cranked up and ready and would be first off the mark with a great story about a great movie that would immediately be embraced by an enraptured public who would follow Stanley where I had, to "Jupiter and Beyond the Infinite." Even Stanley was vulnerable to such untempered optimism, expressed ingenuously by someone who seemed to be in a position to help him, and until New York, he believed me.

The first public screening of *2001: A Space Odyssey* at the Capitol Theater on Broadway was a catastrophe. The audience, who as yet knew nothing of the film and had not even seen a still, sat expectantly through the minimal opening credits, but there was a slight shift of puzzlement, of incipient restlessness, when the title announcing "The Dawn of Man" first appeared. (Another collaboration with Stanley. "Do you think we need a couple of titles to orient people?" he asked me after the first screening. He had, of course, already decided "we" did, so he and I proceeded to write a few. More paper drafts, more SK initialings.)

The first laughter began with the appearance of the first apes. This was only a few months after *Planet of the Apes* had been released and become a big hit, and the Capitol audience must have presumed that the director of the carbolic comedy *Dr. Strangelove* had sprung another kind of mordant surprise on them. The laughter stopped after a time, but the restiveness increased, turning finally to outright mockery and hostility during the Star Gate sequence.

Stanley was watching the film and the audience from the projection booth, which was located at the Capitol in the rear of the orchestra. I was across from the booth, on the aisle, "reading the house," watching streams of people making their way to the exits during the movie's transcendent last minutes. A favorite senior film critic, a man I'd long admired, turned on his way out to see the Star Child fill the screen, snorted derisively—and, I thought, a bit theatrically—and walked out just as the movie ended.

After that, Stanley went to bed for three days. I went to the world premiere in Washington, where various low-level government officials and NASA types reacted to the film as if they were reading a constitutional amendment drafted to protect the rights of unborn extraterrestrials. The reviews, when they started to appear, were almost uniformly devastating. Renata Adler, in *The New York Times*, skewered the film for ambitions she mistook for pretensions, and said the monolith looked like a "1950s chocolate bar," a remark that particularly miffed Stanley not only because it was so derisively wrongheaded but because it was so arcane. The *Time* coverage was quickly canceled, and the review, while recognizing the revolutionary quality of the technical effects, gave the film low marks for metaphysics.

After its first week of release, *2001* seemed like a futuristic folly that would wreck MGM and compromise Stanley's maverick reputation, turning him into a sort of George Pal for the Castaneda crowd. I knew I wasn't wrong about the film. Marty and I went together to the Capitol, and the movie exploded in wonder all around us and over many empty seats. We talked about it for days afterward, and by that time, as I reported to Marty, Stanley had gotten out of bed.

Stanley decided to make cuts. Seventeen minutes (I believe) were excised from the version I'd originally seen, the version screened for the press at the Capitol. The movie had opened in limited release around the world, so it was necessary for Stanley to hire and dispatch film editors to various cities to cut the prints while the negative was reconformed. This was serious surgery and radical procedure. But there were, by that time, a few indications for hope.

Stanley had won the loyalty and support of two young turks in the MGM publicity department in New York, Mike Kaplan and Joanna Ney, and they would meet daily in the office Stanley had managed to wangle at the studio's Manhattan headquarters: a windowless room below street level in a subbasement with fluorescent lights wedged between steam pipes and electrical cables and a small steel desk ringed with stains from old coffee cups. It may have been the office of the head of the building maintenance staff. It was certainly far from Irving Thalberg. Stanley must have noticed, but he showed no signs of minding. He was too busy fighting back.

What good notices the film had received had appeared mostly in what were then known as the "counterculture" papers. On his various visits to the theater, Mike Kaplan noticed that the film's audiences were steady, growing in some cases, and almost always younger than the sixties norm. He also noticed that during the Star Gate sequence, there was a lot of pot smoking.

MGM, which had a considerable investment of cash and prestige in *2001*, was persuaded to hang in a while longer. Stanley reported to his maintenance office five days a week, and I visited frequently. Mike and Joanna kept phoning the press, whipping up controversy, making Stanley accessible for what was probably the last time for a wide range of interviews. Box-office receipts held steady, then began to increase. Critics revisited the film and reassessed. The cosmological conundrums of *2001*, which bid for a time to be its undoing, became instead a selling point and a rallying point. In Mike Kaplan's magical advertising phrase, *2001* became "the ultimate trip," and if you weren't hip enough to take it, you weren't worth being taken seriously. Stanley got to enjoy in fact what he would never have allowed himself in film: a happy ending.

We are on the long lawn of a house on the North Shore that Stanley has rented for Christiane and their three daughters, and we are about to go in to dinner. It is almost summer, and Stanley is preparing to return home to England. This is still 1968, and with the rumored exception of a fast flight to attend the funeral of his second wife, he will not come back to America again.

2001 is a success at last, a pop-culture touchstone that will, in time, become a cornerstone of American film art. Stanley is already talking about his next project, a biography of Napoleon. I have also assisted him in securing the rights to an obscure novel by Arthur Schnitzler that interests him. We have secretly screened a few experimental films with heavy erotic components in a conference room at the Time-Life Building, and have sat, to Stanley's deep bemusement, next to a filmmaker whose loud and enthusiastic couplings on-screen she watches with self-reverential rapture. "Gee, Carolee," Stanley asks ingenuously when the lights come up full, "howdja do that?"

It is never clear to me whether Stanley was talking about the lighting or the position, but weeks later, this late Sunday afternoon on the lawn, he muses, "Wouldn't it be great to make an intimate sexy movie like that, and use a real married couple? I mean, if you could. If they could."

Across Long Island Sound, there is a light blinking on the edge of a dock. We both say something about *Gatsby*, then fall silent. I consider whether to make a remark comparing Gatsby's light and the monolith, talismans of mystery and hope for two generations, but I decide to adopt a more practical, but even bolder, approach. I ask to read the script of *Napoleon* when he's finished. Stanley's answer, as we go in to dinner, is not specific, but it's encouraging at least.

A year later, while I am visiting England and waiting to go out and see him, a package arrives at the hotel. A note from Stanley is enclosed: "This isn't *Napoleon*, but it's helpful to understand what *Napoleon*'s about. See you at 7. I'll send a car." Inside the thick package is a copy of the U.S. Army Officer's Field Service Manual. I look through it for clues. There are none, and taking my cue from that, I start to skate toward what I will recognize only later as the periphery of SK's mutable world, which had managed, in 70mm and Cinerama, to graze the infinite.

Once a film reviewer and music writer for Time, *Jay Cocks, born in the Bronx, is now a screenwriter.*

THE MAKING OF
2001:
A SPACE ODYSSEY

THE PRODUCTION: A CALENDAR

Carolyn Geduld

1948 Arthur C. Clarke writes his short story "The Sentinel." Superman, film's first Star Child, arrives from the planet Krypton in a Columbia movie serial based on the comic strip originally conceived by Jerry Siegel and Joe Schuster in 1938.

1950s **High-water mark for science-fiction films. Directors like George Pal and Byron Haskin in films like *Destination Moon* (1950) and *The Conquest of Space* (1955) ransack the special effects departments in attempts to create authentic-looking space technology consistent with the scientific ideas of the day.**

1960 **The BBC televises a science-fiction serial with close affinities to *2001*—Nigel Kneale's *Quatermass and the Pit* (remade in a film version by Hammer Film Productions as *Five Million Years to Earth* in 1967). In one episode, while excavating to enlarge the London underground, a five-million-year-old alien artifact is discovered. Near it lies the ape ancestors of man whose skulls have been surgically modified to increase intelligence.**

Universe, an award-winning twenty-eight-minute black-and-white animated documentary is produced by the National Film Board of Canada. It is to become the inspiration for *2001*'s panning shots of slowly revolving planets and moving stars in deep space. In 1965, Kubrick tries to hire *Universe*'s special effects team of Wally Gentleman, Herbert Taylor, and James Wilson. Wally Gentleman agrees to do a few months' preparatory work on *2001* before a sudden illness forces him to abandon the project.

1964   *Spring.* Kubrick contacts Clarke and asks him to collaborate on a sci-fi film.

April. Clarke leaves his home in Ceylon for his first meeting with Kubrick in New York. Kubrick suggests the unorthodox procedure of writing a novel together before writing a script, a project that is to take two years to complete.

May. Kubrick agrees to use Clarke's "The Sentinel" as the central idea for the novel. The discovery of the alien artifact on the moon is to be the climax of the story. Meanwhile, Kubrick views every available science-fiction film.

July 31. **Ranger VII sends close-up pictures of the moon back to Earth before crashing on the lunar surface.**

August 6. "Female" computer called Athena written into novel.

November. Gathering of ideas of what is to be the "Dawn of Man" episode. This is intended to be a flashback interrupting the main story.

December 25. Clarke finishes the first fifty-thousand-word draft of the novel, which ends at the Star Gate sequence. Kubrick is able to sell the idea for a film based on this draft to MGM and Cinerama. The film's projected budget is $6 million.

1965   *February 21.* MGM press release announcing forthcoming production of a Kubrick film to be called "Journey Beyond the Stars."

March 18. **Aleksei A. Leonov, a Russian astronaut, becomes the first man to "walk" in space.**

Spring. Clarke revises novel. Kubrick begins to hire staff (35 designers, 20 special effects technicians, a total of 106 people) and cast for the production. "The Sentinel" pyramid is changed to a black tetrahedron, then a transparent cube, finally a black rectangular block—the monolith.

April. Kubrick selects *2001: A Space Odyssey* as the new title for the film.

May. Clarke works on possible endings for the novel.

June 3. **Ed White becomes the first American to "walk" in space, bettering Leonov's feat by twenty minutes.**

June 14. **Mariner IV comes within 6,200 miles of Mars and sends twenty-two photographs of the planet's surface back to Earth.** Kubrick contacts Lloyds of London to price an insurance policy against Martians being discovered before the release of his film.

August. After a brief return to his home in Ceylon, Clarke joins Kubrick at the MGM studios in Boreham Wood near London. There, sets are being built, the most meticulously detailed models ever made for a film are being constructed over a period of months, costumes are being designed and executed with an eye toward fashions thirty-five years in the future, and the ape makeup and costuming are being developed over the course of a year.

October 3. The final decision about the ending of the film is reached. Bowman will turn into an infant.

October 15. Kubrick decides that Bowman should be the only surviving member of Discovery's crew.

December 29. First day of shooting in Shepperton studio near London which is spacious enough to accommodate oversized sets. Kubrick films the scene in the moon excavation in the Tycho crater. The set is a huge 60-by-120-by-60-foot pit constructed on the second largest stage in Europe. Background details of the lunar terrain and the miniature Earth in the sky are added a year later.

1966　*January.* Production moves to the smaller Boreham Wood studios. Kubrick films scenes on board Orion. Clarke finishes draft of novel, adding HAL's rebellion and alien hotel room to plot.

February 2. Makeup tests for Gary Lockwood and Keir Dullea, who remain in the studio for seven months of filming.

February 3. First soft landing on the moon by an unmanned Russian spacecraft.

February 4. Screening of "demonstration film" for Metro-Goldwyn-Mayer, consisting of a few completed scenes, including shots of the interiors of the space station and the moon shuttle. Mendelssohn's *Midsummer Night's Dream* and Vaughan Williams' *Antarctica Symphony* are used on the sound track.

March–April. Shooting inside Discovery's ferris-wheel-shaped centrifuge. The Vickers Engineering Group builds a real one for the production at a cost of $750,000. The wheel is forty feet in diameter and rotates at three miles per hour. A closed circuit television system enables Kubrick to direct the filming from outside the wheel. Inside, two kinds of camera setups are used: either the camera is attached to the set and rotates with it (used when the actors appear to be climbing the centrifuge walls) or the camera is secured to a small dolly which remains with the actors at the bottom of the rotating set (used when Poole jogs). Kubrick plans to put a Chopin waltz on the sound track during the astronauts' routine activities.

May. Clarke visits Hollywood to promote the film and placate worried MGM executives.

June. Clarke returns to Boreham Wood. He tries unsuccessfully to convince Kubrick to allow publication of the novel before the release of the film.

June 2. First soft landing on the moon by an unmanned American spacecraft, Surveyor I.

December. Original target date for film's release.

1967 *January–February.* Composer Alex North records his music for *2001* in London, until Kubrick changes his mind about using an original score for the film.

Most of the year is devoted to completing the film's exacting and complex special effects, a job taking more than eighteen months and costing $6.5 million out of a total budget of

$10.5 million. Two hundred five shots (about half the film) require process work. Each shot involves an average of ten major laboratory steps to complete. Counting the high number of retakes, an estimated sixteen thousand separate shots are taken for the 205 effects. Most of these are "held takes," that is, a portion of a scene is filmed, then the negative is filed away for several months until another element can be filmed and added to the original. (Part of Kubrick's great achievement is that there is no noticeable loss of crispness in the image, despite all the tampering with the negative.) A typical special effects shot might include (1) miniature models of spacecraft shot in extremely slow motion, (2) front or rear projected film for the moving images in the spacecraft's windows, (3) a separately photographed astronaut or pod tumbling in space (both suspended by wires during shooting) "matted" in by hand, (4) a field of moving stars in the background shot on the animation stand along with (5) the moon (a series of actual astronomical plates) and/or an appropriate planet (usually a large painting).

Two techniques developed by Kubrick's special effects team are especially significant for the future of the film industry: (1) *The front-projection system,* seen throughout the "Dawn of Man" episode, is a new way of using a still photograph as a background for a shot. A unique kind of projector throws an image onto a mammoth screen, without being visible on the cast or props in the foreground, making it economically feasible to film large-scale epics in the sound studio without the expense of going "on location." (2) *The Slit-Scan machine,* designed for the Star Gate sequence, produces a fast-moving tunnel of lights and shapes that seems to extend to infinity. The machine keeps the image in focus from a distance of fifteen feet to an incredible one-half inch from the lens.

1968   *March 13.* Kubrick returns to the United States. While the last special effects shots are still coming in, he edits the film. Several scenes are omitted, including the purchase of a bushbaby for Dr. Floyd's daughter, Squirt; routine activities on the moon; shots of the astronauts' families; shots of the Ping-Pong table, shower, and piano in Discovery. After a screening for the MGM executives in Culver City, California, Kubrick cuts the prologue and all voice-over narration from the film.

March 29. Screening of the film for *Life* magazine.

March 31, April 1. Washington press previews.

Early April. Kubrick edits the *2001* trailer.

April. The discovery of a man-like jawbone in southern Ethiopia pushes man's history back to the four-million-year mark.

April 1, 2. New York press previews of the film in Loew's Capitol Cinerama Theatre.

April 3. New York premiere in the Capitol Theatre.

April 4. Los Angeles premiere.

April 4, 5. Kubrick cuts nineteen minutes from the film's original running time of two hours and forty-one minutes, shortening scenes including "Dawn of Man," Orion, Poole jogging in Discovery, and Poole in the pod.

April 6. Final version released in New York in the Cinerama Theatre on Broadway, sixteen months late and at a cost of $4.5 million over the original budget of $6 million.

July. Publication of Clarke's novel, *2001: A Space Odyssey.* The paperback edition sale exceeds one million copies.

December 21. Apollo VIII carries man into a moon orbit for the first time.

1969 *April.* Kubrick receives an Oscar for special effects; three British Film Academy awards for cinematography, art direction, and sound track; and the Italian film industry's David Di Donatello award for the best film from the West.

July 20. Neil Armstrong and Edwin Aldrin walk on the moon.

1970 *April.* Publication of Jerome Agel's *The Making of Kubrick's 2001.*

1971 *November 28.* The first conscious imitation of *2001,* MGM's made-for-TV film, *Earth II,* televised in New York. Gary Lockwood stars and footage, effects, and plot structure are strikingly similar to *2001.*

1972   *January.* Publication of Arthur C. Clarke's *The Lost Worlds of 2001.*

      January 5. Variety puts *2001* in twenty-fourth place in its annual compilation of "All-Time Boxoffice Champs." It estimates that the film has grossed more than $21.5 million in the U.S.-Canada market alone.

      February. Publication of Arthur C. Clarke's *Report on Planet Three.*

      March 2. Pioneer X launched on course toward Jupiter and beyond.

2001   "What we are trying to create is a realistic myth—and we may have to wait until the year 2001 itself to see how successful we have been." (Arthur C. Clarke, *Report on Planet Three,* p. 246.)

CREDITS

Carolyn Geduld

2001: A SPACE ODYSSEY

Metro-Goldwyn-Mayer, Films, Inc., 1968. Super Panavision,
Technicolor and Metrocolor.

Director and Producer	Stanley Kubrick
Screenplay	Stanley Kubrick and Arthur C. Clarke
Production Company	Metro-Goldwyn-Mayer
Special Effects Director	Stanley Kubrick
Special Effects Supervisors	Wally Veevers, Douglas Trumbull, Con Pederson, Tom Howard
Special Effects Photographic Unit	Colin J. Cantwell, Bruce Logan, Bryan Loftus, David Osborne, Frederick Martin, John J. Malick
Production Designers	Tony Masters, Harry Lange, Ernest Archer
Editor	Ray Lovejoy
Wardrobe	Hardy Amies
Director of Photography	Geoffrey Unsworth B.S.C.
Additional Photography	John Alcott

First Assistant Director	Derek Cracknell
Art Director	John Hoesli
Sound Editor	Winston Ryder
Scientific Consultant	Frederick I. Ordway III
Music	Aram Khatchaturian, György Ligeti, Johann Strauss, Richard Strauss

Time: 141 minutes (version in general release)

Filming began on December 29, 1965 in MGM's Shepperton and Boreham Wood Studios in England. First public showing in New York on April 3, 1968.

CAST

Dave Bowman	Keir Dullea
Frank Poole	Gary Lockwood
Dr. Heywood Floyd	William Sylvester
Moon-Watcher	Daniel Richter
Smyslov (the Russian scientist)	Leonard Rossiter
Elena	Margaret Tyzack
Halvorsen	Robert Beatty
Michaels	Sean Sullivan
HAL's voice	Douglas Rain
Mission Control	Frank Miller
Stewardess	Penny Brahms
Poole's Father	Alan Gifford

PREPRODUCTION

Roger Caras, the publicist for *2001,* cabled Arthur C. Clarke, saying:

STANLEY KUBRICK—"DR STRANGELOVE," "PATHS OF GLORY," ET CETERA, INTERESTED IN DOING FILM ON ET'S. INTERESTED IN YOU. ARE YOU INTERESTED? THOUGHT YOU WERE RECLUSE.

Clarke immediately replied:

FRIGHTFULLY INTERESTED IN WORKING WITH ENFANT TERRI-BLE STOP CONTACT MY AGENT STOP WHAT MAKES KUBRICK THINK I'M A RECLUSE.

THE SENTINEL

Arthur C. Clarke

Little did Arthur C. Clarke know in 1950 that his latest short story, "The Sentinel," would be the basis, fifteen years later, for a $10.5 million motion-picture production.

The next time you see the full moon high in the south, look carefully at its right-hand edge and let your eye travel upward along the curve of the disk. Round about two o'clock you will notice a small, dark oval: anyone with normal eyesight can find it quite easily. It is the great walled plain, one of the finest on the Moon, known as the Mare Crisium—the Sea of Crises. Three hundred miles in diameter, and almost completely surrounded by a ring of magnificent mountains, it had never been explored until we entered it in the late summer of 1996.

Our expedition was a large one. We had two heavy freighters which had flown our supplies and equipment from the main lunar base in the Mare Serenitatis, five hundred miles away. There were also three small rockets which were intended for short-range transport over regions which our surface vehicles couldn't cross. Luckily, most of the Mare Crisium is very flat. There are none of the great crevasses so common and so dangerous elsewhere, and very few craters or mountains of any size. As far as we could tell, our powerful caterpillar tractors would have no difficulty in taking us wherever we wished to go.

I was geologist—or selenologist, if you want to be pedantic—in charge of the group exploring the southern region of the Mare. We had crossed a hundred miles of it in a week, skirting the foothills of the mountains along the shore of what was once the ancient sea, some thousand million years before. When life was beginning on Earth, it was already dying here. The waters were retreating down the flanks of those stupendous cliffs, retreating into the empty heart of the Moon. Over the land which we were crossing, the tideless ocean had once been half a mile deep, and now the only trace of moisture was the hoarfrost one could sometimes find in caves which the searing sunlight never penetrated.

We had begun our journey early in the slow lunar dawn, and still had almost a week of Earth-time before nightfall. Half a dozen times a day we would leave our vehicle and go outside in the space suits to hunt for interesting minerals, or to place markers for the guidance of future travelers. It was an uneventful routine. There is nothing hazardous or even particularly exciting about lunar exploration. We could live comfortably for a month in our pressurized tractors, and if we ran into trouble, we could always radio for help and sit tight until one of the spaceships came to our rescue.

I said just now that there was nothing exciting about lunar exploration, but of course that isn't true. One could never grow tired of those incredible mountains, so much more rugged than the gentle hills of Earth. We never knew, as we rounded the capes and promontories of that vanished sea, what new splendors would be revealed to us. The whole southern curve of the Mare Crisium is a vast delta where a score of rivers once found their way into the ocean, fed perhaps by the torrential rains that must have lashed the mountains in the brief volcanic age when the Moon was young. Each of these ancient valleys was an invitation, challenging us to climb into the unknown uplands beyond. But we had a hundred miles still to cover, and could only look longingly at the heights which others must scale.

We kept Earth-time aboard the tractor, and precisely at 22:00 hours the final radio message would be sent out to Base and we would close down for the day. Outside, the rocks would still be burning beneath the almost vertical sun, but to us it would be night until we awoke again eight hours later. Then one of us would prepare breakfast, there would be a great buzzing of electric razors, and someone would switch on the shortwave radio from Earth. Indeed, when the smell of frying sausages began to fill the cabin, it was sometimes hard to believe that we were not back on our own world—everything was so normal and homely, apart from the feeling of decreased weight and the unnatural slowness with which objects fell.

It was my turn to prepare breakfast in the corner of the main cabin that served as a galley. I can remember that moment quite vividly after all these years, for the radio had just played one of my favorite melodies, the old Welsh air "David of the White Rock." Our driver was already outside in his space suit, inspecting our caterpillar treads. My assistant, Louis Garnett, was up forward in the control position, making some belated entries in yesterday's log.

As I stood by the frying pan, waiting, like any terrestrial housewife, for the sausages to brown, I let my gaze wander idly over the mountain walls which covered the whole of the southern horizon, marching out of sight to east and west below the curve of the Moon. They seemed only a mile or two from the tractor, but I knew that the nearest was twenty miles away. On the Moon, of course, there is no loss of detail with distance—none of that almost imperceptible haziness which softens and sometimes transfigures all far-off things on Earth.

Those mountains were ten thousand feet high, and they climbed steeply out of the plain as if ages ago some subterranean eruption had smashed them skyward through the molten crust. The base of even the nearest was hidden from sight by the steeply curving surface of the plain, for the Moon is a very little world, and from where I was standing the horizon was only two miles away.

I lifted my eyes toward the peaks which no man had ever climbed, the peaks which, before the coming of terrestrial life, had watched the retreating oceans sink sullenly into their graves, taking with them the hope and the morning promise of a world. The sunlight was beating against those ramparts with a glare that hurt the eyes, yet only a little way above them the stars were shining steadily in a sky blacker than a winter midnight on Earth.

I was turning away when my eye caught a metallic glitter high on the ridge of a great promontory thrusting out into the sea thirty miles to the west. It was a dimensionless point of light, as if a star had been clawed from the sky by one of those cruel peaks, and I imagined that some smooth rock surface was catching the sunlight and heliographing it straight into my eyes. Such things were not uncommon. When the Moon is in her second quarter, observers on Earth can sometimes see the great ranges in the Oceanus Procellarum burning with a blue-white iridescence as the sunlight flashes from their slopes and leaps again from world to world. But I was curious to know what kind of rock could be shining so brightly up there, and I climbed into the observation turret and swung our four-inch telescope round to the west.

I could see just enough to tantalize me. Clear and sharp in the field of vision, the mountain peaks seemed only half a mile away, but whatever was catching the sunlight was still too small to be resolved. Yet it seemed to have an elusive symmetry, and the summit upon which it rested was curiously flat. I stared for a long time at that glittering enigma, straining my eyes into space, until presently a smell of burning from the galley told me that our breakfast sausages had made their quarter-million-mile journey in vain.

All that morning we argued our way across the Mare Crisium while the western mountains reared higher in the sky. Even when we were out prospecting in the space suits, the discussion would continue over the radio. It was absolutely certain, my companions argued, that there had never been any form of intelligent life on the Moon. The only living things that had ever existed there were a few primitive plants and their slightly less degenerate ancestors. I knew that as well as anyone, but there are times when a scientist must not be afraid to make a fool of himself.

"Listen," I said at last, "I'm going up there, if only for my own peace of mind. That mountain's less than twelve thousand feet high—that's only two thousand under Earth gravity—and I can make the trip in twenty hours at the outside. I've always wanted to go up into those hills, anyway, and this gives me an excellent excuse."

"If you don't break your neck," said Garnett, "you'll be the laughingstock of the expedition when we get back to Base. That mountain will probably be called Wilson's Folly from now on."

"I won't break my neck," I said firmly. "Who was the first man to climb Pico and Helicon?"

"But weren't you rather younger in those days?" asked Louis gently.

"That," I said with great dignity, "is as good a reason as any for going."

We went to bed early that night, after driving the tractor to within half a mile of the promontory. Garnett was coming with me in the morning; he was a good climber, and had often been with me on such exploits before. Our driver was only too glad to be left in charge of the machine.

At first sight, those cliffs seemed completely unscalable, but to anyone with a good head for heights, climbing is easy on a world where all weights are only a sixth of their normal value. The real danger in lunar mountaineering lies in overconfidence; a six-hundred-foot drop on the Moon can kill you just as thoroughly as a hundred-foot fall on Earth.

We made our first halt on a wide ledge about four thousand feet above the plain. Climbing had not been very difficult, but my limbs were stiff with the unaccustomed effort, and I was glad of the rest. We could still see the tractor as a tiny metal insect far down at the foot of the cliff, and we reported our progress to the driver before starting on the next ascent.

Inside our suits it was comfortably cool, for the refrigeration units were fighting the fierce sun and carrying away the body heat of our exertions. We seldom spoke to each other, except to pass climbing instructions and to discuss our best plan of ascent. I do not know what Garnett was thinking, probably that this was the craziest goose chase he had ever embarked upon. I more than half agreed with him, but the joy of climbing, the knowledge that no man had ever gone this way before, and the exhilaration of the steadily widening landscape gave me all the reward I needed.

I don't think I was particularly excited when I saw in front of us the wall of rock I had first inspected through the telescope from thirty miles away. It would level off about fifty feet above our heads, and there on the plateau would be the thing that had lured me over these barren wastes. It would be, almost certainly, nothing more than a boulder splintered ages ago by a falling meteor, and with its cleavage planes still fresh and bright in this incorruptible, unchanging silence.

There were no handholds on the rock face, and we had to use a grapnel. My tired arms seemed to gain new strength as I swung the three-pronged metal anchor round my head and sent it sailing up toward the stars. The first time it broke loose and came falling slowly back when we pulled the rope. On the third attempt, the prongs gripped firmly and our combined weights could not shift it.

Garnett looked at me anxiously. I could tell that he wanted to go first, but I smiled back at him through the glass of my helmet and shook my head. Slowly, taking my time, I began the final ascent.

Even with my space suit, I weighed only forty pounds here, so I pulled myself up hand over hand without bothering to use my feet. At the rim I paused and waved to my companion, then I scrambled over the edge and stood upright, staring ahead of me.

You must understand that until this very moment I had been almost completely convinced that there could be nothing strange or unusual for me to find here. Almost, but not quite; it was that haunting doubt that had driven me forward. Well, it was a doubt no longer, but the haunting had scarcely begun.

I was standing on a plateau perhaps a hundred feet across. It had once been smooth—too smooth to be natural—but falling meteors had pitted and scored its surface through immeasurable eons. It had been leveled to support a glittering, roughly pyramidal structure, twice as high as a man, that was set in the rock like a gigantic, many faceted jewel.

Probably no emotion at all filled my mind in those first few seconds. Then I felt a great lifting of my heart, and a strange, inexpressible joy. For I loved the Moon, and now I knew that the creeping moss of Aristarchus and Eratosthenes was not the only life she had brought forth in her youth. The old, discredited dream of the first explorers was true. There had, after all, been a lunar civilization—and I was the first to find it. That I had come perhaps a hundred million years too late did not distress me; it was enough to have come at all.

My mind was beginning to function normally, to analyze and to ask questions. Was this a building, a shrine—or something for which my language had no name? If a building, then why was it erected in so uniquely inaccessible a spot? I wondered if it might be a temple, and I could picture the adepts of some strange priesthood calling on their gods to preserve them as the life of the Moon ebbed with the dying oceans, and calling on their gods in vain.

I took a dozen steps forward to examine the thing more closely, but some sense of caution kept me from going too near. I knew a little of archaeology, and tried to guess the cultural level of the civilization that must have smoothed this mountain and raised the glittering mirror surfaces that still dazzled my eyes.

The Egyptians could have done it, I thought, if their workmen had possessed whatever strange materials these far more ancient architects had used. Because of the thing's smallness, it did not occur to me that I might be looking at the handiwork of a race more advanced than my own. The idea that the Moon had possessed intelligence at all was still almost too tremendous to grasp, and my pride would not let me take the final, humiliating plunge.

And then I noticed something that set the scalp crawling at the back of my neck—something so trivial and so innocent that many would never have noticed it at all. I have said that the plateau was scarred by meteors; it was also coated inches deep with the cosmic dust that is always filtering down upon the surface of any world where there are no winds to disturb it. Yet the dust and the meteor scratches ended quite abruptly in a wide circle enclosing the little pyramid, as though an invisible wall was protecting it from the ravages of time and the slow but ceaseless bombardment from space.

There was someone shouting in my earphones, and I realized that Garnett had been calling me for some time. I walked unsteadily to the edge of the cliff and signaled him to join me, not trusting myself to speak. Then I went back toward that circle in the dust. I picked up a fragment of splintered rock and tossed it gently toward the shining enigma. If the pebble had vanished at that invisible barrier, I should not have been surprised, but it seemed to hit a smooth, hemispheric surface and slide gently to the ground.

I knew then that I was looking at nothing that could be matched in the antiquity of my own race. This was not a building, but a machine, protecting itself with forces that had challenged Eternity. Those forces, whatever they might be, were still operating, and perhaps I had already come too close. I thought of all the radiations man had trapped and tamed in the past century. For all I knew, I might be as irrevocably doomed as if I had stepped into the deadly, silent aura of an unshielded atomic pile.

I remember turning then toward Garnett, who had joined me and was now standing motionless at my side. He seemed quite oblivious to me, so I did not disturb him but walked to the edge of the cliff in an effort to marshal my thoughts. There below me lay the Mare Crisium— Sea of Crises, indeed—strange and weird to most men, but reassuringly familiar to me. I lifted my eyes toward the crescent Earth, lying in her cradle of stars, and I wondered what her clouds had covered when these unknown builders had finished their work. Was it the steaming jungle of the Carboniferous, the bleak shoreline over which the first amphibians must crawl to conquer the land—or, earlier still, the long loneliness before the coming of life?

Do not ask me why I did not guess the truth sooner—the truth that seems so obvious now. In the first excitement of my discovery, I had assumed without question that this crystalline apparition had been built by some race belonging to the Moon's remote past, but suddenly, and with overwhelming force, the belief came to me that it was as alien to the Moon as I myself.

In twenty years we had found no trace of life but a few degenerate plants. No lunar civilization, whatever its doom, could have left but a single token of its existence.

I looked at the shining pyramid again, and the more I looked, the more remote it seemed from anything that had to do with the Moon. And suddenly I felt myself shaking with a foolish, hysterical laughter, brought on by excitement and overexertion: For I had imagined that the little pyramid was speaking to me and was saying, "Sorry, I'm a stranger here myself."

It has taken us twenty years to crack that invisible shield and to reach the machine inside those crystal walls. What we could not understand, we broke at last with the savage might of atomic power and now I have seen the fragments of the lovely, glittering thing I found up there on the mountain.

They are meaningless. The mechanisms—if indeed they are mechanisms—of the pyramid belong to a technology that lies far beyond our horizon, perhaps to the technology of paraphysical forces.

The mystery haunts us all the more now that the other planets have been reached and we know that only Earth has ever been the home of intelligent life in our Universe. Nor could any lost civilization of our own world have built that machine, for the thickness of the meteoric dust on the plateau has enabled us to measure its age. It was set there upon its mountain before life had emerged from the seas of Earth.

When our world was half its present age, *something* from the stars swept through the Solar System, left this token of its passage, and went again upon its way. Until we destroyed it, that machine was still fulfilling the purpose of its builders; and as to that purpose, here is my guess.

Nearly a hundred thousand million stars are turning in the circle of the Milky Way, and long ago other races on the worlds of other suns must have scaled and passed the heights that we have reached. Think of such civilizations, far back in time against the fading afterglow of Creation, masters of a universe so young that life as yet had come only to a handful of worlds. Theirs would have been a loneliness we cannot imagine, the loneliness of gods looking out across infinity and finding none to share their thoughts.

They must have searched the star clusters as we have searched the planets. Everywhere there would be worlds, but they would be empty or peopled with crawling, mindless things. Such was our own Earth, the smoke of the great volcanoes still staining the skies, when that first ship of the peoples of the dawn came sliding in from the abyss beyond Pluto. It passed the frozen outer worlds, knowing that life could play no part in their destinies. It came to rest among the inner planets, warming themselves around the fire of the Sun and waiting for their stories to begin.

Those wanderers must have looked on Earth, circling safely in the narrow zone between fire and ice, and must have guessed that it was the favorite of the Sun's children. Here, in the distant future, would be intelligence; but there were countless stars before them still, and they might never come this way again.

So they left a sentinel, one of millions they scattered throughout the Universe, watching over all worlds with the promise of life. It was a beacon that down the ages patiently signaled the fact that no one had discovered it.

Perhaps you understand now why that crystal pyramid was set upon the Moon instead of on the Earth. Its builders were not concerned with races still struggling up from savagery. They would be interested in our civilization only if we proved our fitness to survive—by crossing space and so escaping from the Earth, our cradle. That is the chal-

lenge that all intelligent races must meet, sooner or later. It is a double
challenge, for it depends in turn upon the conquest of atomic energy
and the last choice between life and death.

Once we had passed that crisis, it was only a matter of time before
we found the pyramid and forced it open. Now its signals have ceased,
and those whose duty it is will be turning their minds upon Earth. Perhaps they wish to help our infant civilization. But they must be very,
very old, and the old are often insanely jealous of the young.

I can never look now at the Milky Way without wondering from
which of those banked clouds of stars the emissaries are coming. If you
will pardon so commonplace a simile, we have set off the fire alarm
and have nothing to do but to wait.

I do not think we will have to wait for long.

BEYOND THE STARS

Jeremy Bernstein

To most people, including us, the words "science-fiction movie" bring up visions of super-monsters who have flames shooting out of at least one eye while an Adonislike Earthman carries Sylvanna, a stimulating blonde, to a nearby spaceship. It is a prospect that has often kept us at home. However, we are happy to report, for the benefit of science-fiction buffs—who have long felt that, at its best, science fiction is a splendid medium for conveying the poetry and wonder of science—that there will soon be a movie for *them.* We have this from none other than the two authors of the movie, which is to be called *Journey Beyond the Stars*—Stanley Kubrick and Arthur C. Clarke. It is to be based on a forthcoming novel called *Journey Beyond the Stars*, by Arthur C. Clarke and Stanley Kubrick. Mr. Clarke and Mr. Kubrick, who have been collaborating on the two projects for over a year, explained to us that the order of the names in the movie and the novel was reversed to stress Mr. Clarke's role as a science-fiction novelist (he has written dozens of stories, many of them regarded as modern science-fiction classics) and Mr. Kubrick's role as a moviemaker (his most recent film was *Dr. Strangelove*).

Our briefing session took place in the living room of Mr. Kubrick's apartment. When we got there, Mr. Kubrick was talking on a telephone in the next room, Mr. Clarke had not yet arrived, and three lively Kubrick daughters—the eldest is eleven—were running in and out with several young friends. We settled ourself in a large chair, and a few minutes later the doorbell rang. One of the little girls went to the door and asked, "Who is it?" A pleasantly English-accented voice answered, through the door, "It's Clarke," and the girls began jumping up and down and saying, "It's Clark Kent!"—a reference to another well-known science-fiction personality. They opened the door, and in walked Mr. Clarke, a cheerful-looking man in his forties. He was carrying several manila envelopes, which, it turned out, contained parts of *Journey Beyond the Stars*. Mr. Kubrick then came into the room carrying a thick pile of diagrams and charts, and looking like the popular conception of a nuclear physicist who has been interrupted in the middle of some difficult calculations. Mr. Kubrick and Mr. Clarke sat down side by side on a sofa, and we asked them about their joint venture.

Mr. Clarke said that one of the basic problems they've had to deal with is how to describe what they are trying to do. "Science-fiction films have always meant monsters and sex, so we have tried to find another term for our film," said Mr. C.

"About the best we've been able to come up with is a space Odyssey—comparable in some ways to the Homeric *Odyssey*," said Mr. K. "It occurred to us that for the Greeks the vast stretches of the sea must have had the same sort of mystery and remoteness that space has for our generation, and that the far-flung islands Homer's wonderful characters visited were no less remote to them than the planets our spacemen will soon be landing on are to us. *Journey* also shares with the *Odyssey* a concern for wandering, exploration, and adventure."

Mr. Clarke agreed, and went on to tell us that the new film is set in the near future, at a time when the Moon will have been colonized and space travel, at least around the planetary system, will have become commonplace. "Since we will soon be visiting the planets, it naturally occurs to one to ask whether, in the past, anybody has come to Earth to visit us," he said. "In *Journey Beyond the Stars*, the answer is definitely yes, and the Odyssey unfolds as our descendants attempt to make contact with some extraterrestrial explorers. There will be no women among those who make the trip, although there will be some on Earth, some on the Moon, and some working in space."

Relieved, we asked where the film was to be made, and were told that it would be shot in the United States and several foreign countries. "How about the scenes Out There?" we inquired.

Mr. Kubrick explained that they would be done with the aid of a vast assortment of cinematic tricks, but he added emphatically that everything possible would be done to make each scene completely authentic and to make it conform to what is known to physicists and astronomers. He and Mr. Clarke feel that while there will be dangers in space, there will also be wonder, adventure, and beauty, and that space is a source of endless knowledge, which may transform our civilization in the same way that the voyages of the Renaissance transformed the Dark Ages. They want all these elements to come through in the film. Mr. Kubrick told us that he has been a reader of science-fiction and popular-science books, including Mr. Clarke's books on space travel, for many years, and that he has become increasingly disturbed by the barrier between scientific knowledge and the general public. He has asked friends basic questions like how many stars there are in our galaxy, he went on, and has discovered that most people have no idea at all. "The answer is a hundred billion, and sometimes they stretch their imaginations and say maybe four or five million," he said.

Speaking almost simultaneously, Mr. Clarke and Mr. Kubrick said that they hoped their film would give people a real understanding of the facts and of the overwhelming implications that the facts have for the human race.

We asked when the film will be released.

Mr. Kubrick told us that they are aiming for December, 1966, and explained that the longest and hardest part of the job will be designing the "tricks," even though the ones they plan to use are well within the range of modern cinematic technology.

When we had been talking for some time, Mr. Clarke said he had to keep another appointment, and left. After he had gone, we asked Mr. Kubrick how *Dr. Strangelove* had been received abroad. It had been shown all over the world, he told us, and had received favorable criticism everywhere except, oddly, in Germany. He was not sure why this was, but thought it might reflect the German reliance on our nuclear strength and a consequent feeling of uneasiness at any attempt to make light of it. He said that his interest in the whole question of nuclear weapons had come upon him suddenly, when it struck him that here he was, actually in the same world with the hydrogen bomb, and he didn't know how he was learning to live with that fact. Before making *Dr. Strangelove*, he read widely in the literature dealing with atomic warfare.

We said goodbye shortly afterward, and on our way out a phrase of J.B.S. Haldane's came back to us: "The Universe is not only stranger than we imagine; it is stranger than we *can* imagine."

CHRISTMAS, SHEPPERTON

Arthur C. Clarke

When I met Stanley Kubrick for the first time, in Trader Vic's on April 22, 1964, he had already absorbed an immense amount of science fact and science fiction, and was in some danger of believing in flying saucers; I felt I had arrived just in time to save him from this gruesome fate. Even from the beginning, he had a very clear idea of his ultimate goal, and was searching for the best way to approach it. He wanted to make a movie about Man's relation to the universe—something which had never been attempted, still less achieved, in the history of motion pictures.* Of course, there had been innumerable "space" movies, most of them trash. Even the few that had been made with some skill and accuracy had been rather simpleminded, concerned more with the schoolboy excitement of space flight than its profound implications to society, philosophy, and religion.

Stanley was fully aware of this, and he was determined to create a work of art which would arouse the emotions of wonder, awe ... even, if appropriate, terror. How he set about it I have described elsewhere

---

*I once accused my friends in MGM's publicity department of having a special labor-saving key on their typewriters which, when pressed, automatically began to print out: "Never, in the history of motion pictures...."

(see "Son of Dr. Strangelove: or How I Learned to Stop Worrying and Love Stanley Kubrick"—reprinted in *Report on Planet Three,* Harper & Row). His success has been recorded or disputed in millions of spoken and written words, a fair sampling of which will be found in Jerry Agel's entertaining book *The Making of Kubrick's 2001* (New American Library). I am concerned here, however, not with the movie but with the novel, regarded as an independent and self-contained work—even though it was created specifically as the basis for the movie.

This, of course, is the reverse of the usual state of affairs. Most movies are adapted from already existing novels, preferably ones which have proved to be best sellers and so have a built-in box-office guarantee. (Good examples are *Gone with the Wind* and *Doctor Zhivago.*) Other movies are based on screenplays specifically written for them, and no novel version (or even—ugh!—"novelization") ever exists. All of Chaplin's films, *Citizen Kane,* and *Lawrence of Arabia* are in this category. They were conceived purely as movies from start to finish; the only thing that exists on paper is the screenplay and the subsequent shooting script.*

Some directors of genius have even managed to dispense with these. Though it seems incredible, David Wark Griffith is supposed to have carried *Intolerance* entirely in his head. I think that Stanley would like to have done the same with *2001,* and would hesitate to say that, for him, it was theoretically impossible. But it was certainly impossible in practice—if only for the reason that he had to have a fairly complete treatment to show his backers. Banks and movie companies require more than a few notes on scraps of paper before they will disgorge their cherished millions.

Now a screenplay is not a work of art, though its production requires considerable skill. It bears somewhat the same relationship to a movie as the musical score does to a symphonic performance. There are people who can read a musical score and "hear" the symphony—but no two directors will see the same images when they read a movie script. The two-dimensional patterns of colored light

---

*The screenplay gives the dialogue, action, scenes, etc., in the order in which they will actually appear on the screen. But it would be absurd to film them in this order, so the shooting script groups together all the scenes involving the same locations, sets and actors.

involved are far more complex than the one-dimensional thread of sound—which can, in principle, be completely described on paper. A movie can never be pinned down in such a way, though the scriptwriter has to attempt this impossible feat. Unless the writer *is* the director, everything has to be specified in boring detail; no wonder that screenplays are almost as tedious to read as to write. John Fowles has put it very well: "Any novelist who has written scripts knows the appalling restrictions—obligatory detailing of the unnecessary—the cinema imposes. Writing a novel is like swimming in the sea; writing a film script is thrashing through treacle." ("Is the Novel Dead?"—*Books*, Autumn 1970).

Though I was only dimly aware of this in 1964, Stanley knew it very well. It was his suggestion that, before embarking on the drudgery of the script, we let our imaginations soar freely by developing the story in the form of a complete novel. Of course, to do this we would have to generate far more background than could ever be used in the final film. That wouldn't matter. Every good novelist "knows" much more than he writes down: every film maker should be aware of a larger universe than his script.

In theory, therefore, the novel would be written (with an eye on the screen) and the script would be derived from this. In practice, the result was far more complex; toward the end, both novel and screenplay were being written simultaneously, with feedback in both directions. Some parts of the novel had their final revisions after we had seen the rushes based on the screenplay based on earlier versions of the novel...and so on.

After a couple of years of this, I felt that when the novel finally appeared it should be "by Arthur Clarke and Stanley Kubrick; based on the screenplay by Stanley Kubrick and Arthur Clarke"—whereas the movie should have the credits reversed. This still seems the nearest approximation to the complicated truth.

After various false starts and twelve-hour talkathons, by early May 1964 Stanley agreed that "The Sentinel" would provide good story material. But our first concept—and it is hard now for me to focus on such an idea, though it would have been perfectly viable—involved working up to the discovery of an extraterrestrial artifact as the *climax*, not the beginning, of the story. Before that, we would have a series of incidents or adventures devoted to the exploration of the Moon and Planets. For this Mark I version, our private title (never of course intended for public use) was "How the Solar System Was Won."

So once more I went back to my stockpile of short stories, to find material which would fit into this pattern. I returned with five: "Breaking Strain" (from *Expedition to Earth*); "Out of the Cradle, Endlessly Orbiting...," "Who's There?," "Into the Comet," and "Before Eden" (all from *Tales of Ten Worlds*). On May 28, 1964, I sold the lot to Stanley and signed an agreement to work on the projected movie. Our initial schedule was hilariously optimistic: writing script, twelve weeks; discussing it, two weeks; revising, four weeks; fixing deal, four weeks; visuals, art, twenty weeks; shooting, twenty weeks; cutting, editing, twenty weeks— a total of eighty-two weeks. Allowing another twelve weeks before release, this added up to ninety-two, or the better part of two years. I was very depressed by this staggering period of time, since I was (as always) in a hurry to get back to Ceylon; it was just as well that neither of us could have guessed the project's ultimate duration—*four* years....

The rest of 1964 was spent brainstorming. As we developed new ideas, so the original conception slowly changed. "The Sentinel" became the opening, not the finale; and one by one, the other five short stories were discarded. A year later, deciding (not necessarily in this order) that (a) it wasn't fair to Stanley to make him pay for something he didn't need and (b) these stories might make a pretty good movie someday, I bought them back from him....

The announced title of the project, when Stanley gave his intentions to the press, was *Journey Beyond the Stars*. I never liked this, because there had been far too many science-fictional journeys and voyages. (Indeed, the inner-space epic *Fantastic Voyage*, featuring Raquel Welch and a supporting cast of ten thousand blood corpuscles, was also going into production about this time.) Other titles which we ran up and failed to salute were *Universe, Tunnel to the Stars,* and *Planetfall.* It was not until eleven months after we started—April 1965—that Stanley selected *2001: A Space Odyssey.* As far as I can recall, it was entirely his idea.

Despite the unrelenting pressure of work (a mere twelve hours was practically a day off) I kept a detailed log of the whole operation. Though I do not wish to get bogged down in minutiae of interest only

:o fanatical Kubrickologists, perhaps these extracts may convey the flavor of those early days:—

May 28, 1964. Suggested to Stanley that "they" might be machines who regard organic life as a hideous disease. Stanley thinks this is cute and feels we've got something.

May 31. One hilarious idea we *won't* use. Seventeen aliens—featureless black pyramids—riding in open cars down Fifth Avenue, surrounded by Irish cops.

June 20. Finished the opening chapter, "View from the Year 2000," and started on the robot sequence.

July 1. Last day working at Time/Life completing *Man and Space.* Checked into new suite, 1008, at the Hotel Chelsea.

July 2–8. Averaging one or two thousand words a day. Stanley reads first five chapters and says "We've got a best seller here."

July 9. Spent much of afternoon teaching Stanley how to use the slide rule—he's fascinated.

July 11. Joined Stanley to discuss plot development, but spent almost all the time arguing about Cantor's Theory of Transfinite Groups. Stanley tries to refute the "part equals the whole" paradox by arguing that a perfect square is not necessarily identical with the integer of the same value. I decide that he is a latent mathematical genius.

July 12. Now have everything—except the plot.

July 13. Got to work again on the novel and made good progress despite the distraction of the Republican Convention.

July 26. Stanley's birthday. Went to the Village and found a card showing the Earth coming apart at the seams and bearing the inscription: "How can you have a Happy Birthday when the whole world may blow up any minute?"

July 28. Stanley: "What we want is a smashing theme of mythic grandeur."

August 1. Ranger VII impacts on moon. Stay up late to watch the first TV close-ups. Stanley starts to worry about the forthcoming Mars probes. Suppose they show something that shoots down our story line?

[Later, he approached Lloyd's of London to see if he could insure himself against this eventuality.]

August 6. Stanley suggests that we make the computer female and call her Athena.

August 17. We've also got the name of our hero at last—Alex Bowman. Hurrah!

August 19. Writing all day. Two thousand words exploring Jupiter's satellites. Dull work.

September 7. Stanley quite happy: "We're in fantastic shape." He has made up a 100-item questionnaire about our astronauts, e.g. do they sleep in their pajamas, what do they eat for breakfast, etc.

September 8. Upset stomach last night. Dreamed I was a robot, being rebuilt. In a great burst of energy managed to redo two chapters. Took them to Stanley, who was very pleased and cooked me a fine steak, remarking: "Joe Levine doesn't do this for *his* writers."

September 26. Stanley gave me Joseph Campbell's analysis of the myth *The Hero with a Thousand Faces* to study. Very stimulating.

September 29. Dreamed that shooting had started. Lots of actors standing around, but I still didn't know the story line.

October 2. Finished reading Robert Ardrey's *African Genesis.* Came across a striking paragraph which might even provide a title for the movie: "Why did not the human line become extinct in the depths of the Pliocene? . . . We know that but for a gift from the stars, but for the accidental collision of ray and gene, intelligence would have perished on some forgotten African field." True, Ardrey is talking about cosmic-ray mutations, but the phrase "a gift from the stars" is strikingly applicable to our present plot line.

October 6. Have got an idea which I think is crucial. The people we meet on the other star system are humans who were collected from Earth a hundred thousand years ago, and hence are virtually identical with us.

October 8. Thinking of plot all morning, but after a long walk in the sun we ended up on the East River watching the boats. We dumped all our far-fetched ideas—now we're settling for a Galactic Peace Corps and no blood and thunder.

October 17. Stanley has invented the wild idea of slightly fag robots who create a Victorian environment to put our heroes at their ease.

November 20. Went to Natural History Museum to see Dr. Harry Shapiro, head of Anthropology, who took a poor view of Ardrey. Then had a session with Stan, arguing about early man's vegetarian versus carnivorous tendencies. Stan wants our visitors to turn Man into a carnivore; I argued that he always was. Back at the Chelsea, phoned Ike Asimov to discuss the biochemistry of turning vegetarians into carnivores.

November 21. Read Leakey's *Adam's Ancestors.* Getting rather desperate now, but after six hours' discussion Stan had a rather amusing idea. Our E.T.'s arrive on Earth and teach commando tactics to our pacifistic ancestors so that they can survive and flourish. We had an entertaining time knocking this one around, but I don't think it's viable.

November 22. Called Stan and said I didn't think *any* of our flashback ideas were any good. He slowly talked me out of this mood, and I was feeling more cheerful when I suddenly said: "What if our E.T.'s are stranded on Earth and need the ape-men to help them?" This idea (probably not original, but what the hell) opened up whole new areas of plot which we are both exploring.

November 23. Stanley distracted by numerous consultations with his broker, and wants my advice on buying COMSAT.

December 10. Stanley calls after screening H. G. Wells' *Things to Come,* and says he'll *never* see another movie I recommend.

December 21. Much of afternoon spent by Stanley planning his Academy Award campaign for *Dr. Strangelove.* I get back to the Chelsea to find a note from Allen Ginsberg asking me to join him and William Burroughs at the bar downstairs. Do so thankfully in search of inspiration.

December 24. Slowly tinkered with the final pages, so I can have them as a Christmas present for Stanley.

December 25. Stanley delighted with the last chapters, and convinced that we've extended the range of science fiction. He's astonished and delighted because Bosley Crowther of the New York *Times* has placed *Dr. S* on the "Ten Best Films" list, after attacking it ferociously all year. I christen Bosley "The Critic Who Came In from the Cold."

From these notes, it would appear that by Christmas 1964, the novel was essentially complete, and that thereafter it would be a fairly straightforward matter to develop the screenplay. We were, indeed, under that delusion—at least, *I* was. In reality, all that we had was merely a rough draft of the first two-thirds of the book, stopping at the most exciting point. We had managed to get Bowman into the Star Gate, but didn't know what would happen next, except in the most general way. Nevertheless, the existing manuscript, together with his own salesmanship, allowed Stanley to set up the deal with MGM and Cinerama, and "Journey Beyond the Stars" was announced with a flourish of trumpets.

Through the spring of 1965, we continued to revise and extend the novel, and threw away—again and yet again—whole sections which we had once imagined to be final and complete. All this time, Stanley was also hiring staff, checking designs, negotiating with actors and technicians, and coping with the millions of other problems which arise in the production of even the most straightforward movie. The rush of events became far too hectic to enter more than a small fraction of them in my log, and few of them (luckily) concerned me directly. My primary job was still polishing the novel, though I was constantly involved in technical discussions with the artists and production staff. (Sometimes with disastrous results; see entry for November 10, below.)

February 9, 1965. Caught Dali on TV, painting in a Fifth Avenue store window to promote *Fantastic Voyage.* Reported this to Stanley, who replied: "Don't worry—we've already reserved a window for you."

March 8. Fighting hard to stop Stan from bringing Dr. Poole back from the dead. I'm afraid his obsession with immortality has overcome his artistic instincts.

April 6. To COMSAT Headquarters, Washington, for launch of first commercial communications satellite, "Early Bird." Introduced to Vice-President Humphrey, who is also Chairman of the Space Council, and told him we were spending ten million dollars to publicize space. Added that one character in the movie would be the Chairman of the Space Council...thirty years from now. "Oh," said H.H.H. at once, "I still intend to be chairman then."

April 12. Much excitement when Stanley phones to say that the Russians claim to have detected radio signals from space. Rang Walter Sullivan at the New York *Times* and got the real story—merely fluctuations in Quasar CTA 102.

April 14. Reception at Harcourt, Brace and World. Those present included Bill Jovanovich (president), Jeremy Bernstein (*New Yorker* Magazine), Dennis Flanagan (*Scientific American*), Dr. Robert Jastrow (Goddard Space Center), Stanley and Christiane Kubrick, Al Rosenfeld (Science Editor, *Life*), Sylvester (Pat) Weaver, Scott Meredith and many other friends. There was a general belief that the party was to celebrate Harcourt's publication of *Journey Beyond the Stars*, but I explained that this was not definite, and depended upon the size of the mortgage they could raise on the building.

April 19. Went up to the office with about three thousand words Stanley hasn't read. The place is really humming now—about ten people working there, including two production staff from England. The walls are getting covered with impressive pictures and I already feel quite a minor cog in the works.

Some psychotic who insists that Stanley *must* hire him has been sitting on a park bench outside the office for a couple of weeks, and occasionally comes to the building. In self-defense, Stan has secreted a large hunting knife in his briefcase.

May 1. Found that a fire had broken out on the third floor of the Chelsea. Waited anxiously in the lobby while the firemen dealt with it ... visions of the only complete copy of the MS going up in smoke. ...

May 2. Completed the "Universe" chapter—will soon have all Part Three ready for typing, hurrah. ... Stan phoned to say he liked the "Floating Island" sequence. Strange and encouraging how much of the material I thought I'd abandoned fits in perfectly after all.

May 3. Finished first draft of the runaway antenna sequence.

May 25. Now Stanley wants to incorporate the Devil theme from *Childhood's End.* ...

June 7. Bad book review in *Tribune*—says I should stick to science exposition and am an amateur at fiction.

Late June. Read Victor Lyndon's production notes; they left me completely overwhelmed. Glad that's not *my* job. One scene calls for four trained warthogs.

On that note, more or less, I returned to Ceylon after an absence of over a year, and subsequently rejoined Stanley at the MGM studios at Boreham Wood, fifteen miles north of London, in August. His empire had now expanded vastly, the art department was in full swing, and impressive sets were being constructed. My time was now equally divided between the apparently never-ending chore of developing ideas with Stanley, polishing the novel, and almost daily consultations at the studio.

August 25. Suddenly realized how the novel *should* end, with Bowman standing beside the alien ship.

September 25. Visitors from NASA—Dr. George Mueller, Associate Administrator, and "Deke" Slayton (Director of Flight Crew Operations). Gave them the Grand Tour—they were quite impressed. George made several useful suggestions and asked wistfully if he could have the model of *Discovery* for his office when we'd finished with it. Deke was later reported to have said: "Stanley, I'm afraid you've been conned by a used capsule salesman." An improbable story—I suspect the fine Italian hand of Roger Caras, Stanley's vice-president i/c promotion.

October 1. Stanley phoned with *another* ending. I find I left *his* treatment at his house last night—unconscious rejection?

October 3. Stanley on phone, worried about ending . . . gave him my latest ideas, and one of them suddenly clicked—Bowman will regress to infancy, and we'll see him at the end as a baby in orbit. Stanley called again later, still very enthusiastic. Hope this isn't a false optimism: I feel cautiously encouraged myself.

October 5. Back to brood over the novel. Suddenly (I think!) found a logical reason why Bowman should appear at the end as a baby. It's his image of himself at this stage of his development. And perhaps the Cosmic Consciousness has a sense of humor. Phoned these ideas to Stan, who wasn't too impressed, but I'm happy now.

October 15. Stan has decided to kill off *all* the crew of *Discovery* and leave Bowman only. Drastic, but it seems right. After all, Odysseus was the sole survivor. . . .

October 17. For the first time, saw Stan reduced to helpless hysterics as we developed comic ideas. There will be *no one* in the hibernacula—all the trainees chickened out, but the mission had to go ahead regardless.

October 19. Collected by studio car, and spent all day working (or trying to work) with Stan. Despite usual crowds of people getting at him, long phone calls to Hollywood, and a "work-to-rule" the unions called, got a lot done and solved (*again!*) our main plot problems.

October 26. Had a discussion with Stanley over his latest idea—that *Discovery* should be nuclear-pulse-driven. Read a recently declassified report on this and was quite impressed—but the design staff rather upset.

November 10. Accompanied Stan and the design staff into the Earth-orbit ship and happened to remark that the cockpit looked like a Chinese restaurant. Stan said that killed it instantly for him and called for revisions. Must keep away from the Art Department for a few days.

November 16. Long session with Stanley discussing script. Several good ideas, but I rather wish we didn't have any more.

November 18. Feeling rather stale—went into London and saw Carol Reed's film about Michelangelo, *The Agony and the Ecstasy.* One line particularly struck me—the use of the phrase "God made Man in His own image." This, after all, is the theme of our movie.

November 30. To the Oxford and Cambridge Club with Roger Caras and Fred Ordway (Technical Adviser) to meet Dr. Louis Leakey and his son Richard. Dr. Leakey is just as I imagined him—full of enthusiasm and ideas. He thinks that Man now goes back at least four to five million years. He also confided to me that he'd written a play—a fantasy about primitive man which he thought would make a fine movie. It's about a group of anthropologists who are sent back into the past by a witch doctor. I said (breaking all my rules) that I'd be glad to see the MS— which is true.

December 16. My 48th birthday—and Somerset Maugham dies. Trying to make something of this (last of the competition?).

December 25. Christmas Day, ha-ha! Hacked my way to Jupiter—slow but steady going.

December 26. Working all day. Stan phoned to thank me for the presents and sent a driver to collect what I'd written. He called later to say that he didn't think much of the dialogue. I agreed.

That Christmas of 1965 we were really under the gun, and no one had a holiday. Stanley was up against an unbreakable deadline. The enormous set of the TMA 1 excavation, containing the monolith found on the Moon, had been constructed at the Shepperton Studios, in South West London—and it had to be torn down by the first week of the New Year, so that another production could move in. Stanley had only a week to do all his shooting, for the second crucial encounter between Man and Monolith.

It was not until several years later that I remembered another association between Shepperton and space. If you turn to H. G. Wells' masterpiece *The War of the Worlds* you will discover Chapter 12:—"What I saw of the Destruction of Weybridge and Shepperton." This first of all descriptions of armored warfare is still quite terrifying to read:

> The decapitated colossus reeled like a drunken giant; but it did not fall over. It recovered its balance by a miracle, and, no longer heeding its steps and with the camera that fired the Heat-Ray now rigidly upheld, it reeled swiftly upon Shepperton. The living intelligence, the Martian within the hood, was slain and splashed to the four winds of heaven, and the thing was now but a mere intricate device of metal whirling to destruction. It drove along in a straight line, incapable of guidance. It struck the tower of Shepperton Church, smashing it down as the impact of a battering ram might have done, swerved aside, blundered on, and collapsed with tremendous force into the river out of my sight.
>
> A violent explosion shook the air, and a spout of water, steam, mud and shattered metal shot far up into the sky. As the camera of the Heat-Ray hit the water, the latter had immediately flashed into steam. In another moment a huge wave, like a muddy tidal bore but almost scaldingly hot, came sweeping round the bend. . . .

Of course, now we have the heat ray, and we can do a lot better than Wells' feeble Martians with a small tactical atomic bomb. Still, it's not at all bad—for 1898. . . .

SHIPBUILDING

Piers Bizony

Now that the story was beginning to take shape, Kubrick had to start thinking about the visual elements of his project. Nobody really knew for sure what the space vehicles of the year 2001 would look like, or how they would operate. Kubrick wanted absolute realism: he wanted the hardware on screen to look as though it really *worked*. But who would create all this machinery? Traditional film artists and set designers could hardly be expected to know about the arcane details of spaceflight systems. The perfectionist director didn't want his expensive, ambitious movie to be out-guessed by the real future.

Towards the end of January 1965, a good many prominent space writers, scientists and researchers happened to be passing through the New York area all at once, on various errands to do with books, conferences and publicity events. Arthur C. Clarke was in town of course, "brainstorming" with Kubrick and publicizing *Man and Space* for Time-Life; the American Institute of Aeronautics and Astronautics was holding a convention at the New York Hilton; and two men from a small but busy space consultancy company were meeting with publishers in connection with their own book on the theme of extraterrestrial intelligence: Harry Lange and Frederick Ordway.

Harry H-K Lange had already worked for NASA on advanced

space vehicle concepts. Lange was (indeed still is) a superb draughts-man and colourist. He was also fully conversant with the most highly classified details of propulsion systems, radar navigation, docking techniques, and many other matters preoccupying the U.S. aerospace technologists of the day. His job had been to visualize as-yet-unborn vehicle concepts, so that NASA and its associated army of corporate collaborators could communicate their ideas for the future.

Frederick Ordway had what might best be described as the gift of the gab. He had already built an outstanding intellectual and commercial career with NASA, with Lange at the ABMA, and with a wide variety of first-rate industrial, university and research institutions. His scientific expertise was backed up by a persuasive understanding of the public relations processes by which large and complex organizations like NASA try to inform the outside world about their complex activities. Along with Lange (and three other colleagues) he had also founded a specialist company, the General Astronautics Research Corporation, or GARC, which provided consultancy services in the early, heady days of rocket and missile development, when it seemed that just about every major contractor in the country would be involved somewhere in that field.

Ordway found out that Clarke was in New York, and arranged a social gathering at the Harvard Club, where he and Lange were staying. So: what was Arthur doing in town? Oh, publicizing *Man and Space*, and working with a rather talented young movie director called Stanley Kubrick on a film about contact with extra-terrestrials.... Clarke explained that this was going to be *the* space movie, against which all others of its kind would be judged. It would portray humanity facing the enormity of the cosmos, and would consider the possibility of other forms of life out there among the stars.

Oh, really? What a coincidence! Lange and Ordway were putting together a book on that very same theme: *Intelligence in the Universe*, for publishers Prentice-Hall, and they'd just completed another book for Dutton: *Life in Other Solar Systems*. Clarke asked to see some of the artwork which Lange had prepared for the new book. He and Ordway then spent a pleasant half-hour or so showing material to Arthur, who certainly seemed impressed. But a dinner date loomed. Ordway and Lange had to make their excuses and get ready for going out.

A little while later they were standing outside the club, waiting for the doorman to hail a cab. It was snowing heavily (this is always the sort of meteorological detail which people remember after so long). Just as they were about to be driven away, one of the club's employees ran out and told Ordway there was an urgent phone call for him. When he reached the telephone, a voice identified itself on the other end of the line:

"Mr. Ordway? My name is Stanley Kubrick..."

Clarke, it seems, had left the Harvard Club and trudged through the blizzard to a discreet callbox on Sixth Avenue as soon as his friendly chat with Lange and Ordway was over. He had spoken to Kubrick and urged him to call them personally, before they even had time to leave the club for the evening.

Next day, Lange and Ordway spent what the latter has described as "a mentally exhilarating afternoon" discussing concepts with Kubrick and Clarke at the director's Lower East Side apartment, and examining the possibility of collaboration. Then they were asked formally for their assistance. Ordway would become principal technical adviser to the movie project and Lange would map out a range of detailed and realistic spaceship configurations. The two of them signed an initial six-month contract to work in New York, from Kubrick's Polaris Productions offices on Central Park West, where they would help to assemble all the necessary technical material, and keep Kubrick informed about the latest trends in real space research.

Lange chafed at being stuck in New York for so long. Of course, neither he nor Fred Ordway had any idea they would be working alongside Kubrick not just for six months, but for the best part of three years. Nor could they guess they'd end up moving both their families across the Atlantic to England as *2001: A Space Odyssey* came to absorb more and more of their working lives. Both men would emerge from their upcoming adventure very different from when they first began it. Their association with the film would stay with them for the rest of their careers. "He's the guy that worked on *2001*," people would say of each of them from now on.

Ordway began to open up channels of communication with dozens of real aerospace manufacturing companies. He persuaded them just how good it would be for their own publicity if they were seen to take an interest in Mr. Kubrick's new movie. For instance: the Pan American symbol writ large on the side of the *Orion* space liner was not simply the result of some random creative whim. The airline "starred" on screen in return for informing Kubrick and his advisers about their cherished ambitions for the future (presumably, bankruptcy ten years ahead of the new millennium didn't feature in their plans).

NASA, IBM, Honeywell, Boeing, Bell Telephone, RCA, General Dynamics, Chrysler, General Electric, Grumman: all these corporate giants provided tons of documentation and even real hardware. They presented theoretical outlines, drew up instrument panels, and discussed in the minutest detail how astronauts of the future would spend their days: what kind of buttons they would press; how they would wash, eat and sleep; what kind of pyjamas they might wear.

Most of the companies were happy enough with the way things turned out. Except for IBM. They spent many months contributing data to the film, and were less than pleased when HAL 9000 turned out to be such a wrong 'un. The whole mess was exacerbated when the press later noticed that the letters HAL were just one notch along the alphabet from IBM. Undoubtedly this was a genuine coincidence. Even so, the world's biggest computer company didn't welcome their association with *2001*'s maverick mainframe, which was portrayed hijacking its own ship and then ruthlessly "disconnecting" its human end-users. (IBM logos were removed from much of the *Discovery* hardware, though they can still clearly be seen in the *Orion* spaceplane cockpit.)

Kubrick fired questions in every direction, and expected precise answers. What fuel would an interplanetary spaceship use? How big would its radio dish be? How much storage space would be taken up by food and oxygen? What would be the exact sequence of a passenger journey to the moon? How would you rescue people in emergencies? These were tough questions, bearing in mind that NASA and the aerospace companies were only just beginning to work this sort of thing out for themselves. Much of what they told the *2001* team lay on the shadowed boundary between hard knowledge and pure speculation. Meanwhile, a hundred or so miles up in the sky, the early space vehicles were testing out all these fancy theories for real—and for the very first time. Cape Kennedy was struggling to put capsules weighing just a few tons into low Earth orbit for maybe a week or two at a stretch, and Kubrick was demanding to know how a seven-hundred-foot nuclear powered spaceship weighing hundreds of tons might safely be despatched to the far planets, with her crew kept alive and healthy for perhaps years at a time.

And at last, after all this data had been gathered, it had to be made to come alive on screen. Production designer Tony Masters came to New York in April 1965. He was a tall, bumbling British public school chap with a bit of a stutter, and an extraordinary talent for sketching ideas and storyboards with lightning speed. By all accounts a marvellous man. Coming out of the army at the end of the Second World War, an ex-major in the Royal Artillery, he was ideally suited to the marshalling of creative forces in the chaos of a huge film production. His style of command involved great helpings of patience and kindness. Since 1946 he had worked on dozens of films, most notably with John Box on David Lean's *Lawrence of Arabia*, another of MGM's more famous products. Masters took command of the art direction as a whole, particularly the planning of the control decks, passenger compartments, pod bays and so forth. The eerie hotel room at the film's climax was his work. In terms of set design, *2001* was Tony's film— perhaps the greatest achievement of his long and distinguished career. He was ably assisted by John Hoesli, who helped to manage the day-to-day nightmare of set construction and prop-making. (Eventually, thirty draughtsmen would be kept in harness at Borehamwood for more than a year, drawing up thousands of construction plans.) Ernie Archer joined the crew soon afterwards, and created the spectacular African landscape illusions for the film's opening sequences.

With Ordway providing reams of paperwork and material gathered from sources right across the U.S. manufacturing base, Lange mapped out the spaceships, control panels, suits and moonbases during an intense six months in New York, from February up until June 1965, after which he turned several of the main ideas into fully developed technical drawings.

Then the entire production moved across the Atlantic to England.

Just as well, because the Polaris offices on Central Park West were getting pretty crowded. Kubrick's assistant Ray Lovejoy had arrived from London, along with executive producer Victor Lyndon; Roger Caras was gearing up for his lengthy publicity campaign (he'd just quit Columbia after ten years' service in order to join the *2001* team) and various artists and draughtsmen were also on hand, as Tony Masters' creative empire expanded. Artists Richard McKenna and Roy Carnon were already churning out colour pre-production artwork. Later on, space artist Robert McCall would come on board and create his memorable series of publicity illustrations: in particular, his famous space station poster.

By the end of June 1965 most of the crew had transferred to the giant MGM production facility in Borehamwood, north London. Kubrick stayed on in America for another couple of months, and Ordway tied up the remaining schedule of consultancy deals until early August, but by the end of that summer everybody's feet were planted firmly in England. Lange and Ordway ploughed through their great swathes of material: the twenty heavy trunkloads of data which they had shipped over on the S.S. *France*. The special effects teams began gearing up for their long months in harness under the direction of Wally Veevers, Con Pederson, and MGM's in-house expert Tom Howard. (Wally Gentleman was on hand for a while, but retired early with an illness. He wasn't very complimentary about *2001* in subsequent interviews.) Kubrick also hired a very young and enthusiastic Canadian lad called Douglas Trumbull to do a few bits and pieces of artwork.

Tony Masters supervised as the first of the many impressive interior sets started rising up from the studio floors. Harry Lange set about translating the ideas he had come up with into models that could be photographed convincingly. The set designers needed to know very urgently what the *exteriors* were supposed to look like, so that live-action photography would tie in smoothly. There was a constant interchange of information between all the various departments. Plenty of lively lunchtime meetings resulted from the often complicated business of getting everyone working in the same direction. All kinds of animated discussions would break out about the realism or relevance of this or that design, so that even Kubrick, that stickler for authenticity, was occasionally to be heard reminding his overheated experts that this wasn't real—it was only a *movie*.

Lange assembled a team of modelmakers and began the difficult business of turning his drawings into convincing three-dimensional objects. The principal challenge was that the models had to be super-detailed. Kubrick wanted to be able to shoot them from all interesting angles, at all scales and speeds, so that he could choose the best sequences later on during the editing process. Consequently, he demanded that the models look perfect, no matter how close the camera came. In response, Lange decided to use plastic kit components for fine detailing on engines, or in little nooks and crannies.

But the model kits they made so much use of were no cop-out solution. Basic hulls for the vehicles were hand-crafted in wood and fibreglass or custom-moulded plastic. Certain elements had to be fabricated in what amounted to a factory environment: in particular, the *Discovery*'s three massive propulsion housings, her six exhaust nozzles and thirty-odd storage modules (divided among ten vertebrated boom segments) and her nuclear power module with its mass of tiny pipes and gizmos. These separate units were produced with careful attention to consistent detailing. Here in particular, imaginative cannibalization of model kits proved very helpful.

The command module sphere at the front of *Discovery* was a fibreglass ball six feet in diameter. Another plastic sphere was moulded with a diameter that was wider by just fractions of an inch. From this thin-skinned ball, strips were cut to provide a layer of stick-on "panels" for the fibreglass shell. Extra detailing was provided by metal foils and adhesive papers with varying textures. The main model ended up fifty-four feet long. A smaller model for long-shots came in at a still impressive fifteen feet.

The rotating space station owed its shape to the most serious proposals made by Lange's illustrious colleague and friend at NASA, Wernher von Braun. Lange and Kubrick agreed on the famous two-wheel shape so that the rear part of the station could be seen as if still under construction by space workers, with ribs and girders exposed. The eight-foot-diameter model was stuffed full of tiny lightbulbs which glowed behind all the windows of the station's front wheel. There were no fibre optics or LEDs in those days. As often as not, shooting would be interrupted when heat from all the tiny elements threatened to melt and buckle the structure.

The three-foot-diameter *Aries* lunar shuttle vehicle had motorized legs which extended as it came in to land. (Ordway, Caras and others made a special trip to the Grumman plant at Bethpage, New York, to see the emerging Lunar Module's legs under construction.) Compressed air jets in the exhaust nozzles kicked up dust on touchdown, to convincing effect.

At the height of all this construction effort, 103 modelmakers were employed on various projects. They came from all kinds of specialist disciplines. There were boat builders, architectural students, fine artists, sculptors, lithographers, metalworkers, and even some ivory carvers fresh off a whaling boat. This minor army was employed largely on a freelance basis on short-term contracts. Turn-over was high, as more and more of them failed to satisfy the exacting demands of the production's seniors. The only ones who stood the course were the extremely skilled perfectionists, all of whom had to possess the additional quality of being immune to the shocks and disappointments of suddenly having to scrap several weeks' worth of work and start again. This happened quite frequently: the designs were often being altered right up until the very last moment before the models were set in front of the cameras.

Full-size space pods, pressure suits and helmets required the services of independent industrial companies. The suits were manufactured by a well-respected Manchester firm, Frankenstein (Air and Sea Rescue, Division of). The helmets were moulded by a London company, Master Models, along with chest packs and several spacecraft inner shells. The British Hawker Siddeley aircraft company produced pod interiors and instrument layouts to specifications that were so exacting, they might just as well have been working on a genuine aerospace contract. Hawker's team leader Arthur Cole remembers:

> "We were contracted to provide consultancy during the early stages of production, and our responsibility was communications systems, voice, video, radar, navigation and control systems, attitude and orbit, remote manipulators and so on. Between us we derived many instrument layouts and provided advice on the likely shape of various structural features such as antennas, propulsion and control jets, and relevant hatch and docking systems."

Kubrick believed that if *2001* was to be credible on a technical level, then no detail was *too small to consider*. Of course there was the entirely separate problem of whether or not this mass of engineering input could ensure the movie's *historical* plausibility. As we shall see, the world outside Kubrick's studio was changing in ways too complex and subtle to be analysed by even the cleverest Hawker Siddeley expert.

For all her magnificent astronautical realism, *Discovery's* true-life equivalents couldn't expect to be in operation as soon as the year 2001;

and by 1967 this was already becoming evident to some observers of the space business, as the U.S. Congress began for the first time to slash at NASA's budget with a vengeance. However, the optimism of Kubrick's technologists seemed unquenchable. Perhaps, like their counterparts at Cape Kennedy, they were just *too busy* in their intense and closed-off little world to notice Vietnam, Martin Luther King, LSD, the Counter-Culture...?

That September of 1965 though, Ordway's problem on *2001* was the sheer volume of data streaming in from companies like Hawker and its giant American cousins. He was caught in the middle, between Kubrick's ceaseless demands for up-to-the-minute realism and the growing urgency of the production schedule. Everybody was scrabbling to get things ready for the start of main filming by the turn of that year, and all departments were stretched to their very limits.

Suddenly, Kubrick and Clarke decided over a cosy dinner that it might be nice for *Discovery* to go to Saturn instead of Jupiter, so that the planet's ring system could be shown, and Ordway was instructed to come up with a detailed memo outlining current knowledge about Saturn. Clarke loved this new idea so much that he retained Saturn as the destination planet in his novel. He wanted to demonstrate the "perturbation" manoeuvre, whereby the spacecraft would use Jupiter's gravitational field to fling it towards Saturn. Kubrick, for his part, was keen on the rings. So it was agreed. *Discovery* would go to Saturn. But the special effects department was horrified, and spent several tense weeks getting this decision reversed. They'd already spent three hectic months preparing for a visit to Jupiter, and were up against deadline on dozens of different aspects of the movie. They were alarmed at the prospect of having to throw in a Saturnian ring system at short notice (though Trumbull, perhaps pursuing "unfinished business," did just that in his own film, *Silent Running*, in 1972). Lange's team narrowly avoided having to reconfigure *Discovery* yet again. A new mission profile might have involved different engines, fuel pods and so on. Just for once, Kubrick *wasn't* going to get his way.

Or was he? At the end of October, Kubrick became fascinated by a research project called *Orion*, being undertaken by the physicist Freeman Dyson (from Princeton's Institute for Advanced Study) which involved powering a spaceship with pulsed energy from miniaturized nuclear explosions. A giant buffer plate would smooth out the shocks.

Models a few feet long were already being launched a few feet into the air using conventional explosives. Eventually a nuclear treaty would ban the use of such systems; but just then, Kubrick loved the idea that *bombs* should power us to the stars. So *Discovery* was redesigned. Then Kubrick worried, probably quite rightly, that a bomb-driven ship might make too many people think about *Dr. Strangelove*, and anyway, the idea of a spaceship put-put-putting its way across the solar system seemed rather too comical. The redesign was cancelled. (Project *Orion*'s memory survives: the spaceplane bears that name.)

By December 1965, only days away from the start of principal photography, Ordway was frustrated enough to write in his diary:

> We are continually facing difficulties of decision-making.... Whatever U.S. industry comes up with doesn't always please Stanley.... Many design aspects of the vehicles for the film change so regularly that it becomes impossible at times to finalize anything.... The screenplay has a decided tendency to change rather rapidly, even as we are moving forward.... Film experts tell me this is highly unorthodox and produces more difficulties than necessary.

Then there was the occasion when Clarke and Kubrick took a look at the *Orion* flight deck set, and Clarke remarked in passing that it reminded him slightly of a Chinese restaurant. "That kills it for me," Kubrick said, and ordered an immediate redesign of the set. Clarke jotted a chastened note in his diary that he "must keep away from the Art Department for a few days."

The search for perfection was merciless. Mr. H. R. Premaratne was a talented engineer and Clarke's personal assistant at the time. Like many people who worked on the production, he regards his *2001* experience as having been a real adventure, and something to be proud of. But there were obviously some difficult times during the long struggle to get things right:

> I well remember the number of times we detailed the *Discovery* command module, when Mr. Kubrick would come along and, after a critical examination, would order scrapping the whole thing and re-doing it, this time using more convincing materials. Of course we worked under Harry [Lange]'s direction, and when we finally finished the

whole thing, giving it a metallic finish using grained silver adhesive paper, complete with details, it was given a coat of paint obliterating all the metallic effect.

One can surmise that this rethink was the result of NASA's increasing use of ceramics, resins and exotic compounds on their space vehicles. The polished steel skins of traditional sci-fi spaceships were gone forever. But the consequence of all this heartbreaking effort was that *Discovery* would still look convincing thirty years later. (Incidentally, Mr. Premaratne went on to become Sri Lanka's ambassador to Burma. Clarke has wondered which he might have found more difficult: international diplomacy, or working for Stanley Kubrick.)

By and large, of course, everybody was having the time of their lives. The difficulties only added to the fun. And love him or hate him *at the time*, many voices today will testify to Kubrick's perfectionism as the driving engine of their own best work.

The final product of nearly three years' intense effort at Borehamwood was the most realistic space fiction film ever made, bar none. By any standards, *2001* still looks convincing today. In the 1960s, of course, there'd never been anything like it. Senior NASA *Apollo* administrator George Mueller paid a visit to the studios, along with astronaut chief Deke Slayton, and was light-heartedly shocked by all the hardware and detailed documentation piling up everywhere. Mueller dubbed Kubrick's empire "NASA East." Slayton is said to have remarked, "You must've been conned by a used-capsule salesman."

Obviously this not-so-fantastical project was getting things more or less right. Except, maybe, for one thing: a visiting Soviet dignitary, after expressing guarded enthusiasm, looked at all the control panels and said, without the slightest trace of a smile: "Of course, you know all these instructions should be in Russian?"

The *alien* artifacts, however, proved to be even more of a problem than the terrestrial spaceships. Black monoliths were easy enough to describe on paper, but not so easy to film convincingly. Chunks of rock were cut, polished and photographed—only to end up looking like useless chunks of rock. That extra "something" was missing. Painted wooden and plastic structures showed up every warp and flaw under the lights. Matted artwork also failed.

At last a credible technique was devised by which a blacker-than-black finish could be produced on a truly smooth surface. A heavy wooden monolith was sanded, rubbed, sanded again. Then a mixture of black paint and pencil graphite was applied—and rubbed down, applied and rubbed down, over and over, till the slab glowed with an eerie blackness. It shone like silk, yet sucked up light like a black hole. It had a surface texture like nothing on Earth (after all, pencil graphite is not a common element of everyday paint finishes).

Touching this immaculate surface on set with greasy fingers was proclaimed a capital offence. Between scenes, the twelve-foot-high artifact, with its sensitive skin, was swaddled in thick layers of plastic sheeting and cotton wool. Many months would separate its starring performances: in the little clearing outside the apemen's cave; in its trench several metres below the lunar surface; and finally in the dazzling white hotel room. (The slab floating in space above Jupiter was a "miniature.")

Kubrick had wanted to be even more ambitious than this. He had wanted shimmering multi-faceted pictures to appear, deep within a transparent crystalline pillar, as though it was literally showing its primitive pupils the way to a better life. Today, advertisers and movie-makers regularly make use of computer-generated fractal surfaces, glassy reflections and so forth. Kubrick had none of these toys to play with. He decided to experiment by projecting images into slabs of clear perspex, trying to make use of internal reflections. At great expense, a very large and precise block of "Lucite" was moulded by an outside contractor and brought on stage. The newspapers heralded it, probably correctly, as the largest and most precise casting of transparent plastic the world had ever seen. Unfortunately it wasn't optically pure enough to provide the required effect. The perspex experiment was abandoned, very much to the disappointment of the block's all-too-terrestrial manufacturers.

And so it was that a featureless black rectangular box managed to persuade us that we were looking at a sophisticated mechanism from another world. It was the boldest of *2001*'s rich array of illusions. The sheer simplicity of the image, born out of countless experimental failures with more complex ideas, turned out to be just right.

FILMING/
POSTPRODUCTION

There is nothing we wanted to do we couldn't do or wouldn't do. Stanley would say, "If you can describe it, I can film it."

—Arthur C. Clarke, quoted in *Newsweek*

.

First Day of Shooting

Hawk Films Ltd. Amended

CALL SHEET No. 4 (a)

PRODUCTION "2001: A SPACE ODYSSEY" Date: Wednesday
29th December '65

Where Working: Shepperton—STAGE H.
UNIT CALL 8:30 A.M. TMA-1 Excavation Site

Artiste	Character	Portable Dressing Room	Makeup	Ready on set
William Sylvester	Floyd	3 (OH29)	7:45	9:00
Robert Beatty	Halvorsen	6 (OH46)	8:00	9:00
Sean Sullivan	Michaels	10 (OH24)	8:00	9:00
Burnell Tucker	Photographer	2 (OH25)	7:45	9:00
John Swindell	1st Technician	1 (OH25)	7:30	9:00
John Clifford	2nd Technician	1 (OH25)	7:30	9:00
STANDINS:				
John Francis	for Mr. Sullivan		8:00	8:30
Eddie Milburn	for Mr. Beatty		8:00	8:30
Gerry Judge	for Mr. Sylvester		8:00	8:30
Brian Chuter	for Mr. Tucker		8:00	8:30
Tom Sheppard	for Mr. Swindell		8:00	8:30
Robin Dawson- Whisker	for Mr. Clifford		8:00	8:30

SOUND
(1) P. A. System required from 8:30 a.m.
(2) 2 Loud Hailers required from 8:30 a.m.

WARDROBE
(1) Coveralls for all Artistes.
(2) White overalls and crash helmets for Standins.
(3) Floyd's suit for Sc. C150.

PRACTICAL ELECTRICIANS
(1) Heating on Stage H, portable dressing rooms, huts and offices from 7:30 a.m.
(2) On no account should the heating in the Camera Room be switched off over the Christmas period.

CATERING
(1) Breaks in the Tea Hut at 10:00 a.m. and 3:30 p.m. please.
(2) Urns of Bovril and Coffee to be ready for collection at 8:30 a.m. and a constant refill supply to be available please.

PROPS
(1) As per script to include Photographer's camera and equipment.
(2) Please collect the Bovril and Coffee from the Canteen at 8:00 a.m. and thereafter maintain the supply.
(3) Provide litter bins and large ashtrays for set.
(4) Standby with repeat air bottles for space suits.

N.B. TO ALL CONCERNED
(1) In an effort to keep the Stage reasonably warm at all times, will members of the Unit please ensure that the Stage doors are kept shut. If it becomes necessary at any time to open the doors, please advise the Assistant Director.
(2) Please keep the set free of litter and use the bins provided.

SCENE NUMBERS
B42 B38 B44 B46
TV MONITOR MATERIAL FOR SC. NOS. B45 & C151
STANDBY SC. C150

STANDBY SET:
INT. FLOYD'S RECORDED BRIEFING: SC. NO. C150—STAGE K

William Sylvester	Floyd	From above.

TRANSPORT:	Camera, Sound, Prop and Wardrobe vehicles as arranged by departments. Unit Coach will leave M-G-M Studios at 7:05 a.m. sharp.	
LUNCH:	12:45–1:45 p.m.	DEREK CRACKNELL
RUSHES:	Theatre 4–12:45 p.m.	ASSISTANT DIRECTOR

Monoliths and Manuscripts

Arthur C. Clarke

I still have the call sheet for that first day's work at Shepperton on a freezing December 29, 1965. For sentimental reasons—and because it is surely of interest even to the benighted inhabitants of that limbo once called (by one of Hollywood's lady dragons) the "non-celluloid world"—I would like to reproduce it here [see pp. 58–59]. There are few better ways of conveying the behind-the-scenes work that went into every frame of the movie.

My diary records that first day in some detail:

December 29, 1965. The TMA 1 set is huge—the stage is the second largest in Europe, and very impressive. A 150 × 50 × 20-foot hole, with equipment scattered around it. (E.g. neat little electric-powered excavators, bulldozers, etc. which could *really* work on the Moon!) About a hundred technicians were milling around. I spent some time with Stanley, reworking the script—in fact we continued through lunch together. I also met the actors, and felt quite the proper expert when they started asking me astronomical questions. I stayed until 4 p.m.—no actual shooting by then, but they were getting near it. The spacesuits, back-packs, etc. are beautifully done, and TMA 1 is quite impressive—though someone had smeared the black finish and Stanley went on a rampage when I pointed it out to him.

The jet-black slab of the monolith was, of course, an extraordinarily difficult object to light and photograph—and the scene would certainly have been wrecked if naked fingerprints had appeared on the ebon surface, even *before* it had been touched by the gloved hands of the astronauts. (Five years later, in the Smithsonian, I was able to flex my own fingers inside the very glove which had first made contact with the surface of the Moon.)

The famous monolith, which has caused so much controversy and bafflement, was itself the end product of a considerable evolution. In the beginning, the alien artifact had been a black tetrahedron—the simplest and most fundamental of all regular solids, formed of four equal triangles. It was a shape which inspired all sorts of philosophical and scientific speculations (Kepler's cosmography, the carbon atom, Buckminster Fuller's geodesic structures...), and the art department constructed models of various sizes which were set in African and lunar landscapes. But somehow, they never looked right, and there was also the danger that they would arouse wholly irrelevant associations with the pyramids.

For a while, Stanley considered using a transparent cube, but it proved impossible to make one of the required size. So he settled on the rectangular shape, and obtained a three-ton block of lucite—the largest ever cast. Unfortunately, that also looked unconvincing, so it was banished to a corner of the studio and a completely black slab of the same dimensions was substituted. I frantically followed—and occasionally anticipated—all these changes on my typewriter, but must admit that I had a considerably easier job than the Props Department.

Despite such problems as birds (or were they bats?) invading the gigantic stage and flying across the lunar landscape, Stanley completed shooting before the one-week deadline. The monolith was carefully wrapped in cotton wool, and stored in a safe place until it would be needed again—a year or so later, for the confrontation in the final hotel-room sequence. The unit went back to the Borehamwood studios, and I continued to beat out my brains....

January 7, 1966. Realized last night that the Star Gate had to be Iapetus with its six-to-one brightness ratio. Got off a memo to Stan about that.

January 8. Record day—three thousand words, including some of the most exciting in the book. I got quite scared when the computer started going nuts, being alone in the house with my electric typewriter....

January 14. Completed the Inferno chapter and have got Bowman into the hotel room. Now to get him out of it.

January 16. Long talk with Stan and managed to resolve most of the outstanding plot points. Got straight to work and by the time I staggered to bed stupefied had at last almost completed the first draft of the final sequence. Now I really feel the end's in sight—but I've felt *that* twice before.

January 17. About midday got a first draft of the last chapters completed. Have had a headache ever since and my brain's still spinning around. Too exhausted to feel much pleasure—only relief. Trying to unwind all day; luckily I'm off to the studio tomorrow, which will be a break.

January 18. Lord Snowdon on the set, shooting Stanley from all angles for *Life*.

January 19. Stanley phoned to say that he was very happy with the last chapters and feels that the story is now "rock-hard." Delighted, I tried to pin him down at once to agree that the existing version could be typed and sent off to our agent.

February 2. Spent all day with Stan—developed a few new ideas but of course there are endless interruptions, e.g. Gary Lockwood and Keir Dullea with makeup tests (we want them to look thirty-five-ish). I have a sore throat and incipient cold, so Stan kept me at arm's length.

February 4. Saw a screening of a demonstration film in which Stan has spliced together a few scenes to give the studio heads some idea of what's going on. He'd used Mendelssohn's *Midsummer Night's Dream* for the weightless scenes, and Vaughan Williams' *Antarctica Symphony* for the lunar sequence and the Star Gate special effects, with stunning results. I reeled out convinced that we have a masterpiece on our hands—if Stan can keep it up.

A few days after this, I escaped to Ceylon. But not for long:

March 15. Cable from Stan asking for "three minutes of poetic Clarkian narration" about HAL's breakdown. Got it off to him by express in the afternoon. [It was never used....] Also started on the $(last)^n$ revision, and made good progress.

March 20. Worked hard on the novel all day, and by 9 p.m. had completed the messy final draft (what, again!).

April 2. Inserted a couple of hundred final (?) words into the MS, and tucked it away. As far as I'm concerned, it's finished.

Alas, it wasn't. A couple of days later I flew from Ceylon to Lawrence, Kansas, for the centennial celebrations of the University of Kansas. I cabled Stanley to say that I was heading back to London to make final arrangements for the publication of the novel. He replied "Don't bother—it's not ready yet." I retorted that I was coming anyway, and did:

April 19. First full day back at studio—saw shooting in the centrifuge. A portentous spectacle, accompanied by terrifying noises and popping lamp bulbs. Stanley came in during a shooting break and himself raised the subject of publication date. On being challenged, he swore that he didn't want to hold up the novel until release of the movie. He explained that general release would not be until late in 1967 or even 1968. Even if the first showing is in April 1967 [it was actually April 1968] it will be running only in a few Cinerama houses, which will give us some more breathing space.

April 23. Drove with Roger Caras and Mike Wilson to an excellent private zoo near Nuneaton, which had all the big apes. Mike had a very hard time filming the chimps, who kept dashing around and throwing themselves at the camera. I was a bit nervous of the baby gorilla, as it was inclined to nibble with most impressive teeth.... An enjoyable day, and I hope it's given me some ideas about Moon-Watcher and Co.

May 29. Soviet Air Attaché visited set. He looked at all the little instruction plaques on the spaceship panels and said, with a straight face, "You realize, of course, that these should all be in Russian."

At the end of May I flew back to the United States to assist with general promotion on the movie, and did my best to placate the anxious executives of MGM when they asked, "What *is* Stanley up to?" I also paid my first visit to Cape Kennedy, in a very small VIP guided tour conducted by James Webb, the NASA Administrator, to watch the launch of Gemini IX. Like every visitor, I was overwhelmed by the Vehicle Assembly Building and that land-going ship; the 3,000-ton crawler-transporter, with its maximum speed (unloaded) of two miles an hour. I recall watching Representative George Miller, Chairman of the House Committee on Astronautics, as he tried out the controls of the crawler—and warning him not to exceed the speed limit, because Chief Justice Warren was standing right behind him.

Unfortunately, the Atlas-Agena target vehicle, with which Gemini IX was supposed to rendezvous, failed to go into orbit, and so the manned launch was canceled. I admired Administrator Webb's resilience as he took this in his stride and promptly turned to Congressman Miller with the remark, "I'm afraid I'll have to go back to your committee for more money."

The next month, I was once again in London, still trying to convince Stanley that the novel was finished and the MS could go out to market. During one of my more frantic arguments, he remarked, "Things are never as bad as they seem," but I was in no mood to agree.

Stanley's attitude was that he wanted to do some more work on the manuscript, and simply didn't have time because of the overwhelming pressure at the studio. (It *was* overwhelming, and I was continually awed by Stanley's ability to cope with a dozen simultaneous and interlocking crises, any one of which could cost half a million dollars. No wonder he is fascinated by Napoleon....) But I maintained that *I* was the writer and he should rely on my judgment; what would he say if I wanted to edit the film?

In the end we decided on a compromise—Stanley's. He would attempt, during odd moments in the bathroom, or while being ferried home in his Rolls-Royce at the maximum permitted speed of 30 m.p.h., to note down the improvements he wanted me to make. On this basis, Scott Meredith was finally able to draw up an excellent contract with Delacorte Press.

Stanley was as good as his word. I still have a nine-page memorandum of thirty-seven paragraphs, dated June 18, 1966, containing some very acute, and occasionally acerbic, observations:

1. Can you use the word "veldt" in a drought-stricken area?
6. Where do you find bees in a drought-stricken area? What do the bees live on?
9. Do leopards growl?

11. Can a leopard carry a man?

14. Since the book will be coming out before the picture [*sic!*] I don't see why we shouldn't put something in the book that would be preferable if it were achievable in the film. I wish the block had been crystal-clear but it was impossible to make. I would like to have the block black in the novel.

15. I don't think the verb "twittering" seems right. We must decide how these fellows talk.

19. This reference sounds a little bit like a scene from *Bambi.*

22. The literal description of these tests seems completely wrong to me. It takes away all the magic.

24. This scene has always seemed unreal to me and somewhat inconceivable. They will be saved from starvation but they will never become gorged, sleek, glossy-pelted, and content. This has barely happened in 1966. I think that one day the cube should disappear and that Moon-Watcher and his boys passing a large elephant's skeleton which they have seen many times before on the way to forage are suddenly drawn to these bones and begin moving them and swinging them, and that this whole scene is given some magical enchantment both in the writing and then ultimately in the filming, and that from this scene they approach the grazing animals which they usually share fodder with and kill one, etc.

27. I don't understand the meaning of this.

33. I prefer the previous version.... The expression "moons waxed and waned" seems terribly cliché. The expression "toothless thirty-year-olds died" also is a bit awful.

37. I think this is a very bad chapter and should not be in the book. It is pedantic, undramatic and destroys the beautiful transition from man-ape to 2001.

Lest these extracts give a false impression, I should also add that the memorandum contained several highly flattering comments which modesty has forced me to omit. In fact, Stanley sometimes overdid this. He would build up my morale (which often needed it) by unstinted praise of some piece of writing I'd just produced; then, in the course of the next few days, he would find more and more flaws until the whole thing was slowly whittled away. This was all part of his ceaseless search for perfection, which often provoked me to remind him of the aphorism, "No work of art is ever finished; it is only abandoned."

I am afraid I was prepared to abandon ship before he was; but I admired him for his tenacity, even when I wished it was not focused upon me.

Matters came to a climax in the summer of 1966, and I find this pathetic entry in my log:

> *July 19*. Almost all memory of the weeks of work at the Hotel Chelsea seems to have been obliterated, and there are versions of the book that I can hardly remember. I've lost count (fortunately) of the revisions and blind alleys. It's all rather depressing—I only hope the ultimate result is worth it.

The reason for this gloom was understandable. Stanley had refused to sign the contract—after Delacorte had set the book in type and taken an impressive two-page advertisement in *Publisher's Weekly*. He still argued that he wasn't satisfied with the manuscript and wanted to do some more work on it. I considered writing to Dr. Leakey to get the name of a good witchdoctor, and Scott Meredith bought some pins and wax. Delacorte and Co., fighting back corporate tears, broke up the type. I have always felt extremely grateful to them for their forbearance in this difficult matter, and am happy to have given them a modest best seller in *Time Probe*.

It was just as well that no one dreamed that another two years would pass before the book was finally published, by New American Library in the summer of 1968—months after the release of the movie. In the long run, everything came out all right—exactly as Stanley had predicted.

But I can think of easier ways of earning a living.

How About a Little Game?

Jeremy Bernstein

On pleasant afternoons, I often go into Washington Square Park to watch the Master at work. The Master is a professional chess player—a chess hustler, if you will. He plays for fifty cents a game; if you win, you get the fifty, and if he wins, he gets it. In case of a draw, no money changes hands. The Master plays for at least eight hours a day, usually seven days a week; in the winter he plays indoors in one or another of the Village coffeehouses. It is a hard way to make a living, even if you win all your games; the Master wins most of his, although I have seen him get beaten several games straight. It is impossible to cheat in chess, and the only hustle that the Master perpetrates is to make his opponents think they are better than they are. When I saw him one day recently, he was at work on what in the language of the park is called a "potzer"—a relatively weak player with an inflated ego. A glance at the board showed that the Master was a rook and a pawn up on his adversary—a situation that would cause a rational man to resign the game at once. A potzer is not rational (otherwise, he would have avoided the contest in the first place), and this one was determined to fight it out to the end. He was moving pawns wildly, and his hands were beginning to tremble. Since there is no one to blame but yourself, nothing is more rankling than a defeat in chess, especially if you are under the illusion that you are better than your opponent. The Master, smiling as seraph-ically as his hawklike, angular features would allow, said, "You always were a good pawn player—especially when it comes to pushing them," which his deluded opponent took to be a compliment. At a rook and four pawns down, the potzer gave up, and a new game began.

My acquaintance with the Master goes back several years, but it was only recently that I learned of a connection between him and another man I know—the brilliant and original film-maker Stanley Kubrick, who has been responsible for such movies as *Paths of Glory, Lolita,* and *Dr. Strangelove.* The Master is not much of a moviegoer—his profes-sional activities leave little time for it—and, as far as I know, he has never seen one of Kubrick's pictures. But his recollection of Kubrick is nonetheless quite distinct, reaching back to the early nineteen-fifties, when Kubrick, then in his early twenties (he was born in New York City on July 26, 1928), was also squeezing out a small living (he esti-mates about three dollars a day, "which goes a long way if all you are buying with it is food") by playing chess for cash in Washington Square. Kubrick was then living on Sixteenth Street, off Sixth Avenue, and on nice days in the spring and summer he would wander into the park around noon and take up a position at one of the concrete chess tables near Macdougal and West Fourth streets. At nightfall, he would change tables to get one near the street light. "If you made the switch the right way," he recalls, "you could get a table in the shade during the day and one nearer the fountain, under the lights, at night." There was a hard core of perhaps ten regulars who came to play every day and, like Kubrick, put in about twelve hours at the boards, with interrup-tions only for food. Kubrick ranked himself as one of the stronger reg-ulars. When no potzers or semi-potzers were around, the regulars played each other for money, offering various odds to make up for any disparities in ability. The best player, Arthur Feldman, gave Kubrick a pawn—a small advantage—and, as Kubrick remembers it, "he didn't make his living off me." The Master was regarded by the regulars as a semi-potzer—the possessor of a flashy but fundamentally unsound game that was full of pseudo traps designed to enmesh even lesser potzers and to insure the quickest possible win, so that he could collect his bet and proceed to a new customer.

At that time, Kubrick's nominal non-chess-playing occupation (when he could work at it) was what it is now—making films. Indeed, by the time he was twenty-seven he had behind him a four-year career as a staff photographer for *Look,* followed by a five-year career as a film-maker, during which he had made two short features and two full-length films—*Fear and Desire* (1953) and *Killer's Kiss* (1955). By all sociological odds, Kubrick should never have got into the motion-picture business in the first place. He comes from an American Jewish family of Austro-Hungarian ancestry. His father is a doctor, still in active practice, and he grew up in comfortable middle-class surroundings in the Bronx. If all had gone according to form, Kubrick would have attended college and probably ended up as a doctor or a physicist—physics being the only subject he showed the slightest aptitude for in school. After four desultory years at Taft High School, in the Bronx, he graduated, with a 67 average, in 1945, the year in which colleges were flooded with returning servicemen. No college in the United States would even consider his application. Apart from everything else, Kubrick had failed English outright one year, and had had to make it up in the summer. In his recollection, high-school English courses consisted of sitting behind a book while the teacher would say, "Mr. Kubrick, when Silas Marner walked out of the door, what did he see?," followed by a prolonged silence caused by the fact that Kubrick hadn't read *Silas Marner,* or much of anything else.

When Kubrick was twelve, his father taught him to play chess, and when he was thirteen, his father, who is something of a camera bug, presented him with his first camera. At the time, Kubrick had hopes of becoming a jazz drummer and was seriously studying the technique, but he soon decided that he wanted to be a photographer, and instead of doing his schoolwork he set out to teach himself to become one. By the time he left high school, he had sold *Look* two picture stories—one of them, ironically, about an English teacher at Taft, Aaron Traister, who had succeeded in arousing Kubrick's interest in Shakespeare's plays by acting out all the parts in class. After high school, Kubrick registered for night courses at City College, hoping to obtain a B average so that he could transfer to regular undergraduate courses, but before he started going to classes, he was back at *Look* with some more pictures. The picture editor there, Helen O'Brian, upon hearing of his academic troubles, proposed that he come to *Look* as an apprentice photographer. "So I backed into a fantastically good job at the age of seventeen," Kubrick says. Released from the bondage of schoolwork, he also began to read everything that he could lay his hands on. In retrospect, he feels that not going to college and having had the four years to practice photography at *Look* and to read on his own was probably the most fortunate thing that ever happened to him.

It was while he was still at *Look* that Kubrick became a film-maker. An incessant moviegoer, he had seen the entire film collection of the Museum of Modern Art at least twice when he learned from a friend, Alex Singer (now also a movie director), that there was apparently a fortune to be made in producing short documentaries. Singer was working as an office boy at the March of Time and had learned—or thought he had learned—that his employers were spending forty thousand dollars to produce eight or nine minutes of film. Kubrick was extremely impressed by the number of dollars being spent per foot, and even more impressed when he learned, from phone calls to Eastman Kodak and various equipment-rental companies, that the cost of buying and developing film and renting camera equipment would allow him to make nine minutes of film, complete with an original musical score, for only about a thousand dollars. "We assumed," Kubrick recalls, "that the March of Time must have been selling their films at a profit, so if we could make a film for a thousand dollars, we couldn't lose our investment." Thus bolstered, he used his savings from the *Look* job to make a documentary about the middleweight boxer Walter Cartier, about whom he had previously done a picture story for *Look*. Called *Day of the Fight*, it was filmed with a rented spring-wound thirty-five millimetre Eyemo camera and featured a musical score by Gerald Fried, a friend of Kubrick's who is now a well-known composer for the movies. Since Kubrick couldn't afford any professional help, he took care of the whole physical side of the production himself; essentially, this consisted of screwing a few ordinary photofloods into existing light fixtures. When the picture was done—for thirty-nine hundred dollars—Kubrick set out to sell it for forty thousand. Various distributing companies liked it, but, as Kubrick now says ruefully, "we were offered things like fifteen hundred dollars and twenty-five hundred dollars. We told one distributor that the March of Time was getting forty thousand dollars for *its* documentaries, and he said, 'You must be crazy.' The next thing we knew, the March of Time went out of business." Kubrick was finally able to sell his short to R.K.O. Pathé for about a hundred dollars less than it had cost him to make it.

Kubrick, of course, got great satisfaction out of seeing his documentary at the Paramount Theatre, where it played with a Robert Mitchum–Ava Gardner feature. He felt that it had turned out well, and he figured that he would now instantly get innumerable offers from the movie industry—"of which," he says, "I got none, to do anything." After a while, however, he made a second short for R.K.O. (which put up fifteen hundred dollars for it, barely covering expenses), this one about a flying priest who travelled through the Southwest from one Indian parish to another in a Piper Cub. To work on the film, Kubrick quit his job at *Look,* and when the film was finished, he went back to waiting for offers of employment, spending his time playing chess for quarters in the park. He soon reached the reasonable conclusion that there simply wasn't any money to be made in producing documentaries and that there were no film jobs to be had. After thinking about the millions of dollars that were being spent on making feature films, he decided to make one himself. "I felt that I certainly couldn't make one worse than the ones I was seeing every week," he says. On the assumption that there were actors around who would work for practically nothing, and that he could act as the whole crew, Kubrick estimated that he could make a feature film for something like ten thousand dollars, and he was able to raise this sum from his father and an uncle, Martin Perveler. The script was put together by an acquaintance of Kubrick's in the Village, and, as Kubrick now describes it, it was an exceedingly serious, undramatic, and pretentious allegory. "With the exception of Frank Silvera, the actors were not very experienced," he says, "and I didn't know anything about directing *any* actors. I totally failed to realize what I didn't know." The film, *Fear and Desire,* was about four soldiers lost behind enemy lines and struggling to regain their identities as well as their home base, and it was full of lines like "We spend our lives looking for our real names, our permanent addresses." "Despite everything, the film got an art-house distribution," Kubrick says. "It opened at the Guild Theatre, in New York, and it even got a couple of fairly good reviews, as well as a compliment from Mark Van Doren. There were a few good moments in it. It never returned a penny on its investment."

Not at all discouraged, Kubrick decided that the mere fact that a film of his was showing at a theatre at all might be used as the basis for raising money to make a second one. In any case, it was not otherwise apparent how he was going to earn a living. "There were still no offers from anybody to do anything," he says. "So in about two weeks a friend and I wrote another script. As a contrast to the first one, this one, called *Killer's Kiss,* was nothing but action sequences, strung together on a mechanically constructed gangster plot."

Killer's Kiss was co-produced by Morris Bousel, a relative of Kubrick's who owned a drugstore in the Bronx. Released in September, 1955, it, too, failed to bring in any revenue (in a retrospective of his films at the Museum of Modern Art two summers ago, Kubrick would not let either of his first two films be shown, and he would probably be just as happy if the prints were to disappear altogether), so, broke and in debt to Bousel and others, Kubrick returned to Washington Square to play chess for quarters.

The scene now shifts to Alex Singer. While serving in the Signal Corps during the Korean War, Singer met a man named James B. Harris, who was engaged in making Signal Corps training films. The son of the owner of an extremely successful television-film-distribution company, Flamingo Films (in which he had a financial interest), Harris wanted to become a film producer when he returned to civilian life. As Harris recalls it, Singer told him about "some guy in the Village who was going around all by himself making movies," and after they got out of the Army, introduced him to Kubrick, who had just finished *Killer's Kiss.* Harris and Kubrick were both twenty-six, and they got on at once, soon forming Harris-Kubrick Pictures Corporation. From the beginning, it was an extremely fruitful and very happy association. Together they made *The Killing, Paths of Glory,* and *Lolita.* They were going to do *Dr. Strangelove* jointly, but before work began on it, Harris came to the conclusion that being just a movie producer was not a job with enough artistic fulfillment for him, and he decided to both produce and direct. His first film was *The Bedford Incident,* which Kubrick considers very well directed. For his part, Harris regards Kubrick as a cinematic genius who can do anything.

The first act of the newly formed Harris-Kubrick Pictures Corporation was to purchase the screen rights to *Clean Break,* a paperback thriller by Lionel White. Kubrick and a writer friend named Jim Thompson turned it into a screenplay, and the resulting film, *The Killing,* which starred Sterling Hayden, was produced in association with United Artists, with Harris putting up about a third of the production cost. While *The Killing,* too, was something less than a financial success, it was sufficiently impressive to catch the eye of Dore Schary, then head of production for M-G-M. For the first time, Kubrick received an offer to work for a major studio, and he and Harris were invited to look over all the properties owned by M-G-M and pick out something to do. Kubrick remembers being astounded by the mountains of stories that M-G-M owned. It took the pair of them two weeks simply to go through the alphabetical synopsis cards. Finally, they selected *The Burning Secret,* by Stefan Zweig, and Kubrick and Calder Willingham turned it into a screenplay—only to find that Dore Schary had lost his job as a result of a major shuffle at M-G-M. Harris and Kubrick left soon afterward. Sometime during the turmoil, Kubrick suddenly recalled having read *Paths of Glory,* by Humphrey Cobb, while still a high-school student. "It was one of the few books I'd read for pleasure in high school," he says. "I think I found it lying around my father's office and started to read it while waiting for him to get finished with a patient." Harris agreed that it was well worth a try. However, none of the major studios took the slightest interest in it. Finally, Kubrick's and Harris's agent, Ronnie Lubin, managed to interest Kirk Douglas in doing it, and this was enough to persuade United Artists to back the film, provided it was done on a very low budget in Europe. Kubrick, Calder Willingham, and Jim Thompson wrote the screenplay, and in January of 1957 Kubrick went to Munich to make the film.

Seeing *Paths of Glory* is a haunting experience. The utter desolation, cynicism, and futility of war, as embodied in the arbitrary execution of three innocent French soldiers who have been tried and convicted of cowardice during a meaningless attack on a heavily fortified German position, comes through with simplicity and power. Some of the dialogue is imperfect, Kubrick agrees, but its imperfection almost adds to the strength and sincerity of the theme. The finale of the picture involves a young German girl who has been captured by the French and is being forced to sing a song for a group of drunken French soldiers about to be sent back into battle. The girl is frightened, and the soldiers are brutal. She begins to sing, and the humanity of the moment reduces the soldiers to silence, and then to tears. In the film, the girl was played by a young and pretty German actress, Suzanne Christiane Harlan (known in Germany by the stage name Suzanne Christian), and a year after the film was made, she and Kubrick were married.

Christiane comes from a family of opera singers and stage personalities, and most of her life has been spent in the theatre; she was a ballet dancer before she became an actress, and currently she is a serious painter, in addition to managing the sprawling Kubrick household, which now includes three daughters. Later this month, she will have an exhibition at the Grosvenor Gallery, in London.

Paths of Glory was released in November, 1957, and although it received excellent critical notices and broke about even financially, it did not lead to any real new opportunities for Kubrick and Harris. Kubrick returned to Hollywood and wrote two new scripts, which were never used, and worked for six months on a Western for Marlon Brando, which he left before it went into production. (Ultimately, Brando directed it himself, and it became *One-Eyed Jacks.*) It was not until 1960 that Kubrick actually began working on a picture again. In that year, Kirk Douglas asked him to take over the direction of *Spartacus,* which Douglas was producing and starring in. Shooting had been under way for a week, but Douglas and Anthony Mann, his director, had had a falling out. On *Spartacus,* in contrast to all his other films, Kubrick had no legal control over the script or the final form of the movie. Although Kubrick did the cutting on *Spartacus,* Kirk Douglas had the final say as to the results, and the consequent confusion of points of view produced a film that Kubrick thinks could have been better.

While *Spartacus* was being edited, Kubrick and Harris bought the rights to Vladimir Nabokov's novel *Lolita.* There was immense pressure from all sorts of public groups not to make *Lolita* into a film, and for a while it looked as if Kubrick and Harris would not be able to raise the money to do it. In the end, though, the money was raised, and the film was made, in London. Kubrick feels that the weakness of the film was its lack of eroticism, which was inevitable. "The important thing in the novel is to think at the outset that Humbert is enslaved by his 'perversion,' " Kubrick says. "Not until the end, when Lolita is married and pregnant and no longer a nymphet, do you realize—along with Humbert—that he loves her. In the film, the fact that his sexual obsession could not be portrayed tended to imply from the start that he was in love with her."

It was the building of the Berlin Wall that sharpened Kubrick's interest in nuclear weapons and nuclear strategy, and he began to read everything he could get hold of about the bomb. Eventually, he decided that he had about covered the spectrum, and that he was not learning anything new. "When you start reading the analyses of nuclear strategy, they seem so thoughtful that you're lulled into a temporary sense of reassurance," Kubrick has explained. "But as you go deeper into it, and become more involved, you begin to realize that every one of these lines of thought leads to a paradox." It is this constant element of paradox in all the nuclear strategies and in the conventional attitudes toward them that Kubrick transformed into the principal theme of *Dr. Strangelove.* The picture was a new departure for Kubrick. His other films had involved putting novels on the screen, but *Dr. Strangelove,* though it did have its historical origins in *Red Alert,* a serious nuclear suspense story by Peter George, soon turned into an attempt to use a purely intellectual notion as the basis of a film. In this case, the intellectual notion was the inevitable paradox posed by following any of the nuclear strategies to their extreme limits. "By now, the bomb has almost no reality and has become a complete abstraction, represented by a few newsreel shots of mushroom clouds," Kubrick has said. "People react primarily to direct experience and not to abstractions; it is very rare to find anyone who can become emotionally involved with an abstraction. The longer the bomb is around without anything happening, the better the job that people do in psychologically denying its existence. It has become as abstract as the fact that we are all going to die someday, which we usually do an excellent job of denying. For this reason, most people have very little interest in nuclear war. It has become even less interesting as a problem than, say, city government, and the longer a nuclear event is postponed, the greater becomes the illusion that we are constantly building up security, like interest at the bank. As time goes on, the danger increases, I believe, because the thing becomes more and more remote in people's minds. No one can predict the panic that suddenly arises when all the lights go out—that indefinable something that can make a leader abandon his carefully laid plans. A lot of effort has gone into trying to imagine possible nuclear accidents and to protect against them. But whether the human imagination is really capable of encompassing all the subtle permutations and psychological variants of these possibilities, I doubt. The nuclear strategists who make up all those war scenarios are never as inventive as reality, and political and military leaders are never as sophisticated as they think they are."

Such limited optimism as Kubrick has about the long-range prospects of the human race is based in large measure on his hope that the rapid development of space exploration will change our views of ourselves and our world. Most people who have thought much about space travel have arrived at the somewhat ironic conclusion that there is a very close correlation between the ability of a civilization to make significant space voyages and its ability to learn to live with nuclear energy. Unless there are sources of energy that are totally beyond the ken of modern physics, it is quite clear that the only source at hand for really elaborate space travel is the nucleus. The chemical methods of combustion used in our present rockets are absurdly inefficient compared to nuclear power. A detailed study has been made of the possibilities of using nuclear explosions to propel large spaceships, and, from a technical point of view, there is no reason that this cannot be done; indeed, if we are to transport really large loads to, say, the planets, it is essential that it be done. Thus, any civilization that operates on the same laws of nature as our own will inevitably reach the point where it learns to explore space and to use nuclear energy about simultaneously. The question is whether there can exist any society with enough maturity to peacefully use the latter to perform the former. In fact, some of the more melancholy thinkers on this subject have come to the conclusion that the earth has never been visited by beings from outer space because no civilization has been able to survive its own technology. That there *are* extraterrestrial civilizations in some state of development is firmly believed by many astronomers, biologists, philosophers, physicists, and other rational people—a conclusion based partly on the vastness of the cosmos, with its billions of stars. It is presumptuous to suppose that we are its only living occupants. From a chemical and biological point of view, the processes of forming life do not appear so extraordinary that they should not have occurred countless times throughout the universe. One may try to imagine what sort of transformation would take place in human attitudes if intelligent life should be discovered elsewhere in our universe. In fact, this is what Kubrick has been trying to do in his latest project, *2001: A Space Odyssey*, which, in the words of Arthur C. Clarke, the co-author of its screenplay, "will be about the first contact"—the first human contact with extraterrestrial life.

It was Arthur Clarke who introduced me to Kubrick. A forty-eight-year-old Englishman who lives in Ceylon most of the time, Clarke is, in my opinion, by all odds the best science-fiction writer now operating. (He is also an accomplished skin diver, and what he likes about Ceylon, apart from the climate and the isolation, is the opportunities it affords him for underwater exploration.) Clarke, who is highly trained as a scientist, manages to combine scientific insights with a unique sense of nostalgia for worlds that man will never see, because they are so far in the past or in the future, or are in such a distant part of the cosmos. In his hands, inanimate objects like the sun and the moon take on an almost living quality. Personally, he is a large, good-natured man, and about the only egoist I know who makes conversation about himself somehow delightful. We met in New York a few years back, when he was working on a book about the future of scientific ideas and wanted to discuss some of the latest developments in physics, which I teach. Now I always look forward to his occasional visits, and when he called me up one evening two winters ago, I was very happy to hear from him. He lost no time in explaining what he was up to. "I'm working with Stanley Kubrick on the successor to *Dr. Strangelove*," he said. "Stanley is an amazing man, and I want you to meet him." It was an invitation not to be resisted, and Clarke arranged a visit to Kubrick soon afterward.

Kubrick was at that time living, on the Upper East Side, in a large apartment whose décor was a mixture of Christiane's lovely paintings, the effects of three rambunctious young children, and Kubrick's inevitable collection of cameras, tape recorders, and hi-fi sets. (There was also a short-wave radio, which he was using to monitor broadcasts from Moscow, in order to learn the Russian attitude toward Vietnam. Christiane once said that "Stanley would be happy with eight tape recorders and one pair of pants.") Kubrick himself did not conform at all to my expectations of what a movie mogul would look like. He is of medium height and has the bohemian look of a riverboat gambler or a Rumanian poet. (He has now grown a considerable beard, which gives his broad features a somewhat Oriental quality.) He had the vaguely distracted look of a man who is simultaneously thinking about a hard problem and trying to make everyday conversation. During our meeting, the phone rang incessantly, a messenger arrived at the door with a telegram or an envelope every few minutes, and children of various ages and sexes ran in and out of the living room. After a few attempts at getting the situation under control, Kubrick abandoned the place to the children, taking me into a small breakfast room near the kitchen. I was immediately impressed by Kubrick's immense intellectual curiosity. When he is working on a subject, he becomes completely immersed in it and appears to absorb information from all sides, like a sponge. In addition to writing a novel with Clarke, which was to be the basis of the script for *2001,* he was reading every popular and semipopular book on science that he could get hold of.

During our conversation, I happened to mention that I had just been in Washington Square Park playing chess. He asked me whom I had been playing with, and I described the Master. Kubrick recognized him immediately. I had been playing a good deal with the Master, and my game had improved to the point where I was almost breaking even with him, so I was a little stunned to learn that Kubrick had played the Master on occasion, and that in his view the Master was a potzer. Kubrick went on to say that he loved playing chess, and added, "How about a little game right now?" By pleading another appointment, I managed to stave off the challenge.

I next saw Kubrick at the end of the summer in London, where I had gone to a physicists' meeting and where he was in the process of organizing the actual filming of *2001.* I dropped in at his office in the M-G-M studio in Boreham Wood, outside London, one afternoon, and again was confronted by an incredible disarray—papers, swatches of materials to be used for costumes, photographs of actors who might be used to play astronauts, models of spaceships, drawings by his daughters, and the usual battery of cameras, radios, and tape recorders. Kubrick likes to keep track of things in small notebooks, and he had just ordered a sample sheet of every type of notebook paper made by a prominent paper firm—about a hundred varieties—which were spread out on a large table. We talked for a while amid the usual interruptions of messengers and telephone calls, and then he got back to the subject of chess: How about a little game right now? He managed to find a set of chessmen—it was missing some pieces, but we filled in for them with various English coins—and when he couldn't find a board he drew one up on a large sheet of paper. Sensing the outcome, I remarked that I had never been beaten five times in a row—a number that I chose more or less at random, figuring that it was unlikely that we would ever get to play five games.

I succeeded in losing two rapid games before Kubrick had to go back to London, where he and his family were living in a large apartment in the Dorchester Hotel. He asked me to come along and finish out the five games—the figure appeared to fascinate him—and as soon as he could get the girls off to bed and order dinner for Christiane, himself, and me sent up to the apartment, he produced a second chess set, with all the pieces and a genuine wooden board.

Part of the art of the professional chess player is to unsettle one's opponent as much as possible by small but legitimate annoying incidental activities, such as yawning, looking at one's watch, and snapping one's fingers softly—at all of which Kubrick is highly skilled. One of the girls came into the room and asked, "What's the matter with your friend?"

"He's about to lose another game," said Kubrick.

I tried to counter these pressures by singing "Moon River" over and over, but I lost the next two games. Then came the crucial fifth game, and by some miracle I actually won it. Aware that this was an important psychological moment, I announced that I had been hustling Kubrick and had dropped the first four games deliberately. Kubrick responded by saying that the poor quality of those games had lulled him into a temporary mental lapse. (In the course of making *Dr. Strangelove*, Kubrick had all but hypnotized George C. Scott by continually beating him at chess while simultaneously attending to the direction of the movie.) We would have played five more games on the spot, except that it was now two in the morning, and Kubrick's working day on the *2001* set began very early.

"The Sentinel," a short story by Arthur Clarke in which *2001* finds its genesis, begins innocently enough: "The next time you see the full moon high in the south, look carefully at its right-hand edge and let your eye travel upward along the curve of the disk. Round about two o'clock you will notice a small, dark oval: anyone with normal eyesight can find it quite easily. It is the great walled plain, one of the finest on the Moon, known as the Mare Crisium—the Sea of Crises." Then

Clarke adds, unobtrusively, "Three hundred miles in diameter, and almost completely surrounded by a ring of magnificent mountains, it had never been explored until we entered it in the late summer of 1996." The story and the style are typical of Clarke's blend of science and fantasy. In this case, an expedition exploring the moon uncovers, on the top of a mountain, a little pyramid set on a carefully hewed-out terrace. At first, the explorers suppose it to be a trace left behind by a primitive civilization in the moon's past. But the terrain around it, unlike the rest of the moon's surface, is free of all debris and craters created by falling meteorites—the pyramid, they discover, contains a mechanism that sends out a powerful force that shields it from external disturbances and perhaps signals to some distant observer. When the explorers finally succeed in breaking through the shield and studying the pyramid, they become convinced that its origins are as alien to the moon as they are themselves. The astronaut telling the story says, "The mystery haunts us all the more now that the other planets have been reached and we know that only Earth has ever been the home of intelligent life in our Universe. Nor could any lost civilization of our own world have built that machine.... It was set there upon its mountain before life had emerged from the seas of Earth."

But suddenly the narrator realizes the pyramid's meaning. It was left by some far-off civilization as a sentinel to signal that living beings had finally reached it:

Nearly a hundred thousand million stars are turning in the circle of the Milky Way, and long ago other races on the worlds of other suns must have scaled and passed the heights that we have reached. Think of such civilizations, far back in time against the fading afterglow of Creation, masters of a universe so young that life as yet had come only to a handful of worlds. Theirs would have been a loneliness we cannot imagine, the loneliness of gods looking out across infinity and finding none to share their thoughts.

They must have searched the star clusters as we have searched the planets. Everywhere there would be worlds, but they would be empty or peopled with crawling, mindless things. Such was our own Earth, the smoke of the great volcanoes still staining the skies, when that first ship of the peoples of the dawn came sliding in from the abyss beyond Pluto. It passed the frozen outer worlds, knowing that life could play no part in their destinies. It came to rest among the inner planets, warming themselves around the fire of the Sun and waiting for their stories to begin.

These wanderers must have looked on Earth, circling safely in the narrow zone between fire and ice, and must have guessed that it was the favorite of the Sun's children. Here, in the distant future, would be intelligence; but there were countless stars before them still, and they might never come this way again.

So they left a sentinel, one of millions they scattered throughout the Universe, watching over all worlds with the promise of life. It was a beacon that down the ages patiently signaled the fact that no one had discovered it.

The astronaut concludes:

I can never look now at the Milky Way without wondering from which of those banked clouds of stars the emissaries are coming. If you will pardon so commonplace a simile, we have set off the fire alarm and have nothing to do but to wait.

I do not think we will have to wait for long.

Clarke and Kubrick spent two years transforming this short story into a novel and then into a script for *2001,* which is concerned with the discovery of the sentinel and a search for traces of the civilization that put it there—a quest that takes the searchers out into the far reaches of the solar system. Extraterrestrial life may seem an odd subject for a motion picture, but at this stage in his career Kubrick is convinced that any idea he is really interested in, however unlikely it may sound, can be transferred to film. "One of the English science-fiction writers once said, 'Sometimes I think we're alone, and sometimes I think we're not. In either case, the idea is quite staggering,' " Kubrick once told me. "I must say I agree with him."

By the time the film appears, early next year, Kubrick estimates that he and Clarke will have put in an average of four hours a day, six days a week, on the writing of the script. (This works out to about twenty-four hundred hours of writing for two hours and forty minutes of film.) Even during the actual shooting of the film, Kubrick spends every free moment reworking the scenario. He has an extra office set up in a blue trailer that was once Deborah Kerr's dressing room, and when shooting is going on, he has it wheeled onto the set, to give him a certain amount of privacy for writing. He frequently gets ideas for dialogue from his actors, and when he likes an idea he puts it in. (Peter Sellers, he says, contributed some wonderful bits of humor for *Dr. Strangelove*.)

In addition to writing and directing, Kubrick supervises every aspect of his films, from selecting costumes to choosing the incidental music. In making *2001*, he is, in a sense, trying to second-guess the future. Scientists planning long-range space projects can ignore such questions as what sort of hats rocket-ship hostesses will wear when space travel becomes common (in *2001* the hats have padding in them to cushion any collisions with the ceiling that weightlessness might cause), and what sort of voices computers will have if, as many experts feel is certain, they learn to talk and to respond to voice commands (there is a talking computer in *2001* that arranges for the astronauts' meals, gives them medical treatments, and even plays chess with them during a long space mission to Jupiter—"Maybe it ought to sound like Jackie Mason," Kubrick once said), and what kind of time will be kept aboard a spaceship (Kubrick chose Eastern Standard, for the convenience of communicating with Washington). In the sort of planning that NASA does, such matters can be dealt with as they come up, but in a movie everything is immediately visible and explicit, and questions like this must be answered in detail. To help him find the answers, Kubrick has assembled around him a group of thirty-five artists and designers, more than twenty special-effects people, and a staff of scientific advisers. By the time the picture is done, Kubrick figures that he will have consulted with people from a generous sampling of the leading aeronautical companies in the United States and Europe, not to mention innumerable scientific and industrial firms. One consultant, for instance, was Professor Marvin Minsky, of M.I.T., who is a leading authority on artificial intelligence and the construction of automata. (He is now building a robot at M.I.T. that can catch a ball.) Kubrick wanted to learn from him whether any of the things that he was planning to have his computers do were likely to be realized by the year 2001; he was pleased to find out that they were.

Kubrick told me he had seen practically every science-fiction film ever made, and any number of more conventional films that had interesting special effects. One Saturday afternoon, after lunch and two rapid chess games, he and Christiane and I set out to see a Russian science-fiction movie called *Astronauts on Venus*, which he had discovered playing somewhere in North London. Saturday afternoon at a neighborhood movie house in London is like Saturday afternoon at the movies anywhere; the theatre was full of children talking, running up and down the aisles, chewing gum, and eating popcorn. The movie was in Russian, with English subtitles, and since most of the children couldn't read very well, let alone speak Russian, the dialogue was all but drowned out by the general babble. This was probably all to the good, since the film turned out to be a terrible hodgepodge of pseudo science and Soviet propaganda. It featured a talking robot named John and a talking girl named Masha who had been left in a small spaceship orbiting Venus while a party of explorers—who thought, probably correctly, that she would have been a nuisance below—went off to explore. Although Kubrick reported that the effects used were crude, he insisted that we stick it out to the end, just in case.

Before I left London, I was able to spend a whole day with Kubrick, starting at about eight-fifteen, when an M-G-M driver picked us up in one of the studio cars. (Kubrick suffers automobiles tolerably well, but he will under almost no circumstances travel by plane, even though he holds a pilot's license and has put in about a hundred and fifty hours in the air, principally around Teterboro Airport; after practicing landings and takeoffs, flying solo cross-country to Albany, and taking his friends up for rides, he lost interest in flying.) Boreham Wood is a little like the area outside Boston that is served by Route 128, for it specializes in electronics companies and precision industry, and the M-G-M studio is hardly distinguishable from the rather antiseptic-looking factories nearby. It consists of ten enormous sound stages concealed in industrial-looking buildings and surrounded by a cluster of carpenter shops, paint shops, office units, and so on. Behind the buildings is a huge lot covered with bits and pieces of other productions—the façade of a French provincial village, the hulk of a Second World War bomber, and other debris. Kubrick's offices are near the front of the complex in a long bungalow structure that houses, in addition to his production staff, a group of youthful model-makers working on large, very detailed models of spacecraft to be used in special-effects photography; Kubrick calls their realm "Santa's Workshop." When we walked into his private office, it seemed to me that the general disor-

der had grown even more chaotic since my last visit. Tacked to a bul-
letin board were some costume drawings showing men dressed in odd-
looking, almost Edwardian business suits. Kubrick said that the
drawings were supposed to be of the business suit of the future and
had been submitted by one of the innumerable designers who had
been asked to furnish ideas on what men's clothes would look like in
thirty-five years. "The problem is to find something that looks different and that might reflect new developments in fabrics but that isn't so
far out as to be distracting," Kubrick said. "Certainly buttons will be
gone. Even now, there are fabrics that stick shut by themselves."

Just then, Victor Lyndon, Kubrick's associate producer (he was also
the associate producer of *Dr. Strangelove* and, most recently, of *Darling*),
came in. A trim, athletic-looking man of forty-six, he leans toward the
latest "mod" styling in clothes, and he was wearing an elegant green but-
tonless, self-shutting shirt. He was followed by a young man wearing
hair down to his neck, a notably non-shutting shirt, and boots, who was
introduced as a brand-new costume designer. (He was set up at a drawing table in Santa's Workshop, but that afternoon he announced that the
atmosphere was too distracting for serious work, and left; the well-
known British designer Hardy Amies was finally chosen to design the
costumes.) Lyndon fished from a manila envelope a number of shoulder
patches designed to be worn as identification by the astronauts. (The
two principal astronauts in the film were to be played by Keir Dullea,
who has starred in *David and Lisa* and *Bunny Lake Is Missing,* and Gary
Lockwood, a former college-football star and now a television and
movie actor.) Kubrick said that the lettering didn't look right, and suggested that the art department make up new patches using actual NASA
lettering. He then consulted one of the small notebooks in which he lists
all the current production problems, along with the status of their solutions, and announced that he was going to the art department to see how
the drawings of the moons of Jupiter were coming along.

The art department, which occupies a nearby building, is presided
over by Tony Masters, a tall, Lincolnesque man who was busy working
on the Jupiter drawings when we appeared. Kubrick told me that the
department, which designs and dresses all sets, was constructing a
scale model of the moon, including the back side, which had been
photographed and mapped by rocket. Looking over the Jupiter drawings, Kubrick said that the light in them looked a little odd to him, and

suggested that Masters have Arthur Clarke check on it that afternoon when he came out from London.

Our next stop was to pick up some papers in the separate office where Kubrick does his writing—a made-over dressing room in a quiet part of the lot. On our way to it, we passed an outbuilding containing a number of big generators; a sign reading DANGER!—11,500 VOLTS! was nailed to its door. "Why eleven thousand five *hundred*?" Kubrick said. "Why not twelve thousand? If you put a sign like that in a movie, people would think it was a fake." When we reached the trailer, I could see that it was used as much for listening as for writing, for in addition to the usual battery of tape recorders (Kubrick writes rough first drafts of his dialogue by dictating into a recorder, since he finds that this gives it a more natural flow) there was a phonograph and an enormous collection of records, practically all of them of contemporary music. Kubrick told me that he thought he had listened to almost every modern composition available on records in an effort to decide what style of music would fit the film. Here, again, the problem was to find something that sounded unusual and distinctive but not so unusual as to be distracting. In the office collection were records by the practitioners of *musique concrète* and electronic music in general, and records of works by the contemporary German composer Carl Orff. In most cases, Kubrick said, film music tends to lack originality, and a film about the future might be the ideal place for a really striking score by a major composer.

We returned to the main office, and lunch was brought in from the commissary. During lunch, Kubrick signed a stack of letters, sent off several cables, and took a long-distance call from California. "At this stage of the game, I feel like the counterman at Katz's delicatessen on Houston Street at lunch hour," he said. "You've hardly finished saying 'Half a pound of corned beef' when he says 'What else?,' and before you can say 'A sliced rye' he's saying 'What else?' again."

I asked whether he ever got things mixed up, and he said rarely, adding that he thought chess playing had sharpened his naturally retentive memory and gift for organization. "With such a big staff, the problem is for people to figure out what they should come to see you about and what they should *not* come to see you about," he went on. "You invariably find your time taken up with questions that aren't important and could have easily been disposed of without your opinion.

To offset this, decisions are sometimes taken without your approval that can wind up in frustrating dead ends."

As we were finishing lunch, Victor Lyndon came in with an almanac that listed the average temperature and rainfall all over the globe at every season of the year. "We're looking for a cool desert where we can shoot some sequences during the late spring," Kubrick said. "We've got our eye on a location in Spain, but it might be pretty hot to work in comfortably, and we might have trouble controlling the lighting. If we don't go to Spain, we'll have to build an entirely new set right here. More work for Tony Masters and his artists." (Later, I learned that Kubrick did decide to shoot on location.)

After lunch, Kubrick and Lyndon returned to a long-standing study of the space-suit question. In the film, the astronauts will wear space suits when they are working outside their ships, and Kubrick was very anxious that they should look like the space suits of thirty-five years from now. After numerous consultations with Ordway and other NASA experts, he and Lyndon had finally settled on a design, and now they were studying a vast array of samples of cloth to find one that would look right and photograph well. While this was going on, people were constantly dropping into the office with drawings, models, letters, cables, and various props, such as a model of a lens for one of the telescopes in a spaceship. (Kubrick rejected it because it looked too crude.) At the end of the day, when my head was beginning to spin, someone came by with a wristwatch that the astronauts were going to use on their Jupiter voyage (which Kubrick rejected) and a plastic drinking glass for the moon hotel (which Kubrick thought looked fine). About seven o'clock, Kubrick called for his car, and by eight-thirty he had returned home, put the children to bed, discussed the day's events with his wife, watched a news broadcast on television, telephoned Clarke for a brief discussion of whether nuclear-powered spacecraft would pollute the atmosphere with their exhausts (Clarke said that they certainly would today but that by the time they actually come into use somebody will have figured out what to do about poisonous exhausts), and taken out his chess set. "How about a little game?" he said in a seductive tone that the Master would have envied.

On December 29, 1965, shooting of the film began, and in early March the company reached the most intricate part of the camerawork, which was to be done in the interior of a giant centrifuge. One of the problems in space travel will be weightlessness. While weightlessness has, because of its novelty, a certain glamour and amusement, it would be an extreme nuisance on a long trip, and probably a health hazard as well. Our physical systems have evolved to work against the pull of gravity, and it is highly probable that all sorts of unfortunate things, such as softening of the bones, would result from exposure to weightlessness for months at a time. In addition, of course, nothing stays in place without gravity, and no normal activity is possible unless great care is exercised; the slightest jar can send you hurtling across the cabin. Therefore, many spacecraft designers figure that some sort of artificial gravity will have to be supplied for space travellers. In principle, this is very easy to do. An object on the rim of a wheel rotating at a uniform speed is subjected to a constant force pushing it away from the center, and by adjusting the size of the wheel and the speed of its rotation this centrifugal force can be made to resemble the force of gravity. Having accepted this notion, Kubrick went one step further and commissioned the Vickers Engineering Group to make an actual centrifuge, large enough for the astronauts to live in full time. It took six months to build and cost about three hundred thousand dollars. The finished product looks from the outside like a Ferris wheel thirty-eight feet in diameter and can be rotated at a maximum speed of about three miles an hour. This is not enough to parallel the force of gravity—the equipment inside the centrifuge has to be bolted to the floor—but it has enabled Kubrick to achieve some remarkable photographic effects. The interior, eight feet wide, is fitted out with an enormous computer console, an electronically operated medical dispensary, a shower, a device for taking an artificial sunbath, a recreation area, with a Ping-Pong table and an electronic piano, and five beds with movable plastic domes—hibernacula, where astronauts who are not on duty can, literally, hibernate for months at a time. (The trip to Jupiter will take two hundred and fifty-seven days.)

I had seen the centrifuge in the early stages of its construction and very much wanted to observe it in action, so I was delighted when chance sent me back to England in the early spring. When I walked through the door of the *2001* set one morning in March, I must say that the scene that presented itself to me was overwhelming. In the middle of the hangarlike stage stood the centrifuge, with cables and lights hanging from every available inch of its steel-girdered superstructure. On the floor to one side of its frame was an immense electronic console (not a prop), and, in various places, six microphones and three television receivers. I learned later that Kubrick had arranged a closed-circuit-television system so that he could watch what was going on inside the centrifuge during scenes being filmed when he could not be inside himself. Next to the microphone was an empty canvas chair with "Stanley Kubrick" painted on its back in fading black letters. Kubrick himself was nowhere to be seen, but everywhere I looked there were people, some hammering and sawing, some carrying scripts, some carrying lights. In one corner I saw a woman applying makeup to what appeared to be an astronaut wearing blue coveralls and leather boots. Over a loudspeaker, a pleasantly authoritative English voice—belonging, I learned shortly, to Derek Cracknell, Kubrick's first assistant director—was saying, "Will someone bring the Governor's Polaroid on the double?" A man came up to me and asked how I would like my tea and whom I was looking for, and almost before I could reply "One lump with lemon" and "Stanley Kubrick," led me, in a semi-daze, to an opening at the bottom of the centrifuge. Peering up into the dazzlingly illuminated interior, I spotted Kubrick lying flat on his back on the floor of the machine and staring up through the viewfinder of an enormous camera, in complete concentration. Keir Dullea, dressed in shorts and a white T-shirt, and covered by a blue blanket, was lying in an open hibernaculum on the rising curve of the floor. He was apparently comfortably asleep, and Kubrick was telling him to wake up as simply as possible. "Just open your eyes," he said. "Let's not have any stirring, yawning, and rubbing."

One of the lights burned out, and while it was being fixed, Kubrick unwound himself from the camera, spotted me staring openmouthed at the top of the centrifuge, where the furniture of the crew's dining quarters was fastened to the ceiling, and said, "Don't worry—that stuff is bolted down." Then he motioned to me to come up and join him.

No sooner had I climbed into the centrifuge than Cracknell, who turned out to be a cheerful and all but imperturbable youthful-looking man in tennis shoes (all the crew working in the centrifuge were wearing tennis shoes, not only to keep from slipping but to help them climb the steeply curving sides; indeed, some of them were working while clinging to the bolted-down furniture halfway up the wall), said, "Here's your Polaroid, Guv," and handed Kubrick the camera. I asked Kubrick what he needed the Polaroid for, and he explained that he used it for checking subtle lighting effects for color film. He and the director of photography, Geoffrey Unsworth, had worked out a correlation between how the lighting appeared on the instantly developed Polaroid film and the settings on the movie camera. I asked Kubrick if it was customary for movie directors to participate so actively in the photographing of a movie, and he said succinctly that he had never watched any other movie director work.

The light was fixed, and Kubrick went back to work behind the camera. Keir Dullea was reinstalled in his hibernaculum and the cover rolled shut. "You better take your hands from under the blanket," Kubrick said. Kelvin Pike, the camera operator, took Kubrick's place behind the camera, and Cracknell called for quiet. The camera began to turn, and Kubrick said, "Open the hatch." The top of the hibernaculum slid back with a whirring sound, and Keir Dullea woke up, without any stirring, yawning, or rubbing. Kubrick, playing the part of the solicitous computer, started feeding him lines.

"Good morning," said Kubrick. "What do you want for breakfast?"

"Some bacon and eggs would be fine," Dullea answered simply.

Later, Kubrick told me that he had engaged an English actor to read the computer's lines in the serious dramatic scenes, in order to give Dullea and Lockwood something more professional to play against, and that in the finished film he would dub in an American-accented voice. He and Dullea went through the sequence four or five times, and finally Kubrick was satisfied with what he had. Dullea bounced out of his hibernaculum, and I asked him whether he was having a good time. He said he was getting a great kick out of all the tricks and gadgets, and added, "This is a happy set, and that's something."

When Kubrick emerged from the centrifuge, he was immediately surrounded by people. "Stanley, there's a black pig outside for you to look at," Victor Lyndon was saying. He led the way outside, and, sure enough, in a large truck belonging to an animal trainer was an enormous jet-black pig. Kubrick poked it, and it gave a suspicious grunt.

"The pig looks good," Kubrick said to the trainer.

"I can knock it out with a tranquillizer for the scenes when it's supposed to be dead," the trainer said.

"Can you get any tapirs or anteaters?" Kubrick asked.

The trainer said that this would not be an insuperable problem, and Kubrick explained to me, "We're going to use them in some scenes about prehistoric man."

At this point, a man carrying a stuffed lion's head approached and asked Kubrick whether it would be all right to use.

"The tongue looks phony, and the eyes are only marginal," Kubrick said, heading for the set. "Can somebody fix the tongue?"

Back on the set, he climbed into his blue trailer. "Maybe the company can get back some of its investment selling guided tours of the centrifuge," he said. "They might even feature a ride on it." He added that the work in the machine was incredibly slow, because it took hours to rearrange all the lights and cameras for each new sequence. Originally, he said, he had planned on a hundred and thirty days of shooting for the main scenes, but the centrifuge sequences had slowed them down by perhaps a week. "I take advantage of every delay and breakdown to go off by myself and think," he said. "Something like playing chess when your opponent takes a long time over his next move."

At one o'clock, just before lunch, many of the crew went with Kubrick to a small projection room near the set to see the results of the previous day's shooting. The most prominent scene was a brief one that showed Gary Lockwood exercising in the centrifuge, jogging around its interior and shadowboxing to the accompaniment of a Chopin waltz—picked by Kubrick because he felt that an intelligent man in 2001 might choose Chopin for doing exercise to music. As the film appeared on the screen, Lockwood was shown jogging around the complete interior circumference of the centrifuge, which appeared to me to defy logic as well as physics, since when he was at the top he would have needed suction cups on his feet to stay glued to the floor. I asked Kubrick how he had achieved this effect, and he said he was definitely, absolutely not going to tell me. As the scene went on, Kubrick's voice could be heard on the sound track, rising over the Chopin: "Gain a little on the camera, Gary!...Now a flurry of lefts and rights!...A little more vicious!" After the film had run its course, Kubrick appeared quite pleased with the results, remarking, "It's nice to get two minutes of usable film after two days of shooting."

Later that afternoon, I had a chance to see a publicity short made up of some of the most striking material so far filmed for *2001*. There were shots of the space station, with people looking out of the windows at the earth wheeling in the distance; there was an incredible sequence, done in red, showing a hostess on a moon rocket appearing to walk on the ceiling of the spaceship; there was a solemn procession of astronauts trudging along on the surface of the moon. The colors and the effects were extremely impressive.

When I got back to the set, I found Kubrick getting ready to leave for the day. "Come around to the house tomorrow," he said. "I'll be working at home, and maybe we can get in a little game. I still think you're a complete potzer. But I can't understand what happens every fifth game."

He had been keeping track of our games in a notebook, and the odd pattern of five had indeed kept reappearing. The crucial tenth game had been a draw, and although I had lost the fifteenth, even Kubrick admitted that he had had an amazingly close call. As for the games that had not been multiples of five, they had been outright losses for me. We had now completed nineteen games, and I could sense Kubrick's determination to break the pattern.

The next morning, I presented myself at the Kubricks' house, in Hertfordshire, just outside London, which they have rented until *2001* is finished. It is a marvellous house and an enormous one, with two suits of armor in one of the lower halls, and rooms all over the place, including a panelled billiard room with a big snooker table. Christiane has fixed up one room as a painting studio, and Kubrick has turned another into an office, filled with the inevitable tape recorders and cameras. They moved their belongings from New York in ninety numbered dark-green summer-camp trunks bought from Boy Scout headquarters—the only sensible way of moving, Kubrick feels. The house is set in a lovely bit of English countryside, near a rest home for horses, where worthy old animals are sent to live out their declining years in tranquillity. Heating the house poses a major problem. It has huge picture windows, and Arthur Clarke's brother Fred, who is a heating engineer, has pointed out to Kubrick that glass conducts heat so effectively that he would not be much worse off (except for the wind) if the glass in the windows were removed entirely. The season had produced a tremendous cold spell, and in addition to using electric heaters in every corner of the rooms, Kubrick had acquired some enormous thick blue bathrobes, one of which he lent me. Thus bundled up, we sat down at the inevitable chessboard at ten in the morning for our twentieth game, which I proceeded to win on schedule. "I can't understand it," Kubrick said. "I know you are a potzer, so why are you winning these fifth games?"

A tray of sandwiches was brought in for lunch, and we sat there in our blue bathrobes like two figures from Bergman's *The Seventh Seal*, playing on and taking time out only to munch a sandwich or light an occasional cigar. The children, who had been at a birthday party, dropped in later in the day in their party dresses to say hello, as did Christiane, but the games went on. I lost four in a row, and by late afternoon it was time for the twenty-fifth game, which, Kubrick announced, would settle the matter once and for all. We seesawed back and forth until I thought I saw a marvellous chance for a coup. I made as if to take off one of Kubrick's knights, and Kubrick clutched his brow dramatically, as though in sharp pain. I then made the move ferociously, picking off the knight, and Kubrick jumped up from the table.

"I knew you were a potzer! It was a trap!" he announced triumphantly, grabbing my queen from the board.

"I made a careless mistake," I moaned.

"No, you didn't," he said. "You were hustled. You didn't realize that I'm an actor, too."

It was the last chess game we have had a chance to play, but I did succeed in beating him once at snooker.

FILMING *2001: A SPACE ODYSSEY*

Herb A. Lightman

During my last trip to London a year and a half ago arrangements were made for me to meet with producer-director Stanley Kubrick who was at M-G-M's Borehamwood studio working on his futuristic Super-Panavision spectacle, *2001: A Space Odyssey.* I was looking forward to talking with him and perhaps standing by during the filming of a scene or two of this production, which was being filmed in great secrecy but which had already become a kind of legend among those working on it.

On the morning of the day set for our get-together, I received a call from Kubrick's secretary. It seemed that he had encountered a crisis in the cutting room which would keep him tied up for the entire day. Would it be all right if we switched our appointment to the following day, she wanted to know. Unfortunately it wouldn't, because I was scheduled to leave England the next morning.

The upshot was that I didn't get a chance to talk with him in depth about the production until after I had sat enthralled through a preview screening of the final cut. I was stunned by the scope and sheer visual beauty of this 70mm filmic excursion into the future, by the magnificent photography of Geoffrey Unsworth and John Alcott, by the technical perfection of its multitude of enormously complex special effects—but most of all by the uncompromising dedication of the creative genius who had devoted four years of his life and unstinting effort to the realization of this dream on film. Listening to him tell about how it was made, I found myself caught up by his enthusiasm, and tremendously impressed with the wealth of creative imagination which had been required to put it onto the screen.

2001 is no mere science-fiction movie. In truth, to be really accurate, it is more like "science-fact" simply extended a few decades into the future. In his quest for complete authenticity in terms of present and near-future technology, Kubrick consulted constantly with more than thirty technical experts and the results, with the possible exception of an "up-tight" computer, are an accurate forecast of things to come.

A STORY FAR OUT IN TIME AND TECHNIQUE

In order that the enormity of the challenge may be fully appreciated, it is necessary, briefly, to synopsize the story of the film.

The picture opens with an awesome prologue entitled "The Dawn of Man" in which apelike pre-humans are seen (during an era occurring four million years ago) in action against spectacular natural backgrounds. Out of this rugged terrain there arises one morning a smooth, black, rectilinear monolith which first frightens the ape-men and then attracts them.

The time of the film then flashes forward to the year 2001, A.D. A United States envoy is sent on a secret mission to the moon to investigate a strange "made" object uncovered in an excavation of the crater Tycho. It turns out to be the same large monolith which we have seen in the previous sequence—except that now it is emitting a high-pitched signal apparently beamed at the planet Jupiter.

It is decided to send an immense spacecraft, the *Discovery,* to Jupiter for purposes of investigation. The gigantic vehicle is manned by two superbly self-controlled young astronauts (played by Keir Dullea and Gary Lockwood), with a back-up crew of three others resting in a state of quick-frozen suspended animation within "hibernaculums" that resemble mummy cases. The sixth personality aboard the spacecraft is an almost-human computer named HAL that talks in a dreamy voice and ultimately goes off the neurotic deep-end.

The main area of the *Discovery* is a huge centrifuge which rotates at the rate of three miles-per-hour to nullify the weightless effect by means of artificial gravity. Inside their space-age ferris wheel the astronauts do their roadwork and casually walk upside down.

When HAL makes an error in mechanical judgment, the astronauts decide to disconnect all but his most basic functions. However, the computer discovers the plot and, in a fit of all-too-human self-preservative frenzy, kills one of the astronauts when he goes outside of the mother ship to make repairs, executes the deep-frozen trio in their sarcophagi by cutting off their life support, and attempts to prevent the remaining astronaut from re-entering the *Discovery*. This plot is foiled when the cool young man, caught outside without his helmet, blasts his way through the vacuum of space into an air-lock of the mother ship.

With almost surgical objectivity he then proceeds to lobotomize the rebellious (and now contrite) computer by pulling out its "brain cells" one-by-one. Left as the sole survivor, he steers his course toward Jupiter. Approaching the huge planet he is drawn into a vortex of "psychedelic" color, rushing geometric corridors of infinite length and a galaxy of magnificently hued starbursts. Finally, he steps from the one-man pod into a lavish living-bedroom suite that boasts a luminous floor and Louis XVI furniture. He sees himself aging progressively until, as a very ancient senior citizen he reaches out in supplication toward the by-now-familiar monolith which stands at the foot of his bed.

The last sequence in the film shows a "starchild" embryo with glowing eyes which seems to emerge from the fusion of planets to go soaring through space in cosmic concert with the monolith.

THE BEHIND-THE-SCENES OF A GREAT FILM ADVENTURE

Knowing of the air-tight security which had attended filming of the special effects for this production, I was a bit apprehensive about asking Stanley Kubrick to discuss the intricate technology involved.

However, in my lengthy discussion with him (an occurrence which some journalists might aptly refer to as an "exclusive interview"), I found him to be completely cooperative. He answered my questions fully and often volunteered additional information, seeming actually eager to share his considerable know-how with the professional film-makers who constitute the great majority of the *American Cinematographer* readership.

I had heard about the elaborate "command post" which had been set up at Borehamwood during the production of *2001*. It was de-scribed to me as a huge, throbbing nerve center of a place with much the same frenetic atmosphere as a Cape Kennedy blockhouse during the final stages of Countdown.

"It was a novel thing for me to have such a complicated informa-tion-handling operation going, but it was absolutely essential for keep-ing track of the thousands of technical details involved," Kubrick explained. "We figured that there would be 205 effects scenes in the picture and that each of these would require an average of ten major steps to complete. I define a 'major step' as one in which the scene is handled by another technician or department. We found that it was so complicated to keep track of all of these scenes and the separate steps involved in each that we wound up with a three-man sort of 'opera-tions room' in which every wall was covered with swing-out charts in-cluding a shot history for each scene. Every separate element and step was recorded on this history—information as to shooting dates, expo-sure, mechanical processes, special requirements and the technicians and departments involved. Figuring ten steps for two hundred scenes equals two thousand steps—but when you realize that most of these steps had to be done over eight or nine times to make sure they were perfect, the true total is more like sixteen thousand separate steps. It took an incredible number of diagrams, flow-charts and other data to keep everything organized and to be able to retrieve information that somebody might need about something someone else had done seven months earlier. We had to be able to tell which stage each scene was in at any given moment—and the system worked."

THE IDEAL OF THE "SINGLE-GENERATION LOOK"

A film technician watching *2001* cannot help but be impressed by the fact that the complex effects scenes have an unusually sharp, crisp and grain-free appearance—a clean "single-generation look," to coin a phrase. This is especially remarkable when one stops to consider how many separate elements had to be involved in compositing some of the more intricate scenes.

This circumstance is not accidental, but rather the result of a deliberate effort on Kubrick's part to have each scene look as much like "original" footage as possible. In following this pursuit he automatically ruled out process shots, ordinary traveling matte shots, blue-backings and most of the more conventional methods of optical printing.

"We purposely did all of our duping with black and white, three-color separation masters," he points out. "There were no color inter-positives used for combining the shots, and I think this is principally responsible for the lack of grain and the high degree of photographic quality we were able to maintain. More than half of the shots in the picture are dupes, but I don't think the average viewer would know it. Our separations were made, of course, from the original color negative and we then used a number of bi-pack camera-printers for combining the material. A piece of color negative ran through the gate while, contact-printed onto it, actually in the camera, were the color separations, each of which was run through in turn. The camera lens 'saw' a big white printing field used as the exposure source. It was literally just a method of contact printing. We used no conventional traveling mattes at all, because I feel that it is impossible to get original-looking quality with traveling mattes."

SMOOTH TRIPS FOR STAR·VOYAGERS

A recurring problem arose from the fact that most of the outer-space action had to take place against a star-field background. It is obvious that as space vehicles and tumbling astronauts moved in front of these stars they would have to "go out" and "come back on" at the right times—a simple matter if conventional traveling mattes were used. But how to do it a better way?

The better way involved shooting the foreground action and then making a 70mm print of it with a superimposed registration grid and an identifying frame number printed onto each frame. The grid used corresponded with an identical grid inscribed on animation-type platens.

Twenty enlargers operated by twenty girls were set up in a room and each girl was given a five or six-foot segment of the scene. She would place one frame at a time in the enlarger, line up the grid on the frame with the grid on her platen and then trace an outline of the foreground subject onto an animation cel. In another department the area enclosed by the outline would be filled in with solid black paint.

The cels would then be photographed in order on the animation stand to produce an opaque matte of the foreground action. The moving star background would also be shot on the animation stand, after which both the stars and the matte would be delivered to Technicolor Ltd. for the optical printing of a matted master with star background. Very often there were several foreground elements, which meant that the matting process had to be repeated for each separate element.

THE MECHANICAL MONSTER
WITH THE DELICATE TOUCH

In creating many of the effects, especially those involving miniature models of the various spacecraft, it was usually necessary to make multiple repeat takes that were absolutely identical in terms of camera movement. For this purpose a camera animating device was constructed with a heavy worm-gear twenty feet in length. The large size of this worm-gear enabled the camera mount of the device to be moved with precise accuracy. A motorized head permitted tilting and panning in all directions. All of these functions were tied together with selsyn motors so that moves could be repeated as often as necessary in perfect registration.

For example, let us assume that a certain scene involved a fly-by of a spaceship with miniature projection of the interior action visible through the window. The required moves would be programmed out in advance for the camera animating device. A shot would then be made of the spaceship miniature with the exterior properly lighted, but with the window area blacked out. Then the film would be wound back in the camera to its sync frame and another identical pass would be made. This time, however, the exterior of the spacecraft would be covered with black velvet and a scene of the interior action would be front-projected onto a glossy white card exactly filling the window area. Because of the precision made possible by the large worm-gear and the selsyn motors, this exact dual maneuver could be repeated as many times as necessary. The two elements of the scene would be exposed together in perfect registration onto the same original piece of negative with all of the moves duplicated and no camera jiggle.

Often, for a scene such as that previously described, several elements would be photographed onto held-takes photographed several months apart. Since light in space originates from a sharp single point source, it was necessary to take great pains to make sure that the light sources falling on the separate elements would match exactly for angle and intensity.

Also, since the elements were being photographed onto the same strip of original negative, it was essential that all exposures be matched precisely. If one of them was off, there would be no way to correct it without throwing the others off. In order to guard against this variation in exposure very precise wedge-testing was made of each element, and the wedges were very carefully selected for color and density. But even with all of these precautions there was a high failure rate and many of the scenes had to be redone.

"We coined a new phrase and began to call these 're-don'ts,' " says Kubrick, with a certain post-operative amusement. "This refers to a re-do in which you don't make the same mistake you made before."

FILMING THE ULTIMATE IN SLOW MOTION

In the filming of the spacecraft miniatures, two problems were encountered which necessitated the shooting of scenes at extremely slow frame rates. First, there was the matter of depth-of-field. In order to hold both the forward and rear extremities of the spacecraft models in sharp focus, so that they would look like full-sized vehicles and not miniatures, it was necessary to stop the aperture of the lens down to practically a pin-hole. The obvious solution of using more light was not feasible because it was necessary to maintain the illusion of a single bright point light source. Secondly, in order to get doors, ports and other movable parts of the miniatures to operate smoothly and on a "large" scale, the motors driving these mechanisms were geared down so far that the actual motion, frame by frame, was imperceptible.

"It was like watching the hour hand of a clock," says Kubrick. "We shot most of these scenes using slow exposures of four seconds per frame, and if you were standing on the stage you would not see anything moving. Even the giant space station that rotated at a good rate on the screen seemed to be standing still during the actual photography of its scenes. For some shots, such as those in which doors opened and closed on the space ships, a door would move only about four inches during the course of the scene, but it would take five hours to shoot that movement. You could never see unsteady movement, if there was unsteadiness, until you saw the scene on the screen—and even then the engineers could never be sure exactly where the unsteadiness had occurred. They could only guess by looking at the scene. This type of thing involved endless trial and error, but the final results are a tribute to M-G-M's great precision machine shop in England."

IT'S ALL DONE WITH WIRES—BUT YOU CAN'T SEE THEM

Scenes of the astronauts floating weightlessly in space outside the *Discovery*—and especially those showing Gary Lockwood tumbling off into infinity after he has been murdered by the vengeful computer—required some very tricky maneuvering.

For one thing, Kubrick was determined that none of the wires supporting the actors and stunt men would show. Accordingly, he had the ceiling of the entire stage draped with black velvet, mounted the camera vertically and photographed the astronauts from below so that their own bodies would hide the wires.

"We established different positions on their bodies for a hip harness, a high-back harness and a low-back harness," he explains, "so that no matter how they were spinning or turning on this rig—whether feet-first, headfirst or profile—they would always cover their wires and not get fouled up in them. For the sequence in which the one-man pod picks Lockwood up in its arms and crushes him, we were shooting straight up from under him. He was suspended by wires from a track in the ceiling and the camera followed him, keeping him in the same position in the frame as it tracked him into the arms of the pod. The pod was suspended from the ceiling also, hanging on its side from a tubular frame. The effect on the screen is that the pod moves horizontally into the frame to attack him, whereas he was actually moving toward the pod."

To shoot the scene in which the dead astronaut goes spinning off to become a pin-point in space took a bit of doing. "If we had actually started in close to a six-foot man and then pulled the camera back until he was a speck, we would have had to track back about two thousand feet—obviously impractical," Kubrick points out. "Instead we photographed him on 65mm film simply tumbling about in full frame. Then we front-projected a six-inch image of this scene onto a glossy white card suspended against black velvet and, using our worm-gear arrangement, tracked the camera away from the miniature screen until the astronaut became so small in the frame that he virtually disappeared. Since we were re-photographing an extremely small image there was no grain problem and he remained sharp and clear all the way to infinity."

The same basic technique was used in the sequence during which the surviving astronaut, locked out of the mother ship by the computer, decides to pop the explosive bolts on his one-man pod and blast himself through the vacuum of space into the air-lock. The air-lock set, which appears to be horizontal on the screen, was actually built vertically so that the camera could shoot straight up through it and the astronaut would cover with his body the wires suspending him.

First a shot was made of the door alone, showing just the explosion. Then an over-cranked shot of the astronaut was made with him being lowered toward the camera at a frame rate which made him appear to come hurtling horizontally straight into the lens. The following shot was over-cranked as he recovered and appeared to float lazily in the air-lock.

A FASCINATING FERRIS WHEEL

2001: A Space Odyssey abounds in unusual settings, but perhaps the most exotic of them all is the giant centrifuge which serves as the main compartment of the *Discovery* spacecraft and is, we are told, an accurate representation of the type of device that will be used to create artificial gravity for overcoming weightlessness during future deep-space voyages.

Costing $750,000, the space-going "ferris wheel" was built by the Vickers-Armstrong Engineering Group. It was thirty-eight feet in diameter and about ten feet in width at its widest point. It rotated at a maximum speed of three miles per hour and had built into it desks, consoles, bunks for the astronauts and tomb-like containers for their hibernating companions.

All of the lighting units, as well as the rear-projectors used to flash readouts onto the console scopes, had to be firmly fixed to the centrifuge structure and be capable of functioning while moving in a 360° circle. The magazine mechanisms of the Super-Panavision cameras had to be specially modified by Panavision to operate efficiently even when the cameras were upside down.

"There were basically two types of camera set-ups used inside the centrifuge," Kubrick explains. "In the first type the camera was mounted stationary to the set, so that when the set rotated in a 360° arc, the camera went right along with it. However, in terms of visual orientation, the camera didn't 'know' it was moving. In other words, on the screen it appears that the camera is standing still, while the actor walks away from it, up the wall, around the top and down the other side. In the second type of shot the camera, mounted on a miniature dolly, stayed with the actor at the bottom while the whole set moved past him. This was not as simple as it sounds because, due to the fact that the camera had to maintain some distance from the actor, it was necessary to position it about twenty feet up the wall—and have it *stay* in that position as the set rotated. This was accomplished by means of a steel cable from the outside which connected with the camera through a slot in the center of the floor and ran around the entire centrifuge. The slot was concealed by rubber mats that fell back into place as soon as the cable passed them."

Kubrick directed the action of these sequences from outside by watching a closed-circuit monitor relaying a picture from a small vidicon camera mounted next to the film camera inside the centrifuge. Of the specific lighting problems that had to be solved, he says:

"It took a lot of careful pre-planning with the Lighting Cameraman, Geoffrey Unsworth, and Production Designer Tony Masters to devise lighting that would look natural, and, at the same time, do the job photographically. All of the lighting for the scenes inside the centrifuge came from strip lights along the walls. Some of the units were concealed in coves, but others could be seen when the camera angle was wide enough. It was difficult for the cameraman to get enough light inside the centrifuge and he had to shoot with his lens wide open practically all of the time."

Cinematographer Unsworth used an unusual approach toward achieving his light balance and arriving at the correct exposure. He employed a Polaroid camera loaded with ASA 200 black-and-white film (because the color emulsion isn't consistent enough) to make still photographs of each new set-up prior to filming the scene. He found this to be a very rapid and effective way of getting an instant check on exposure and light balance. He was working at the toe end of the film latitude scale much of the time, shooting in scatter light and straight into exposed practical fixtures. The ten thousand Polaroid shots taken during production helped him considerably in coping with these problems.

"FILM-MAKING" IN THE PUREST SENSE OF THE TERM

To say that *2001: A Space Odyssey* is a spectacular piece of entertainment, as well as a technical *tour de force,* is certainly true, but there is considerably more to it than that.

In its larger dimension, the production may be regarded as a prime example of the *auteur* approach to film-making—a concept in which a single creative artist is, in the fullest sense of the word, the *author* of the film. In this case, there is not the slightest doubt that Stanley Kubrick is that author. It is *his* film. On every 70mm frame *his* imagination, *his* technical skill, *his* taste and *his* creative artistry are evident. Yet he is the first to insist that the result is a group effort (as every film must be) and to give full credit to the 106 skilled and dedicated craftsmen who worked closely with him for periods of up to four years.

Among those he especially lauds are: screenplay co-author Arthur C. Clarke, Cinematographers Geoffrey Unsworth and John Alcott, and Production Designers Tony Masters, Harry Lange and Ernie Archer.

He also extends lavish praise to Special Effects Supervisors Wally Veevers, Douglas Trumbull, Con Pederson and Tom Howard.

The praise, it would seem, is not all one-sided. M-G-M's Post-production Administrator Merle Chamberlin worked with Kubrick for a total of twenty weeks, both in London and in Hollywood, on the final phases of the project. A man not given to rash compliments, Chamberlin has this to say of the endeavor: "Working with Stanley Kubrick was a wonderful experience—a tremendously pleasant and educational one. He knows what he wants and how to get it, and he will not accept anything less than absolute perfection. One thing that surprised me is his complete lack of what might be called 'temperament.' He is always calm and controlled no matter what goes wrong. He simply faces the challenge with incredible dedication and follows it through to his objective. He is a hard taskmaster in that he holds no brief for inefficiency—and it has been said that he knows nothing of the proper hours for sleeping—but he is a fantastic film-maker with whom to work. I have been privileged to work very closely with David Lean on *Doctor Zhivago*, with John Frankenheimer on *Grand Prix*, with Michelangelo Antonioni on *Blow-up* and with Robert Aldrich on *The Dirty Dozen*—all terrific people and wonderful film-makers. But as a combination of highly skilled cinema technician and creative artist, Kubrick is absolutely tops."

From my own relatively brief contact with the creator of *2001: A Space Odyssey* I would say that this praise is not over-stated, for Stanley Kubrick, Film Author, epitomizes that ideal which is so rare in the world today: Not merely "Art for the sake of Art"—but vastly more important, "Excellence for the sake of Excellence."

FRONT-PROJECTION FOR *2001: A SPACE ODYSSEY*

Herb A. Lightman

Perhaps the most significant single technique utilized in M-G-M's *2001: A Space Odyssey*—considered in terms of its potential value to the film industry as a whole—is Stanley Kubrick's extensive use of a completely new departure in the application of front-projection for background transparencies.

This advanced technology evolved out of the dramatic demands of his "Dawn of Man" prologue which called for hordes of ape-men to be shown against vast natural terrain backgrounds of primeval beauty. A perfect location in a remote area of Southwest Africa had been found and Kubrick was anxious to use this spectacular setting for his opening sequence.

"The geology in that area was completely different from anything else I'd seen," he explains. "The rocks didn't look like 'Bible' rocks and they didn't look like 'Western' rocks. They were really quite unique."

To capture this setting on film the way he envisioned it there were several options open to him. The first, most obviously, would have been to take a large cast and crew on location to the actual site. However, aside from the enormous cost involved, the company would most likely have found itself at the mercy of inclement and ever-changing weather.

Another obvious alternative would have been the use of a painted backdrop, which, in this case, would have had to be 40 feet high and 110 feet wide. The main drawback was not the size, but rather the fact that such backdrops all too often look like exactly what they are.

In theory, the blue-screen matting system could have been used, or even a king-size adaptation of the standard rear-projection process method. In actual practice, however, each of these approaches, applied on such a vast scale, might not have produced quite the illusion of reality which the director hoped to achieve.

He elected, instead, to use front-projection on a scale never before attempted. The front-projection concept is not, in itself, new. The method has, in fact, been in practical use for several years, mainly by still photographers and in television studios. It had not, however, up until now, been used to any great extent in the motion picture industry.

The largest format utilized to date had been a 4 × 5-inch Ektachrome transparency, but it was felt that the grand-scale requirements of this particular space epic would demand an even larger transparency.

"I had made a test using a four-by-five still and it was almost good enough, so I was positive that with an eight-by-ten the effect would be perfect," Kubrick comments. "The trickiest part would be balancing the foreground illumination to match the intensity of the front-projected background. Now that it's over I'm convinced that if a still transparency is to be used for the background scene an eight-by-ten is essential, because if you don't have a surplus of resolution you are going to get a degradation of the projected background image."

The only drawback at the time was that there existed no such device as an 8 × 10 projector—let alone one powerful enough to throw a bright image across 90 feet of foreground area onto a screen 110 feet wide. Working in close cooperation with M-G-M Special Effects Supervisor Tom Howard, Kubrick set about building his own superpowerful 8 × 10 projector, with a condenser pack eighteen inches thick made up of condensers from standard 8 × 10 enlargers. The most powerful water-cooled arc available was employed as a light source and it was necessary to use slides of heat-resistant glass in front of the condensers in order to prevent the heat from peeling the magenta layer of emulsion right off of the transparency. At least six of the rear condensers cracked because of the heat during the filming, but this was usually due to a draft of cold air hitting the projector when someone opened the door of the sound stage while the projector was operating.

In order to conserve the transparencies as much as possible, the projector was only turned on during the one to five minutes at a time needed to make an actual take with the camera. For purposes of aligning the equipment a reject plate was used. Since any dust or dirt appearing on the surface of the plate would be magnified on the giant screen many times and become clearly apparent, the most careful precautions had to be taken. Anti-static devices were used and the plates were loaded under "antiseptic" conditions. The operator who loaded plates into the projector used editing gloves, and even wore a surgical mask so that his breath would not fog the mirror.

In aligning the camera-projector configuration for front-projection the projector was set up at right angles to the camera with the projected image beamed onto a partially-silvered 36-inch-wide mirror mounted at a 45° angle about 8 inches in front of the camera lens. The camera photographed through the mirror, the front surface of which bounced the projected image onto the screen. A heavy steel rig with micrometer adjustment was engineered to assure the very critical alignment between camera and projector in order that there would be no possibility of "fringing." A nodal camera head made it possible to pan across the mirror in scenes where the camera lens was fielding a composition that included less than the full screen.

A key requirement in front-projection is that the camera and projector be so precisely aligned that, in terms of physics, the projected light source and the center of the camera lens are located at the same point. Or, in more graphic terms, as if the light source were inside the camera. This is essential because of the peculiar uni-directional reflectivity of the screen material used, which produces a phenomenal gain in brilliance—but only when projected light is reflected *directly* back to its source.

The surfacing material used for the giant screen was a special 3M fabric coated with very tiny mirrored beads of glass. It has the incredible capability of reflecting one hundred times the amount of light that is projected onto it, so that, theoretically, if the light falling onto the screen gave an incident light reading of one foot-candle, the light reflected back to the camera would measure one hundred foot-candles.

This special lenticular 3M material comes in rolls and an effort was made to surface the screen by mounting it in hundred-foot strips. However, because of a slight variation in reflectivity between rolls, seams were frequently visible under projected light. An attempt to match strips exactly proved unsuccessful, so the material was finally torn into small, jagged, irregular shapes which were mounted in a "camouflage" mosaic, shape on top of shape, so that there was no longer any visible variation in reflectivity.

It is natural that certain obvious questions should come to mind in relation to the front-projection technique.

Firstly, since the projected image is falling upon the foreground subject *as well* as upon the screen in the background, why is that projected image not at least partially visible spilling onto the foreground subject—particularly in view of the fact that such a subject is much closer to the camera than the background screen? The answer is that exposure of the entire scene must be gauged to the extremely brilliant image reflected from the screen and which, because of the incredible reflectivity of the 3M screen material, is one hundred times brighter than any light image reflected from the foreground subject. This would pertain even if the foreground subject were a person wearing a silver suit; he would still show up on the film as a black figure silhouetted against the brilliant background image. Even though the faint image falling upon the foreground subject might be dimly visible to someone present on the set, it would be too faint for the film to "see"—because there simply does not exist an emulsion with a wide enough latitude to accommodate such an extreme brightness contrast range. In addition, a tremendous amount of light is needed to balance the foreground subject with the extremely bright image reflected from the screen. This light would effectively "wash out" any residue of front-projected image falling upon the foreground subject.

The second question that might logically be asked is: Why aren't the shadows of foreground objects visible on the background screen? The answer is that, since the light source and the camera lens are precisely aligned on a common axis, the foreground subject exactly "fits" its own shadow, covering it completely. So perfect is the match that even if a front-projected close-up were made of a girl with her hair blowing in the wind, each individual hair would completely cover, and therefore "hide," its own shadow.

In order to photograph the magnificent vistas used as backgrounds for the "Dawn of Man" sequence, Kubrick had three still camera crews operating in Southwest Africa for several months with 8 × 10 view cameras. In addition to the spectacular terrain itself, the dramatic cloud formations evoke images of an Earth millions of years younger, still in the lingering spasms of creative convulsion, a sphere of savage and violent beauty.

"This sequence was especially well suited to the use of front-projection because all of the backgrounds were desert scenes in which nothing had to move," says Kubrick. "Our location still photographers were able to wait for just the right moment and shoot a scene in light that would remain exactly that way for perhaps only five minutes out of a whole day. But on the stage we could shoot the sequence at our own pace in constant light of the type you could never maintain on location, no matter how much money you might spend."

In addition to the "Dawn of Man" prologue, the front-projection system was used to establish scenes of the astronauts walking on the lunar surface. Onto the background screen was projected a photograph of a miniature set representing the vast American Moon-base within the crater Clavius. The foreground action shows the astronauts amid huge lunar rocks that apparently tower above the base.

The main lighting key of the front-projected sequences was geared to the amount of light that could be poured on to reflect from the background screen. The lighting of the foreground and the actors moving in that area was then keyed to balance naturally with that of the background scene.

An enormous amount of basic light was needed to produce the "cloudy bright" simulated daylight illumination for the foreground areas in the "Dawn of Man" sequence, and this was provided by covering almost the entire ceiling of the sound stage with a total of fifteen hundred RFL-2 lamps.

"Each of these lamps had its own individual switch so that we could maintain very delicate control of the foreground lighting," Kubrick points out. "This was necessary not only in order to match it with the background lighting, but also because the height of the set varied. In some areas the 'hills' were closer to the ceiling than the surrounding terrain. The individual switches made it possible to turn off any one light all by itself and to literally *shape* the light to the contours of the set. We could do this very, very quickly and with the greatest flexibility."

While Brute arcs with straw-colored gels in front of them were used to provide a hint of modeling and relieve the basically flat effect, no attempt was made to create a strong point source suggesting direct sunlight.

"There's simply no really effective way to realistically simulate a single light source when you're shooting such a huge area in a high lighting key," Kubrick explains, "but if you're shooting for an effect of cloudy weather or spotty sunlight, you can match it perfectly to the background. And that kind of lighting looks better anyway, in my opinion, than full, direct, 'Kodak Brownie' sunlight."

The ghostly night scenes in the "Dawn of Man" sequence were photographed by using basically the same techniques that are routinely employed for shooting day-for-night exteriors in the true outdoors—namely, a couple of stops of under-exposure and printing through a light blue filter.

One stunning effect that invariably brings gasps from the audience was achieved quite unexpectedly and may be regarded as a sort of "bonus" to the production. During the prologue a lithe leopard is seen moving among the rocks. As the big cat turns its head full into camera its eyes seem literally to light up with a brilliant, fluorescent orange glow. The impact is startling.

"A happy accident," shrugs Kubrick. "I can only conjecture that the cat's eyes must contain some substance having a reflectivity similar to that of the 3M material used on our screen, because the eyes picked up the front-projected light and reflected it almost as brightly as the screen itself."

In order to utilize the full scope of the front-projection screen, the normal shooting combination paired a 75mm lens on the film camera with a 14-inch lens on the 8 × 10 projector. However, it was possible, by "cheating" a bit, to record scenes with an even wider scope. This was accomplished by using a 50mm lens on the camera and extending the sides of the composition beyond the limits of the screen with foreground elements such as a boulder or a river bank.

There is no doubt that the superlative quality of the front-projection sequences in *2001: A Space Odyssey* will lead to a widespread adoption of the technique within the film industry. "In my opinion it will revolutionize what we used to call 'transparency photography' because of its great flexibility and scope," comments M-G-M Post-production Administrator Merle Chamberlin. "Because it affords the capability of projecting a sharp, clear background onto such a huge screen, it will be possible to achieve tremendous production value at a relatively low cost. You can create almost any locale quite realistically right on the sound stage, and march a whole army through it if you choose—in one door of the stage and out the other."

Already the process is being used in the production of another M-G-M super-spectacle, *Where Eagles Dare*, which is currently shooting in London, and Special Effects expert Tom Howard is adapting it to the use of moving backgrounds by devising a special 65mm motion picture movement that will accommodate a frame twenty sprocket holes wide. This movement will transport the film horizontally (much in the manner of Vista-Vision) and will make possible the front-projection of a very large and clear motion picture scene to be used as a background.

If for no other reason than this, the production of *2001* might be considered a cinematic milestone—but there are a great many *more* reasons!

CREATING SPECIAL EFFECTS FOR

2001: A SPACE ODYSSEY

Douglas Trumbull

2001: A Space Odyssey was an extremely complex and difficult film to make, and naturally there are many interesting stories connected with the production. Probably the most important aspect of the film is its special effects, and in this article I shall try to relate some of the specific problems encountered in a production of this type, some of the techniques we used to create the effects, and a few other interesting points about the production as a whole.

One of the most serious problems that plagued us throughout the production was simply keeping track of all ideas, shots, and changes and constantly re-evaluating and updating designs, storyboards, and the script itself. To handle all of this information, a "control room," constantly manned by several people and with walls covered by PERT charts, flow diagrams, progress reports, log sheets, punch cards, and every conceivable kind of filing system, was used to keep track of all progress on the film.

With a half-dozen cameras shooting simultaneously, some on twenty-four-hour shifts, and different aspects of many sequences being executed at once, the problem of keeping apprised of each shot's progress was difficult at best. For the purpose of being able to discuss a shot without referring to a storyboard picture, each scene had a name as well as a number. For example, all scenes in the Jupiter sequence were named after football plays—"deep pass," "kickoff," "punt return," etc. Each of these terms called to mind a certain scene which related in some way to the name.

Early in production we began to realize that storyboards were useful only to suggest the basic scene idea, and as soon as a particular model or effect would come before the camera, something new would suggest itself and the scene would be changed. This change would often influence subsequent scenes. As each element of a shot was completed, a frame clip of the 35mm rush print would be unsqueezed and blown up to storyboard size with prints distributed to all of the people concerned. It was necessary to keep such an accurate record so that work could begin on other elements of the same shot. For example, each scene of the *Discovery* spacecraft required a different angle and speed of star movement, and a different positioning and action of the miniature rear-projected image in the cockpit.

All moving images in the windows of the various spacecraft were rear projected either at the time of photography of the model, although as a separate exposure, or later after the model image had been duped using Technicolor Yellow-Cyan-Magenta Masters, or "YCM's."

A few scenes show a miniature rear-projected image in the window of a spacecraft as the spacecraft is matted over an image of the moon. For this effect the foreground spacecraft was a still photograph mounted on glass and, using a bi-pack camera, the masters of the background image could be printed with a white backing behind the still photo—the photo silhouette producing its own matte. Then the photo and the rear-projected image could be shot as separate exposures onto the same negative. To produce exactly the same movement on each successive exposure, all movement drives and film advances were selsyn synchronized. The mammoth device designed to produce this effect we nicknamed the "Sausage Factory," because we expected the machine to crank out shots at a very fast rate. This turned out to be wishful thinking, however, and shooting became very painstaking and laborious work. Another drawback to printing masters in this way was the fact that lens flaring caused by the white backing would partially print the image within the silhouette. Therefore only very dark backgrounds could be used for these shots.

One of our first serious special effects problems presented itself during the live action shooting. The interior set of the *Orion* spacecraft (which flew from the earth to the space station) and the interior set of the *Aries* spacecraft (which flew from the space station to the moon) were both equipped with pinhole star backgrounds outside the windows. These backgrounds were made of thin sheet metal with each star individually drilled, and were mounted on tracks to produce an apparent motion from inside. As shooting began it became apparent that when the stars had the correct intensity in the 35mm print-down, they were much too bright in a 70mm print. And, when the stars looked correct in the 70mm version, they would disappear altogether in 35mm. So star brightness became a compromise, and after all the problems encountered in trying to accurately control star intensity on the set, almost all stars shot subsequent to those interiors were photographed on the animation stand.

The Oxberry animation stand equipped with a 65mm Mitchell camera was used for shooting backgrounds of stars, Earth, Jupiter, the Moon, as well as for rotascoping and shooting high contrast mattes. All stars shot on the animation stand were spatter-airbrushed onto glossy black paper backing and were shot at field sizes of from six to twenty-four inches wide. Extensive tests were made to find the optimum star speed for each shot and great care was taken to control the action so that the stars wouldn't strobe. In almost all shots it was necessary for the stars to be duped, but this became a simpler problem because they required only one record instead of the usual three YCM's.

Backgrounds of the Earth, Jupiter, Jupiter's moons, and others were back-lit Ektachrome transparencies ranging in size from 35mm to eight by ten inches, and these were shot from much larger painted artwork. The Moon was a series of actual astronomical glass plates produced by the Lick Observatory. These plates were used only after nearly a year of effort at the studio to build a moon model—several attempts, in fact, by different artists, and all were unsuccessful.

It may be noted that in only a few effects shots in space does one object overlap another. The reason for this is that normal matting techniques were either difficult or impossible to use. The rigging to suspend the models was so bulky and complex that the use of the blue screen technique would have been very awkward. Also, the blue screen would have tended to reflect fill light into the subtle shadow side of the white models. It became a monumental task merely to matte the spacecraft over the stars, and the final solution to this was meticulously rotascoped, hand-painted mattes.

Since we couldn't afford to tie up the animation stand, or any camera, for very laborious and time-consuming rotascope jobs on so many shots, a unique rotascoping system was devised. Using ordinary darkroom enlargers, equipped with carriers for rolls of 70mm film, each frame-by-frame image was projected onto specially marked animation peg boards, to which the projected image of the perforations had to be visually aligned.

We found that a star could not be allowed to penetrate the edge of any spacecraft image even to the very slightest degree, although it was unnoticeable if the star was extinguished several frames before reaching that image. So to account for the poor tolerances in our visually registered system, each rotascoped cel was painted with a slightly oversized image.

All special effects work involves the standard problems of film steadiness, color correction, and matting, and *2001* was no exception. Since every effects shot necessitated the combining of multiple separate images onto one negative, absolute film steadiness was essential. After trying for months to find some rhyme or reason as to why some shots were steady and some weren't, we began the tedious task of comprehensive steady-tests on every roll of raw stock, every set of YCM's, and every roll of 35mm print-downs.

Another problem that gave us many headaches was the loss of black density due to multiple duped images being exposed onto one negative, and in a space film like *2001* the retention of blacks was very important. Part of this problem could be solved by ordering very dense sets of YCM masters to retain maximum contrast. Most original negatives were shot slightly over-exposed so that a higher printer light would be required to reproduce the image. This helped a little, but if carried too far would take the brilliance out of the whites. These precautions were only partially helpful and any shot involving more than two or three sets of masters would suffer a noticeable greying of the blacks.

The solution was to make at least one element in the scene an original unduped image. Aside from helping to retain the blacks, an original image is naturally preferable to a duped one, and in many cases great pains were taken to keep all elements of an entire scene on the original negative.

The first live action shooting on *2001* took place in the giant moon excavation set built on Stage H at Shepperton Studios. The set itself only included a small portion of terrain at one end for the astronauts to walk on, so shots that included the complete Moon terrain, stars, and Earth, were held undeveloped for nearly a year until these other elements could be completed, tested, and then exposed onto the held original negative.

The "held take" shots at the Moon excavation were relatively simple compared to the held takes of moving live action miniature projections. Many shots required that a weightless, gyrating astronaut be moving through space, matted over the stars. For this effect, a 65mm shot of the astronaut was projected onto a small white card, and the camera moved relative to that card to produce the apparent motion. Since this miniature projection was already a form of duping, although it remained sharp and brilliant due to the extreme reduction in size, it was important that this image not go through a further dupe generation. In order to retain the miniature projection as a held take, four separate but identical takes would be shot, using the "Sausage Factory" selsyn system to retain absolute synchronization. Only one of these takes would be sent to the lab for processing, where a 35mm rush print would be made to check color and movement, and a 70mm print would be made so that the rotascoping process could begin. Later, the other duped elements of the shot and the matted stars would be exposed onto one of the held takes, still leaving two more takes to iron out any problems which might have arisen in the first "marry-up."

The models in *2001* are probably the most precisely detailed ever constructed for a film. As soon as the overall design was completed on each model, construction was begun to produce the basic form of that spacecraft, and this process often took several months. Then the arduous task of detailing and painting the model would begin. Massive crews of model detailers worked around the clock for several more months to produce the finished results. Basic construction was of wood, fiberglass, Plexiglas, steel, brass, and aluminum. The fine detailing was made up of specially heat-formed plastic cladding, flexible metal foils of different textures and thicknesses, wire, tubing, and thousands of tiny parts carefully selected from hundreds of every conceivable kind of plastic model kit, from boxcars and battleships to airplanes and Gemini spacecraft. A delegation from the production was sent to an international model exhibition in Germany to select the best kits available.

Every minute facet of each model had to be perfect, so that photography would not be restricted in any way, and during shooting the cameras came relentlessly close with no loss of detail or believability.

Each spacecraft was built to a scale which best suited that particular model, without any particular regard to scale relationship between models. Only the *Discovery* spacecraft and the pod were on the same scale, since they had to work so closely together. Very tricky calculating had to be done for the approach of the *Orion* spacecraft to the space station because both models couldn't be built to the same scale. Roughly, the *Orion* was three feet long, the space station eight feet in diameter, the *Aries* two feet in diameter, the Moon rocket-bus two feet long, and the *Discovery* fifty-four feet long with a thirteen-inch diameter pod. The main "command module" ball of *Discovery* was six feet in diameter, and for long shots another complete model of *Discovery* was built to a length of fifteen feet. All moving parts on the models were motor driven and extremely geared-down since most shooting was at a very slow rate due to the necessity for stopping down to small lens apertures to obtain maximum depth-of-field.

The Moon terrain models required considerable depth-of-field also, and in order to keep the distance from foreground to infinity within a focusable range, they were built with extremely forced perspective. Detail was graduated from very large foreground rocks and rubble to tiny mountain peaks and plains on the horizon in a total actual depth of about five feet. To reproduce in model form exactly what a drawing required, the drawing would be photographed as a 70mm-size transparency and projected onto the work area from the exact point at which the Super Panavision camera would be shooting, and with the same focal-length lens. In some cases we still couldn't hold the depth-of-field even with forced perspective, so the model would be shot as two four-by-five black-and-white stills, one focused on the foreground and one focused on the background. Large prints were made of each, cut out, retouched, pasted together, and then shot on the animation stand.

During the filming of what are probably best termed the "psychedelic" effects for the end sequence, we all joked that *2001* would probably attract a great number of "Hippies" out to get the trip of their lives. It seems now that what was once a joke is fast becoming reality, and as of this writing, I understand that each showing draws an increasing number of these people, who would probably prefer to just see the last two reels over and over again.

Stanley Kubrick strongly emphasized to all members of the production crew that he wished the specific techniques used in the last sequence to remain as unpublicized as possible, so out of respect for his wishes and in appreciation of the wonderful opportunity he gave me and others to experiment and produce these very costly effects, I will describe them only briefly without specific details.

As the black monolith vanishes into a strangely symmetrical alignment of Jupiter and its moons, the camera pans up and the "Stargate" engulfs the screen. For this infinite corridor of lights, shapes, and enormous speed and scale, I designed what I called the Slit-Scan machine. Using a technique of image scanning as used in scientific and industrial photography, this device could produce two seemingly infinite planes of exposure while holding depth-of-field from a distance of fifteen feet to one and one-half inches from the lens at an aperture of F/1.8 with exposures of approximately one minute per frame using a standard 65mm Mitchell camera.

After the Stargate, there follows a series of fantastically delicate, apparently astronomical cataclysms. The images implied exploding stars, vast galaxies, and immense clouds of interstellar dust and gas. Without revealing too much detail, I'll merely say that these effects involved the interactions of certain chemicals within a camera field of a size no larger than a pack of cigarettes.

The final series of shots before Keir Dullea ends up in his unusual predicament were done by shooting some fairly unusual aerial scenes, and then juggling the color filters in the YCM duping process. It took months of experimentation to find the key to this technique.

The live action sequences in *2001* involved so many different trick sets, rear projections, and stunts, that the only approach to writing about them is to handle each in the order in which it occurs in the film.

Filming of the "Dawn of Man" sequence took place entirely on only one stage at the studio. Distant backgrounds for all the action were front-projected eight-by-ten Ektachrome transparencies, using probably the largest front-projection device ever made, and constructed specially for *2001*. The projector consisted of a specially intensified arc source with water-cooled jaws to hold the oversized carbons, special heat-absorbing glass, giant condensing lenses which would occasionally shatter under the intense heat, special eight-by-ten glass plate holders and positioning mounts, an extremely delicate semi-silvered mirror, and a specially built nodal point head so that the camera could pan, tilt, and zoom without fringing of the image.

To camouflage the varying light transmission rates between rolls of the front projection screen material on the giant forty-by-ninety-foot screen, the material was cut up into small, irregular pieces and pasted up at random so that slight variations in the transmission rates would merge with cloud shapes or be lost altogether in brilliant sunlight effects. Since the screen occupied an entire wall of the stage, and the front-projection rig was delicate and cumbersome, the sets were built on a giant rotating platform which covered most of the stage floor. Widely varying camera angles could then be obtained with no movement of the screen, and little movement of the projection rig.

During the testing of this front-projection system, it was found that the intense light and heat being poured through the transparency would burn off layers of emulsion in a matter of minutes. Additional heat filters were installed but the only real solution was to expose the plate only during the critical moments that the camera was running. Duplicate plates were used for various line-ups, tests, and rehearsals. Even with such an intense light source, the long throw from projector to screen required lens apertures of around $F/2$.

The first live action shots in the space sequence took place on board the *Orion* spacecraft during its journey to the space station. For long shots of the apparently weightless floating in mid-air, the pen was simply suspended on thin monofilament nylon strands. For the close-up reverse angle shots the entire end of the set was floated away, and an eight-foot diameter rotating glass was moved into position with the pen lightly glued to it. The stewardess merely had to pluck it off.

The movie being shown on the TV set in front of the sleeping passenger was a little more complicated. Kubrick wanted shots of a futuristic car, and close-ups of a love scene taking place inside. A crew was dispatched to Detroit to shoot a sleek car of the future which was provided by, I believe, the Ford Motor Company. The exteriors were shot in 35mm, but the interiors were shot without seats or passengers, as four-by-five Ektachrome transparencies. Using these as background plates for a normal rear-projection set-up, an actor and actress were seated in dummy seats and Kubrick directed the love scene. Shot on 35mm, this was cut together with the previous exterior shots, and projected onto the TV screen using a first-surface mirror.

In the cockpit of the *Orion* spacecraft, during its approach to the space station we begin to see a few of the 35mm animated, rear-projected computer displays on multiple screens. Throughout the space sequences these displays depict the activities of computers on board the *Orion, Aries,* Moon rocket-bus, *Discovery,* and Pod spacecraft.

To produce thousands of feet of continually changing graphic readouts to cover the multitude of screens in *2001* would have been an impossibly long job using ordinary animation techniques. We terminated work with the local animation camera service, set up our own 35mm Mitchell camera with stop-motion motor, and with the help of a very talented and artistically oriented cameraman, we began the job of pasting up and juggling around artwork under the camera as we were shooting. In this way sometimes as much as a thousand feet of active, colorful, diagram animation could be produced in one day. Specific readouts showing docking alignments taking place, testing procedures under way, and other specific story points were not as fast and easy to shoot, however, and the job of producing all of the readouts for *2001* took nearly a year.

The interior of the space station was a giant curved set over three hundred feet long, and sloping up at one end to nearly forty feet. It may be noticeable that in the long shot of two men approaching the camera from the far end, their pace is slightly awkward, and this was due to the very steep slope at that end of the set. Most action took place in the more comfortable area at the bottom. The Earth image seen through the window of the space station was a rear-projected four-by-five transparency in a special rotating mount.

Aboard the *Aries* spacecraft on its trip to the moon, in the passenger compartment a stewardess is watching another TV screen, and again the action was directed and edited by Stanley Kubrick. The galley scene of this spacecraft where the stewardess comes in, picks up a tray,

and then walks up the wall to exit upside down, was filmed using a rotating set with all lights and the camera secured to the rotating structure. The stewardess merely remained upright as the set and camera
rotated around her.

The *Discovery* spacecraft included the most exciting sets of the production, and the most spectacular of these was the giant centrifuge. At
a cost of over $750,000 the massive forty-foot diameter structure could
rotate like a ferris-wheel. With the actors either standing, walking, or
even running at the bottom of the set, cleverly thought-out camera
angles made it appear that the actors could stand upright at any angle
around the circular set.

In one of the most difficult shots Gary Lockwood was strapped into
his seat and had to hang upside-down pretending to eat glued-down
food while Keir Dullea climbed down the ladder at an angle 180 degrees opposed to Gary. As Keir began to walk around the centrifuge
toward Gary, the centrifuge was slowly rotated until Keir and Gary
were together at the bottom. The camera, which was locked down to
the centrifuge floor, was then at the top. For other shots the camera was
mounted on a specially made 360-degree tilting platform which was
bolted to the floor of the centrifuge, and the camera operator sat in a
ferris-wheel type seat which kept him upright at all times. Other shots
were done with the camera mounted on a small rubber-tired dolly,
which would be pulled by grips frantically clambering up the inside of
the centrifuge as it rotated, trying to keep ahead of an actor shadow
boxing at the bottom.

All lights and large banks of 16mm projectors also rotated with the
set, so that exploding bulbs, loose junk, and reels of film constituted a
serious hazard to people nearby. Hard hats had to be worn by everyone
involved, and the control area from where the centrifuge was driven,
and action directed by closed-circuit television, was netted over with
chicken wire and heavy plastic.

The cylindrical corridor which linked the hub of the centrifuge to
the rest of the ship, was constructed of two separately rotating sections, with the camera mounted securely to the corridor end. With the
hub end rotating, the actors could walk down the static corridor and
then step onto the hub as the port came to a position at the bottom. As
soon as they stepped across onto the hub, it would stop and the corridor would begin to rotate in the opposite direction. From the camera's

point of view the apparent rotation remained constant, but the actors seemed to be completely defying the law of gravity.

Other apparently weightless effects, which took place during the excursions outside the spacecraft, and in the "Brain Room," were created by suspending the astronaut on wires and then shooting from directly below so that he would cover his own means of support.

Several versions of the full-sized pod were used during the *Discovery* sequence. Three dummy pods were used in the pod-bay, two of which had operational doors, but only roughly mocked-up interiors. A separate interior pod set was built which included all the instrumentation, controls, and readout displays. Finally, a full-sized pod was built with completely motorized, articulated arms. It took ten or twelve men at long control consoles to simultaneously control the finger, wrist, forearm, elbow, and shoulder actions of the two pod arms, and the interior of that pod was a maze of servos, actuators, and cables.

Possibly one of the most unusual aspects of the live action photography on the interior sets of *2001* is that almost all lighting was an actual integral part of the set itself, and additional lighting was used only for critical close-ups.

TESTIMONIES

Frederick I. Ordway, scientific and technical consultant

My association with the film and with Stanley Kubrick was perhaps the most unplanned major project in my life. It all began in January, 1965, on an extended trip to the Northeast from Huntsville. On the twentieth, I attended the Inaugural Ball of President Lyndon B. Johnson, and on the twenty-first was in Philadelphia attending meetings at the Franklin Institute. The next day I reached New York and lunched with Paul Mathias, New York bureau chief of *Paris Match;* Leland Hayward, the Broadway producer; and Maria Cooper, daughter of Gary Cooper, who is married to pianist Byron Janis. In the afternoon, I rang Arthur C. Clarke, an old friend of mine, and asked him to join Harry Lange and me for drinks at the Harvard Club on Forty-fourth Street. During the course of conversations, Clarke related to us that he had been approached by Stanley Kubrick with the view of coming up with a screenplay dealing with the general theme of extrasolar (beyond the solar system) intelligence. I had never heard of Stanley Kubrick and was unaware of his stature as a filmmaker, and therefore, my first reaction was that Arthur's ideas would not come across well on the screen. I recall saying to Arthur that "You have your extrasolar project, and we have ours," and then telling him about the MacGowan-Ordway book, *Intelligence in the Universe*, then in an advanced state of preparation; Harry Lange had done all the artwork for it, and the manuscript, or at least most of it, was already in the hands of Prentice-Hall, the publisher.

About 8 P.M. we bade good-bye to Arthur and went upstairs to get our topcoats to go out to a dinner party on Park Avenue. It was snowing hard, and we had a bit of trouble getting a cab. While we were waiting in front of the club, the doorman called me and said there was a telephone call. I went in, and discovered to my great surprise that Stanley Kubrick was calling. Arthur had rung him and spoken to him of Harry and me, and obviously raised his interest. We discussed a whole gamut of problems of relating to intelligence beyond our solar system, my experience with NASA on advanced Mars exploration craft, and so on. He asked if Harry Lange and I could meet him at his penthouse the next day with Arthur, which we subsequently did.

I soon discovered that Kubrick had read voraciously on the subjects of science fiction and space science and technology, and had developed quite a lingo—he would often surprise me with a new acquisition. He would often suggest a "systems" approach to this or that problem, ask for parameters, and state that he had just "locked on" to an idea. He was particularly fascinated with computers of the voice input-output type, and would talk about logic elements, neural nets, central processors, integrated computer networks, heuristic systems, etc.

On the fifth of August, 1965, shortly after making a whirlwind trip to Minneapolis, Chicago, and Philadelphia on behalf of the film, my family and I departed with dozens of trunks full of drawings and technical data for England and production of *2001*.

Ordway advice to Kubrick after the film was released:

1. The "Dawn of Man" scene should be shortened, and above all *narrated*. The importance of this cannot be overemphasized. No one with whom I talked understood the real meaning of this visually beautiful and deeply significant sequence. Its intended impact was lost. Certainly, some reviewers, aided by press releases and Arthur Clarke's

lucid comments, knew what it was all about, but the audience doesn't. And the audience not only has a right but a need to know, if the sequence is to have relevance.

Go back to the splendid words of narration:

> The remorseless drought had lasted now for ten million years, and would not end for another million. The reign of the terrible lizards had long since passed, but here on the continent which would one day be known as Africa, the battle for survival had reached a new climax of ferocity, and the victor was not yet in sight. In this dry and barren land, only the small or the swift or the fierce could flourish, or even hope to exist. The man-apes of the field had none of these attributes, and they were on the long, pathetic road to racial extinction.

The sequence now has real meaning. We are concerned with nothing less than racial extinction, the end of a line that eventually evolved into man. The audience cannot help but identify itself with this struggle for survival, and feel haunting rapport with these primitive creatures across the awesome chasm of time.

Narration is also essential to cast Moon-Watcher into a mold of reality.

> As he looks out now upon the hostile world, there is already something in his gaze beyond the capacity of any ape. In those dark, deep-set eyes is a dawning awareness—the first intimations of an intelligence that would not fulfill itself for another four million years.

Narration can also reveal that the man-apes were starving in the midst of plenty because they had not yet learned to consume meat. After the artifact appears, they mysteriously learn—or rather, are taught—to use bone weapons and to eat the animals they soon will slaughter. The narrator's words softly tell us:

> They have no conscious memory of what they had seen; but that night, as he sits brooding at the entrance of his lair, his ears attuned to the noises of the world around him, Moon-Watcher feels the first twinges of a new and potent emotion—the urge to kill. He has taken his first step toward humanity.

The terminal narration of the "Dawn of Man" sequence leads to anticipation. As he throws the bone, his new weapon, up and down, Moon-Watcher thinks:

Now he was the master of the world, and he was not sure what to do next. But he would think of something.

2. Without warning, we cut to the orbiting bombs. And to a short, introductory narration, missing in the present version.

3. The Orion III sequences are satisfactory and the Space Station-V portion came through well, though I was disappointed that the picturephone automated information request scene was deleted. The Aries-IB scenes were good as far as they went, but their effectiveness was lost by the deletion of (1) narration at the beginning (only a few lines are necessary), (2) the delightful dialogue between the stewardess, captain, and copilot, (3) the brief dialogue between the captain and Floyd, and (4) the following narration for the landing sequence:

The laws of Earthly aesthetics did not apply here; this world had been shaped and molded by other than terrestrial forces, operating over eons of time unknown to the young, verdant Earth, with its fleeting ice-ages, its swiftly rising and falling seas, its mountain ranges dissolving like mists before dawn. Here was age inconceivable—but not death, for the Moon had never lived until now.

4. Consider what was lost after the TMA-1 artifact emitted its burst of electromagnetic energy:

Radiation detectors analyzed incoming cosmic rays from the galaxy and points beyond … gusts and hurricanes of the solar winds, as the sun breathed million-mile-an-hour blasts of plasma into the faces of its circling children … but now a deep-space monitoring probe had noted something strange … the faint yet unmistakable disturbance rippling across the solar system, and quite unlike any natural phenomena it had ever observed in the past.

With these missing, but available, pieces, the great symphony becomes coherent. In an age of super science, of incredible information-processing and display devices, of computer-assisted thinking and delicately tuned responses, nothing less than total understanding can be tolerated. We are now on the Discovery midway between Earth and Jupiter. And the audience must know why. Fuzzy thinking, incomplete explanations, lost coupling scenes, missing bits of essential information have no place in *2001*.

5. I was fairly content with the Discovery portion of the film, but only fairly. Impressive though it was, there is too much exercising around the centrifuge for Poole, and the pod EVA sequences could be shortened—particularly since there are two of them. Indispensable dialogue regarding the three hibernating astronauts was lacking; see particularly C12, where Bowman and Poole first become aware that "there is something about the mission the sleeping beauties know and that we don't know...." These few words are probably the most critical to the logic structure of the entire film, and lead to a valid reason why HAL breaks down. Yet they were inexplicably cut out. Poole tells HAL that there is

> something about this mission that we weren't told. Something the rest of the crew know and that you know. We would like to know whether this is true.

HAL enigmatically answers:

> I'm sorry, Frank, but I don't think I can answer that question without knowing everything that all of you know.

Several pages of superb and absolutely required dialogue follow, without which nothing that happens later can make much sense.

From the moment HAL reports the failure of the antenna's azimuth control unit, the film progresses well, but because of unfortunate cutting of key preceding material, much is lost to even the most perceptive members of the audience. It's like a marvelously complicated and beautiful puzzle that has taken years to prepare. Yet, when one sits down to put it together, one finds that many of the pieces are missing. There is nothing striking, intellectually or visually, about gaping empty spaces where gaping empty spaces don't belong.

6. Another point. The dialogue by Simonson, over the mission con-

trol circuit in C148, and that of Floyd in C150, must be reinserted as applicable to the revised script. And the narration in D1. With it, the interstellar sequence can proceed without change, but will mean so much more to the viewers when they see the mysterious artifact once again:

> For four million years, it had circled Jupiter, awaiting a moment of destiny that might never come. Now, the long wait was ending. On yet another world intelligence had been born and was escaping from its planetary cradle. An ancient experiment was about to reach its climax.

Alex North, film composer

I was living in the Chelsea Hotel in New York (where Arthur Clarke was living) and got a phone call from Kubrick from London asking me of my availability to come over and do a score for *2001*. He told me that I was the film composer he most respected, and he looked forward to working together. I was ecstatic at the idea of working with Kubrick again (*Spartacus* was an extremely exciting experience for me), as I regard Kubrick as the most gifted of the younger-generation directors, and that goes for the older as well. And to do a film score where there were about twenty-five minutes of dialogue and no sound effects! What a dreamy assignment, after *Who's Afraid of Virginia Woolf?*, loaded with dialogue.

I flew over to London for two days in early December to discuss music with Kubrick. He was direct and honest with me concerning his desire to retain some of the "temporary" music tracks which he had been using for the past years. I realized that he liked these tracks, but I couldn't accept the idea of composing part of the score interpolated with other composers. I felt I could compose music that had the ingredients and essence of what Kubrick wanted and give it a consistency and homogeneity and contemporary feel. In any case, I returned to London December 24th [1967] to start work for recording on January 1, after having seen and discussed the first hour of film for scoring. Kubrick arranged a magnificent apartment for me on the Chelsea Embankment, and furnished me with all the things to make me happy: record player, tape machine, good records, etc. I worked day and night to meet the first recording date, but with the stress and strain, I came down with muscle spasms and back trouble. I had to go to the recording in an ambulance, and the man who helped me with the orchestration, Henry Brant, conducted while I was in the control room. Kubrick was present, in and out; he was pressured for time as well. He made very good suggestions, musically. I had written two sequences for the opening, and he was definitely favorable to one, which was my favorite as well. So I assumed all was going well, what with his participation and interest in the recording. But somehow I had the hunch that whatever I wrote to supplant Strauss' *Zarathustra* would not satisfy Kubrick, even though I used the same structure but brought it up to date in idiom and dramatic punch. Also, how could I compete with Mendelssohn's Scherzo from *Midsummer Night's Dream?* Well, I thought I did pretty damned well in that respect.

In any case, after having composed and recorded over forty minutes of music in those two weeks, I waited around for the opportunity to look at the balance of the film, spot the music, etc. During that period I was rewriting some of the stuff that I was not completely satisfied with, and Kubrick even suggested over the phone certain changes that I could make in the subsequent recording. After eleven tense days of waiting to see more film in order to record in early February, I received word from Kubrick that no more score was necessary, that he was going to use breathing effects for the remainder of the film. It was all very strange, and I thought perhaps I would still be called upon to compose more music; I even suggested to Kubrick that I could do whatever necessary back in L.A. at the M-G-M studios. Nothing happened. I went to a screening in New York, and there were most of the "temporary" tracks.

Well, what can I say? It was a great, frustrating experience, and despite the mixed reaction to the music, I think the Victorian approach with mid-European overtones was just not in keeping with the brilliant concept of Clarke and Kubrick.

Con Pederson, special photographic effects supervisor

I'll always feel we might have done one more major thing. A lot of time went into a section of the book that would have explained a good deal of the film—the history of the extraterrestrials and their blocks, their wonderful machines. I spent several months designing some possible visual material for this; Stanley was keen for portraying their story, and he talked about what magical things may lie beyond our ken. It was not to be; it could have been too much. We did do a few of the things, and they filtered into the collection of "trip" scenes, but as a cohesive sequence, again relying on narration, it was too much to cope with. Well, it would have added about ten minutes—one reel—but the work to make it credible...who knows? If you read the novel, you'll sense the obstacles of just making the scenes more than *Star Trek*. It is almost as hard to portray the alien world as the alien himself, because the audience is less prepared to accept it in a highly literal but non-story-oriented (a contradiction, really) form. If the styles were more impressionistic, one might get away with it. Nothing—but nothing—has ever been produced in a science-fiction movie that is an artfully done, beautifully alien world or alien being. Not even remotely. I think they're trying to tell us something out there.

But what *has* been done, and has worked, and has really produced emotional responses is the clever use of the ordinary, the commonplace. Even H. G. Wells, in *The Time Machine*, describes the most distant point in the future in terms that relate to a very mundane situation—and one could visualize it working in a film as well as in words: the empty, desolate beach and the gigantic crustaceans grubbing around. Our minds respond to familiar events and use our own images to build on. I think, to be successful, it is wise for a maker of this kind of picture to be prudent in selecting imagery. Stanley certainly was.

Douglas Trumbull, special photographic effects supervisor

Completion often involved the addition of many different elements which may have included miniature projection, stars, Earth or Jupiter, the sun, and quite often the addition of a second model matched in scale and motion to the first, such as the Orion spacecraft approaching the space station or the pod moving relative to the Discovery spacecraft. All of the movements and exposures of the additional elements would be keyed to match the first original photography of the main model shooting.

Throughout the shooting, meticulous care was taken to keep track of minute details concerning camera movement, speed, shutter speed, and exposure. Thousands of rolls of Polaroid film were used to check basic exposures and lighting setups; they were filed for reference. In addition, every single separate element was wedge-tested for exposure, running the gamut from several stops overexposed to no exposure at all, in increments of one-quarter of a stop. At the end of each take, each element would be rewedged. Every take of every element that went before the cameras was meticulously wedged and checked against previous and subsequent wedges to ascertain that lighting conditions, color, temperatures, etc., remained absolutely constant throughout.

One of the most interesting aspects of this complex combination of models, matted stars, Earth, Moon, sun, etc., was that few if any of these shots were preplanned or designed in advance. Each shot merely grew from its first element. Subsequent elements were added and tested for speed, exposure, movement, etc., and were accepted or rejected according to their merits for that shot, with little or no regard to that shot's relationship to any previous or subsequent shots. In most cases, shots would be matted, combined, and completed in their entirety, even though only a few feet or seconds would be used in the final cut of the film. Although this technique may have seemed wasteful, time-consuming, and expensive, it was the only way that latitude could be available in the final cutting of the film. The special effects could be cut just like live action, in that each particular action or story-point was covered by a multitude of angles and shots, each of which was carried to completion.

By the time we got to Jupiter, we started to use football terminology to keep things straight: Kick-off...Fourth Down...Strong Side II... Punt Return...Nearly There...Deep Pass. Then we ran out of that and started getting more oblique. These were always based on some imagined compositional correlation: Pawnbroker...50 Free Games... See How They Run...Vertigo...On the Brink. The last two Jupiter shots were later combined into one long shot called Vertibrink, which later was extended to add Discovery and was then called Vertilong.

Repeated attempts to create a truly believable-looking extraterrestrial constantly ran into the Coefficient of Difficulty. We had to ask ourselves for a definition of what was possible to depict—it may well be there are many things that simply cannot be done to a certain standard. The asymptotic curve annihilates you in the quest for the perfect ion—that is, you can approach it, get infinitely closer all the time, but never reach it. All the while the Coefficient of Difficulty is expanding. If only we'd had a few more years....

Con Pederson

Working with Kubrick is great. I never have enjoyed working more. He is remarkable, with characteristics that tend to make many people defensive, but I couldn't imagine any director tolerating everything. He really is stupendous.

Gordon Moore, art director, TV Times, London, who selected stills for publicity purposes

I was immensely impressed with the absolute perfection Stanley was trying to obtain. There has never been a film, surely where the dominance and single-minded character of the director was so obvious in every frame. His attention to detail was legend. He even involved himself in the making of the cardboard frames that went around the stills I chose. I saw him working seven days a week in the gloom of his cutting room with music sounding incessantly, but he was very approachable. He was looking very haggard toward the end of production, racing against time as he was editing the film. There were lots of visitors to the studios, as Stanley is a magnet to talent, but he was being cautious with his film. I was not allowed to see several takes, and his colleagues were pretty tight-lipped.

Freeman Dyson of the Institute for Advanced Study, Princeton, one of the experts interviewed for a proposed prologue that never made it into the film

When I saw Kubrick at work on *Space Odyssey* in London, I was immediately struck by the fact that he was interested in gadgetry rather than in the people. Watching the finished movie, I found the lack of human characterization even more remarkable. It seemed that Kubrick was forcing himself with iron self-discipline to avoid the brilliant character-sketching and fast dialogue that made *Strangelove* great. The result was for me unsatisfactory. As a scientist, I took the gadgetry for granted, and I wished we had had a chance to see Keir Dullea act.

I was pleasantly surprised to find that the reaction of my teen-age children and their friends to the movie was quite different. They found it exciting and moving. I conclude from this that Kubrick knew what he was doing. He was pitching the message to the young people, not middle-aged professors, and the message got through. . . .

After seeing *Space Odyssey,* I read Arthur Clarke's book. I found the book gripping and intellectually satisfying, full of the tension and clarity the movie lacks. All the parts of the movie that are vague and unintelligible, especially the beginning and the end, become clear and convincing in the book. So I recommend to my middle-aged friends who find the movie bewildering that they should read the book; their teen-aged kids don't need to.

Douglas Trumbull

I didn't realize until production just got under way that Stanley intended to keep the star-child in the movie. *2001* could have been the funniest movie ever made. Stanley's alternative scenes were hilarious. At an early stage, all the astronauts were to make it to the room in the penultimate scene. I told Stanley to kill all except Bowman, and he told me I was ridiculously stupid.

Frederick I. Ordway

The only time in all those years that I didn't hear Kubrick talk about *2001* was during the Israeli-Arab War in 1967, when he kept saying, "Where are the Russian advisers? Where are the Russian advisers?" Stanley, always the general. You can criticize old Kubrick, but it took a genius to put *2001* all together.

ANECDOTES

Peter Bogdanovich

KEIR DULLEA

I was always aware that he knew exactly what he wanted. He would invite Gary Lockwood and myself to have dinner at his beautiful home. And he would invite a lot of other people from all walks of life and different disciplines—art historians, authors and intellectuals. And he was as informed as anybody about their disciplines. He was like an onion—every layer you peeled off there were two new ones to be exposed.

We worked very long hours. But he was very generous—telling me he was feeling bad that he hadn't created a good enough environment, taking the blame for some scene not working for me. If Stanley had been an octopus, with that many arms, he would have held his own camera, done his own makeup, he would have built his own sets. But I had a feeling that he wouldn't have acted in his own films.

JERRY LEWIS (ACTOR·DIRECTOR·WRITER; EDITED A FILM AT SAME STUDIO KUBRICK WAS EDITING *2001*)

He's in the cutting room and I'm watching this man investigate his work, and it was fascinating. He was intrigued with the fact that I did more than one thing. He was a very big fan of "hyphenates." I think he would have loved to have written *2001* without Arthur Clarke. But he did have a high regard for people who directed their own material.

I was in my cutting room around one in the morning, and he strolls in smoking a cigarette and says, "Can I watch?" I said: "Yeah, you can watch. You wanna see a Jew go down? Stand there." That was the night I coined the expression, "You cannot polish a turd." And then Kubrick looked at me and said, "You can if you freeze it."

RELEASE

2001. I see it every week.

—John Lennon

ORIGINAL PRESS RELEASE

Courtesy of Piers Bizony

For Release Tuesday, February 23, 1965

STANLEY KUBRICK TO FILM
"JOURNEY BEYOND THE STARS"
IN CINERAMA FOR MGM

Stanley Kubrick, who received world-wide acclaim as the director of "Lolita" and most recently "Dr. Strangelove," will bring "Journey Beyond the Stars" to the screen for Metro-Goldwyn-Mayer. The picture, which will begin production on August 16th with a cast of international importance, will be filmed in the Cinerama process, and in color. The announcement was made in New York today (23) by MGM President Robert H. O'Brien.

Based on a novel to be published this winter by Arthur C. Clarke and Stanley Kubrick, "Journey Beyond the Stars" will be filmed on locations in Britain, Switzerland, Africa, Germany and the United States. Interior scenes will be filmed at the MGM Studio in London. The screenplay for the production will be written by Kubrick and Clarke.

Describing the production, Kubrick stated:

" 'Journey Beyond the Stars' is an epic story of adventure and exploration, encompassing the Earth, the planets of our Solar System, and a journey light-years away to another part of the Galaxy. It is a scientifically-based yet dramatic attempt to explore the infinite possibilities that space travel now opens to mankind. The great biologist J.B.S. Haldane said: 'The Universe is not only stranger than we imagine; it is stranger than we *can* imagine.' When you consider that in our Galaxy there are a hundred *billion* stars, of which our Sun is a perfectly average specimen, and that present estimates put the number of Galaxies in the visible Universe at a hundred *million*, Haldane's statement seems rather conservative.

"Space is one of the great themes of our age, yet, it is one still almost untouched in serious art and literature.

"Now that the first man-carrying spaceships are actually being built, and the United States is spending over $10,000,000 a day to reach the Moon, and robot probes have already been launched to Mars and Venus, it is time to break away from the cliches of Monsters and Madmen. There will be dangers in space—but there also will be wonder, adventure, beauty, opportunity, and sources of knowledge that will transform our civilization, as the voyages of the Renaissance brought about the end of the Dark Ages.

"During the last few years, some of the world's best minds have applied themselves to questions such as: Since *we* are about to explore space, has anyone already visited Earth? If so, did they come 100, 1,000 or 1,000,000 years ago? Does intelligent life exist on other planets of this Sun, such as Mars or Venus—or will we have to span the million-times greater distance to the other *stars* before we encounter intelligent beings?

"The story of 'Journey Beyond the Stars' opens in the year 2001, when permanent bases have been established on the Moon, manned expeditions have visited Mars, and automatic probes have been sent to all the major planets of this Solar System. Enough has been discovered to make it certain that only the Earth, of all the Sun's children, has ever brought forth intelligence; there are simple life forms on Mars, but that is all. Mankind is alone in the Solar System.

"Then, unexpectedly, and from uncomfortably close at hand, comes the electrifying discovery of extra-terrestrial intelligence."

Clarke is credited in official Communications Satellite Corporation histories as the first person to describe in detail, in Wireless World, October 1945, the communications satellite system. He has written 29 fiction and non-fiction works in addition to "Man and Space," which he wrote in collaboration with the Editors of Life Magazine. Currently engaged in underwater photography on the Great Barrier Reef of Australia and the coast of Ceylon, Clarke is President of the Ceylon Astronomical Society and Past Chairman of the British Interplanetary Society. In 1961 he was awarded the UNESCO-Kalinga £1,000 Prize and in 1963 the Stuart Ballantine Gold Medal (Franklin Institute).

REVIEWS

Pauline Kael (Harper's)

2001 is a movie that might have been made by the hero of *Blow-Up*, and it's fun to think about Kubrick really doing every dumb thing he wanted to do, building enormous science-fiction sets and equipment, never even bothering to figure out what he was going to do with them. Fellini, too, had gotten carried away with the Erector Set approach to movie-making, but his big science-fiction construction, exposed to view at the end of *8½*, was abandoned. Kubrick never really made his movie either but he doesn't seem to know it. Some people like the American International Pictures stuff because it's rather idiotic, and maybe some people love *2001* just because Kubrick did all that stupid stuff, acted out a kind of super sci-fi nut's fantasy. In some ways it's the biggest amateur movie of them all, complete even to the amateur-movie obligatory scene—the director's little daughter (in curls) telling daddy what kind of present she wants.

There was a little pre-title sequence in *You Only Live Twice* with an astronaut out in space that was in a looser, more free style than *2001*—a daring little moment that I think was more fun than all of *2001*. It had an element of the unexpected, of the shock of finding death in space lyrical. Kubrick is carried away by the idea. The secondary title of *Dr. Strangelove,* which we took to be satiric, "How I learned to stop worrying and love the bomb," was not, it now appears, altogether satiric for Kubrick. *2001* celebrates the invention of tools of death, as an evolutionary route to a higher order of *non-human* life. Kubrick literally learned to stop worrying and love the bomb; he's become his own butt—the Herman Kahn of extraterrestrial games theory. The ponderous blurry appeal of the picture may be that it takes its stoned audience out of this world to a consoling vision of a graceful world of space, controlled by superior godlike minds, where the hero is reborn as an angelic baby. It has the dreamy somewhere-over-the-rainbow appeal of a new vision of heaven. *2001* is a celebration of cop-out. It says man is just a tiny nothing on the stairway to paradise, something better is coming, and it's all out of your hands anyway. There's an intelligence out there in space controlling your destiny from ape to angel, so just follow the slab. Drop up.

It's a bad, bad sign when a movie director begins to think of himself as a myth-maker, and this limp myth of a grand plan that justifies slaughter and ends with resurrection has been around before. Kubrick's story line—accounting for evolution by an extraterrestrial intelligence—is probably the most gloriously redundant plot of all time. And although his intentions may have been different, *2001* celebrates the *end of man;* those beautiful mushroom clouds at the end of *Strangelove* were no accident. In *2001: A Space Odyssey,* death and life are all the same: no point is made in the movie of Gary Lockwood's death—the moment isn't even defined—and the hero doesn't discover that the hibernating scientists have become corpses. That's unimportant in a movie about the beauties of resurrection. Trip off to join the cosmic intelligence and come back a better mind. And as the trip in the movie is the usual psychedelic light show, the audience doesn't even have to worry about getting to Jupiter. They can go to heaven in Cinerama.

It isn't accidental that we don't care if the characters live or die; if Kubrick has made his people so uninteresting, it is partly because characters and individual fates just aren't big enough for certain kinds of big movie directors. Big movie directors become generals in the arts; and they want subjects to match their new importance. Kubrick has announced that his next project is *Napoleon*—which, for a movie director, is the equivalent of Joan of Arc for an actress. Lester's "savage" comments about affluence and malaise, Kubrick's inspirational banality about how we will become as gods through machinery, are big-shot show-business deep thinking. This isn't a new show-business phenomenon; it belongs to the genius tradition of the theatre. Big entrepreneurs, producers, and directors who stage big spectacular shows, even designers of large sets have traditionally begun to play the role of visionaries and thinkers and men with answers. They get too big for art. Is a work of art possible if pseudoscience and the technology of movie-making become more important to the "artist" than man? This is central to the failure of *2001*. It's a monumentally unimaginative movie: Kubrick, with his $750,000 centrifuge, and in love with gigantic hardware and control panels, is the Belasco of science fiction. The special effects—though straight from the drawing board—are good and big and awesomely, expensively detailed. There's a little more that's good in the movie, when Kubrick doesn't take himself too seriously—like the comic moment when the gliding space vehicles begin their Johann Strauss waltz; that is to say, when the director shows a bit of a sense of proportion about what he's doing, and sees things momentarily as comic—when the movie doesn't take itself with such idiot solemnity. The light-show trip is of no great distinction; compared to the work of experimental filmmakers like Jordan Belson, it's third-rate. If big film directors are to get credit for doing badly what others have been doing brilliantly for years with no money, just because they've put it on a big screen, then businessmen are greater than poets and theft is art.

Renata Adler (The New York Times)

Even the M-G-M lion is stylized and abstracted in Stanley Kubrick's *2001: A Space Odyssey*, a film in which infinite care, intelligence, patience, imagination and Cinerama have been devoted to what looks like the apotheosis of the fantasy of a precocious, early nineteen-fifties city boy. The movie, on which Kubrick collaborated with the British science-fiction author Arthur C. Clarke, is nominally about the finding, in the year 2001, of a camera-shy sentient slab on the Moon and an expedition to the planet Jupiter to find whatever sentient being the slab is beaming its communications at.

There is evidence in the film of Clarke's belief that men's minds will ultimately develop to the point where they dissolve in a kind of world mind. There is a subplot in the old science-fiction nightmare of man at terminal odds with his computer. There is one ultimate science-fiction voyage of a man (Keir Dullea) through outer and inner space, through the phases of his own life in time thrown out of phase by some higher intelligence, to his death and rebirth in what looked like an intergalactic embryo.

But all this is the weakest side of a very complicated, languid movie—in which almost a half-hour passes before the first man appears and the first word is spoken, and an entire hour goes by before the plot even begins to declare itself. Its real energy seems to derive from that bespectacled prodigy reading comic books around the block. The whole sensibility is intellectual fifties child: chess games, body-building exercises, beds on the spacecraft that look like camp bunks, other beds that look like Egyptian mummies, Richard Strauss music, time games, Strauss waltzes, Howard Johnson's birthday phone calls. In their space uniforms, the voyagers look like Jiminy Crickets. When they want to be let out of the craft, they say, "Pod bay doors open," as one might say "Bomb bay doors open" in every movie out of World War II.

When the voyagers go off to plot against HAL, the computer, it might be HAL, the camper, they are ganging up on. When HAL is expiring, he sings "Daisy." Even the problem posed when identical twin computers, previously infallible, disagree is the kind of sentence-that-says-of-itself-I-lie paradox, which—along with the song and the nightmare of ganging up—belongs to another age. When the final slab, a combination Prime Mover slab and coffin lid, closes in, it begins to resemble a fifties candy bar.

The movie is so completely absorbed in its own problems, its use of color and space, its fanatical devotion to science-fiction detail, that it is somewhere between hypnotic and immensely boring. (With intermission, it is three hours long.) Kubrick seems as occupied with the best use of the outer edge of the screen as any painter, and he is particularly fond of simultaneous rotations, revolving, and straight for-

ward motions—the visual equivalent of rubbing the stomach and pat-
ting the head. All kinds of minor touches are perfectly done: there are
carnivorous apes that look real; when they throw their first bone
weapon into the air, Kubrick cuts to a spacecraft; the amiable HAL begins most of his sentences with "Well," and his answer to "How's everything?" is, naturally, "Everything's under control."

There is also a kind of fanaticism about other kinds of authenticity:
space travelers look as sickly and exhausted as travelers usually do;
they are exposed in space stations to depressing canned music; the
viewer is often made to feel that the screen is the window of a spacecraft and as Kubrick introduces one piece of unfamiliar apparatus after
another—a craft that looks, from one angle, like a plumber's helper
with a fist on the end of it, a pod that resembles a limbed washing
machine—the viewer is always made aware of exactly how it is used
and where he is in it.

The special effects in the movie—particularly a voyage, either
through Dullea's eye or through the slab and over the surface of Jupiter-
Earth and into a period bedroom—are the best I have ever seen; and the
number of ways in which the movie conveys visual information (there is
very little dialogue) drives it to an outer limit of the visual.

And yet the uncompromising slowness of the movie makes it hard
to sit through without talking—and people on all sides when I saw it
were talking almost throughout the film. Very annoying. With all its
attention to detail—a kind of reveling in its own I.Q.—the movie ac-
knowledged no obligation to validate its conclusion for those, me for
example, who are not science-fiction buffs. By the end, three unrecon-
ciled plot lines—the slabs, Dullea's aging, the period bedroom—are
simply left there like a Rorschach, with murky implications of theol-
ogy. This is a long step outside the convention, some extra scripts seem
required, and the all-purpose answer, "relativity," does not really serve
unless it can be verbalized.

Charles Champlin (Los Angeles Times)

Stanley Kubrick's *2001: A Space Odyssey* is the picture which science-
fiction enthusiasts of every age and in every corner of the world have
prayed (sometimes forlornly) that the industry might one day give them.

It is an ultimate statement of the science-fiction film, an awesome realization of the spatial future. As a technical achievement—a graduation exercise in ingenuity and the making of film magic—it surpasses anything I've ever seen. In that sense, it is a milestone, a landmark for a spacemark, in the art of film.

A spacecraft resembling a vast Cubist centipede glides noiseless through deep space toward Jupiter. Men walk in space, and tumble in death toward an eternal orbit. Weightlessness is shown to be an accustomed state.

The Pan American commuter craft makes its ordinary way to the busy Moon, in this day only thirty-three years from now. So ordinary is the experience that the soundtrack is the old-fashioned "Blue Danube" waltz (which is only one of Kubrick's inventive strokes).

Daddy makes a visionphone call from the Moon station to chat with a daughter whose Earthly birthday party he's missing. The waiting lounge looks even more like a plastic vision of limbo than those already in existence, and indeed Kubrick and co-author Arthur C. Clarke are at frequent pains to contrast these lofty experiences with the rather mundane words and worries of those involved in them.

How it is all done I don't begin to know, but it's done in part with mirrors; that I do know. No matter; the effects are stunning. Keeping fit on the Jupiter voyage, Gary Lockwood runs in the vast centrifuge, which is rather like an enclosed Ferris wheel. He runs 360 degrees, 720 degrees: no cuts, no sign of a camera, no problems of gravity. Fantastic.

I spent the first half of the film nudging my wife black and blue and saying again and again, "I don't believe it."

The detail—down to the operating plaque for the Zero Gravity Toilet—is immense and unimpeachable, I'm sure. This must be the best-informed dream ever.

There is a plot, of course, and for my money it is right here that the pocketa-pocketa-queeps of malfunction become audible. (Let me be clear: I don't think the sci-fi-faithful will even hear the queeps of plotting, but the nonaddict with a more literal turn of mind may be in greater or lesser degree exasperated.)

The film begins with a fairly pretentious title: "The Dawn of Man," introducing a long—interminable—sequence (like everything else, beautifully photographed) in which our grandfathers, the apes, achieve the beginnings of humanity. They divide into warring camps and discover that an old bone makes a killing cudgel. In the desert the apes ponder a curious tall, black monolith, not natural, not theirs, not Earthly.

In 2001, a similar black monolith has been found buried beneath the Moon's surface. It's hushed up, for it can only mean the existence of other intelligent life in space, maybe unfriendly. Clues point to Jupiter (I guess; things begin to get very elliptical and obscure). A spacecraft manned by Keir Dullea and Gary Lockwood, three hibernating scientists (to economize on life-support commodities) and a rather epicene talking computer named HAL ("Open the door, please, HAL") takes off for Jupiter.

Whether they make it, I honestly don't know. The computer turns villain (confirming a widely held suspicion) and at last Dullea enters into a very psychedelic-looking trip, the aurora borealis viewed from within, and absolutely dazzling, whatever it is meant to mean.

Ultimately the monolith reappears in a Regency drawing room; Dullea confronts himself in various stages of antiquity and our last view is of a thoughtful green embryo with huge haunting eyes. Like *Blow-Up,* this ending may be a kind of Cinerama inkblot test, in which there are no right answers to be deciphered but only ourselves to be revealed by our speculations. It is a kind of metaphysics that seems deeply a part of science-fiction's attraction.

One can read anything or nothing into the wordless last half-hour of *Space Odyssey.* Dullea, still in spacesuit, is a withered old man exploring an Earthlike house, his space pod parked in the bedroom. A mirror civilization, a periodicity of the whole human experience?

I don't know, and I confess to finding this evasion of a statement, this deliberate obscurantism, just that. There're certainly not any answers, but there is reasonable question whether the questions themselves must be murky.

However, any annoyance over the ending—if indeed it is widely felt—cannot really compromise Kubrick's epic achievement, his mastery of the techniques of screen sight and screen sound to create impact and illusion.

Some of next year's Academy Awards are already bespoken.

Tim Hunter, with Stephen Kaplan and Peter Jaszi (Harvard Crimson)

This review of 2001: A Space Odyssey *is said to be the longest film review ever published in the* Harvard Crimson.

As a film about progress—physical, social, and technological—Stanley Kubrick's huge and provocative *2001: A Space Odyssey* remains essentially linear until its extraordinary ending. In the final transfiguration, director Kubrick and co-author Arthur Clarke (*Childhood's End*) suggest that evolutionary progress may in fact be cyclical, perhaps in the shape of a helix formation. Man progresses to a certain point in evolution, then begins again from scratch on a higher level. Much of *2001*'s conceptual originality derives from its being both anti-Christian *and* anti-evolutionary in its theme of man's progress controlled by an ambiguous extraterrestrial force, possibly both capricious and destructive.

If the above seems a roundabout way to open a discussion of an eleven-million-dollar Cinerama spectacular, it can only be said that Kubrick's film is as personal as it is expensive, and as ambitious an attempt at metaphysical philosophy as it is at creating a superb science-fiction *genre* film. Consequently, *2001* is probable commercial poison. A sure-fire audience baffler guaranteed to empty any theater of ten percent of its audience, *2001* is even now being reedited by Kubrick to shorten the 165-minute length by 15-odd minutes. *2001*, as it is being shown in Boston now, is in a transitional stage, the theater currently exhibiting a splice-ridden rough-cut while awaiting new prints from the M-G-M labs.

Although some sequences are gone, most of the cutting consists of shortening lengthy shots that dwelled on the slow and difficult operation of space-age machinery. Kubrick probably regrets his current job of attempting to satisfy future audiences: the trimming of two sequences involving the mechanics of entering and controlling "space pods," one-man spaceships launched from the larger craft, may emphasize plot action but only at the expense of the eerie and important continuity of technology that dominates most of the film. *2001* is, among other things, a slow-paced intricate stab at creating an aesthetic from natural and material things we have never seen before: the film's opening, "The Dawn of Man," takes place four million years ago (with a cast composed solely of australopithecines, tapirs, and a prehistoric leopard), and a quick cut takes us past the history of man into the future.

Kubrick's dilemma in terms of satisfying an audience is that his best work in *2001* is plotless slow-paced material, an always successful creation of often ritualistic behavior of apes, men, and machines with whom we are totally unfamiliar. In the longer version, the opening of Astronaut Poole's (Gary Lockwood) pod scene is shot identically to the preceding pod scene with astronaut Bowman (Keir Dullea), stressing standardized operational method by duplicating camera setups. This laborious preparation may appear initially repetitive until Poole's computer-controlled pod turns on him and murders him in space, thus justifying the prior duplication by undercutting it with a terrifyingly different conclusion. Throughout *2001*, Kubrick suggests a constantly shifting balance between man and his tools, a dimension that largely vanishes from this particular scene in cutting the first half and making the murder more abrupt dramatically than any other single action in the film.

Even compromised in order to placate audiences, Kubrick's handling of the visual relationship between time and space is more than impressive. He has discovered that slow movement (of spacecraft, for example) is as impressive on a Cinerama screen as fast movement (the famous Cinerama roller-coaster approach), also that properly timed sequences of slow movement actually appear more real—sometimes even faster—than equally long long sequences of fast motion shots. No film in history achieves the degree of three-dimensional depth maintained consistently in *2001* (and climaxed rhapsodically in a shot of a pulsating stellar galaxy); Kubrick frequently focuses our attention to one side of the wide screen, then introduces an element from the opposite corner, forcing a reorientation which heightens our sense of personal observation of spontaneous reality.

His triumph, both in terms of film technique and directorial approach, is in the audience's almost immediate acceptance of special effects as reality: after we have seen a stewardess walk up a wall and across the ceiling early in the film, we no longer question similar amazements and accept Kubrick's *new world* without question. The credibility of the special effects established, we can suspend disbelief, to use a justifiable cliché, and revel in the beauty and imagination of Kubrick/Clarke's space. And turn to the challenging substance of the excellent screenplay.

2001 begins with a shot of an eclipse condition: the Earth, Moon, and sun in orbital conjunction, shown on a single vertical plane in center screen. The image is central and becomes one of three prerequisites for each major progression made in the film.

The initial act of progress is evolutionary. A series of brief scenes establishes the life cycle of the australopithecine before its division into what became both ape and man—they eat grass, are victimized by carnivores, huddle together defensively. One morning they awake to find in their midst a tall, thin, black rectangular monolith, its base embedded in the ground, towering monumentally above them, plainly not a natural formation. They touch it, and we note at that moment that the Moon and sun are in orbital conjunction.

In the following scene, an australopithecine discovers what we will call the *tool*, a bone from a skeleton which, when used as an extension of the arm, adds considerably to the creature's strength. The discovery is executed in brilliant slow-motion montage of the pre-ape destroying the skeleton with the bone, establishing Kubrick and Clarke's subjective anthropological notion that the discovery of the tool was identical to that of the *weapon*. The "dawn of man," then, is represented by a coupling of progress and destruction; a theme of murder runs through *2001* simultaneously with that of progress. Ultimately, Kubrick shows an ambiguous spiritual growth *through* physical death.

The transition from prehistory to future becomes a simple cut from the bone descending in the air to a rocket preparing to land at a space station midway between Earth and Moon. A classic example of Bazin's "associative montage," the cut proves an effective, if simplistic, method of bypassing history and setting up the link between bone and rocket as the spectral tools of man, one primitive and one incredibly sophisticated.

On the Moon, American scientists discover an identical black monolith, apparently buried over four million years before, completely inert save for the constant emission of a powerful radio signal directed toward Jupiter. The scientists examine it (touching it tenta-

tively as the apes did) at a moment when the Earth and sun are in con-
junctive orbit. They conclude that some form of life on Jupiter may
have placed the monolith there and, fourteen months later, an expedition is sent to Jupiter to investigate.

Two major progressions have been made: an evolutionary progression
in the discovery of the tool, and a technological progression inherent
in the trip to Jupiter. The discovery of the monolith has preceded
each advance, and with it the conjunction of the sun and moons of a
given planet, as well as the presence of ape or human at a stage of development where they are *ready* to make the significant progression.
The monolith, then, begins to represent something of a deity; for our
own purposes, we will assume that, given the three conditions, the
inert monolith actually teaches or inspires ape and man to make the
crucial advance. Therefore, it becomes a major force in man's evolution: man is *not* responsible for his own development, and perhaps the
monolith even *brings* the men to it at the precise moment of the con-
junctive orbits.

   To Kubrick, this dehumanization is more than the result of the un-
defined force exerted by the monolith and proves a direct consequence of advanced technology. Kubrick is no stranger to the subject:
The Killing and *Lolita* both involve man's self-expression through the
automobile; Spartacus's defeat comes because he is not adequately
prepared to meet the advanced military technology of the Roman
army; *Dr. Strangelove,* of course, contains a running motif of machines
assuming human characteristics (the machine sexuality of its opening
titles) while humans become machinelike, a theme carried further in
2001. The central portion of *2001,* the trip to Jupiter, can, as an odyssey
toward a final progression of man, concern itself largely with Kubrick's
persistent preoccupation of the relationship between man and his
tools.

Kubrick prepares us for the ultimate emotional detachment of Bowman and Poole; his characterization of Dr. Floyd, the protagonist of
the Moon sequence and the initiator of the Jupiter expedition, stresses
his coldness, noticeably in a telephone conversation with his young
daughter, a dialogue which suggests a reliance on manipulating her
more than it demonstrates any love for her. These men, all profes-

sional, are no longer excited by space travel: they sleep during flights and pay no attention to the what-we-consider-extraordinary phenomenon occurring before their eyes (the rapid rotation of the Earth in the background during the telephone scene).

Bowman and Poole are inhuman. Their faces register no emotion and they show no tension; their few decisions are always logical and the two always agree; Poole greets a televised birthday message from his gauche middle-class parents on Earth with complete lack of interest—he is, for practical purposes, no longer their child. With subtle humor, Kubrick separates one from the other only in their choice of food from the dispensing machine: Poole chooses food with clashing colors and Bowman selects a meal composed entirely within the ochre-to-dark-brown range. In a fascinating selection of material, Kubrick omits the actual act of Poole's murder, cutting to his body in space directly after the mechanical pod-hands sever his air hose, thus taking emphasis off any identification we might suddenly feel and turning the murder into cold, further dehumanized abstraction.

The only human in the film is HAL 9000, the super-computer which runs the ship and exhibits all the emotional traits lacking in Bowman and Poole. The script development is, again, linear: the accepted relationship of man using machine is presented initially, then discarded in favor of an equal balance between the two (HAL, for example, asks Bowman to show him some sketches, then comments on them). This equilibrium where men and machine perversely share characteristics shatters only when HAL mistakenly detects a fault in the communications system. The HAL computers *cannot* make mistakes and a confirmation of the error would necessitate disconnection. At this point the balance shifts again: Bowman asks HAL to explain his mistake and HAL denies it, attributing it to "human error"; we are reminded of the maxim, "a bad workman blames his tools," and realize HAL is acting from a distinctly human point of view in trying to cover up his error.

As the only human in the film HAL proves a greater murderer than any of the men. Returning *2001* to the theme of inherent destruction in social and technological progress, Kubrick's chilling last-shot-before-the-intermission (a shot from HAL's point-of-view, lip-reading a conversation of Bowman and Poole deciding to dismantle him if the mistake is confirmed) suggests the potential of machine to control man, the ultimate reversal of roles in a situation where man makes machines in his own image. HAL's success is partial; he murders Poole, and the three doctors on the ship in a state of induced hibernation. The murder of the sleeping doctors is filmed almost entirely as closeups of electronically controlled charts, a pulsating coordination of respiration regulators, cardiographs, and encephalographs. HAL shuts his power off gradually and we experience the ultimate dehumanization of watching men die not in their bed-coffins but in the diminished activity of the lines on the charts.

In attempting to reenter the ship from the pod he has used to retrieve Poole's corpse, Bowman must *improvise*—for the first time— ad-lib emergency procedures to break in against HAL's wishes. His determination is perhaps motivated by the first anger he has shown, and is certainly indicative of a crucial reassertion of man over machine, again shifting the film's balance concerning the relationship between man and tool. In a brilliant and indescribable sequence, preceded by some stunning low-angle camera gyrations as Bowman makes his way toward HAL's controls, the man performs a lobotomy on the computer, dismantling all except its mechanical functions. Symbolically, it is the murder of an equal, and HAL's "death" becomes the only empathy-evoking scene in *2001.* Unlike any of the humans, HAL dies a natural human death at Bowman's hand, slowing down into senility and second childhood, until he remembers only his first programmed memory, the song "Daisy," which he sings until his final expiration.

Bowman's complex act parallels that of the australopithecus: his use of the pod ejector to reenter the craft was improvisational, the mechanism undoubtedly designed for a different purpose—this referring to the use of bone as weapon-tool. Finally in committing murder, Bowman has essentially lost his dehumanization and become an archetypal new being: one worthy of the transcendental experience that follows. For the last part of the film, we must assume Bowman an individual by virtue of his improvised triumph over the complex computer.

Left alone in the spaceship, Bowman sees the monolith slab floating in space in Jupiter's atmosphere and takes off in a pod to follow it; knowing by now the properties of the pod, we can conjure images of the mechanical arms controlled by Bowman reaching to touch the monolith as did the australopithecines and the humans. The nine moons of Jupiter are in orbital conjunction (a near-impossible astronomical occurrence) and the monolith floats into that orbit and disappears. Bowman follows it and enters what Clarke calls the *timespace warp*, a zone "beyond the infinite" conceived cinematically as a five-minute three-part light show, and intercut with frozen details of Bowman's reactions.

If the monolith has previously guided man to major evolutionary and technological progression, it leads Bowman now into a realm of perception man cannot conceive, an experience unbearable for him to endure while simultaneously marking a new level in his progress. The frozen shots intercut with the light sequences show, debatably, Bowman's horror in terms of perception and physical ordeal, and his physical death: the last of many multicolored solarized close-ups of his eye appears entirely flesh-colored, and, if we are justified in creating a color metaphor, the eye is totally wasted, almost subsumed into a pallid flesh. When man journeys far enough into time and space, Kubrick and Clarke are saying, man will find things he has no right to see.

But this is not, as Clarke suggests in *Life*, the end of an Ahab-like quest on the part of men driven to seek the outer reaches of the universe. Bowman is led into the time warp by the monolith. The Moon monolith's radio signals directed toward Jupiter were not indicative of life as we know it on Jupiter, but were a roadmap, in effect, to show Bowman how to find his way to the monolith that guides him toward transcendent experience.

At the end, Bowman, probably dead (if we are to interpret makeup in conventional terms), finds himself in a room decorated with Louis XVI period furniture with fluorescent-lighted floors. He sees himself at different stages of old age and physical decay. Perhaps he is seeing representative stages of what his life would have been had he not been drawn into the infinite. As a bed-ridden dying man, the monolith appears before him and he reaches out to it. He is replaced by a glowing embryo on the bed and, presumably, reborn or transfigured into an embryo-baby enclosed in a sphere in our own solar system, watching Earth. He has plainly become an integral part of the cosmos, perhaps as *Life* suggests, as a "star-child" or, as Penelope Gilliatt suggests, as the first of a species of mutant that will inhabit the Earth and begin to grow. What seemed a linear progression may ultimately be cyclical, in that the final effect of the monolith on man can be interpreted as a progress ending in the beginning of a new revolutionary cycle on a vastly higher plane. But the intrinsic suggestiveness of the final image is such that any consistent theory about the nature of *2001* can be extended to apply to the last shot: there are no clear answers.

Several less-than-affirmative ideas can be advanced. The monolith is a representation of an extraterrestrial force which keeps mankind (and finally Bowman) under observation, and manipulates it at will. Man's progress is not of his own making, but a function of the monolith—man cannot predict, therefore, the ensuing stages of his own evolution. That the initiation of man into higher stages of development involves murder casts ambiguity as to the nature of the monolith force. In its statement that man cannot control his destiny, *2001* is antihumanistic—this also in the concept that what we consider humanity is actually a finite set of traits reproducible by machines.

The final appearance of the Louis XVI room suggests that Bowman was, in fact, being observed as if he were a rat in a maze, perhaps to test his readiness for a further progression, this time a transcendence. The decor of the room is probably not significant, and is either an arbitrary choice made by the observers, or else a projection of Bowman's own personality (the floor and the food are specifically within Bowman's immediate frame of reference).

If Kubrick's superb film has a problem, it may simply be that great philosophical-metaphysical films about human progress and man's relationship to the cosmos have one strike against them when they attempt to be literally just that. Rossellini's radiant religious films or Bresson's meditative asceticism ultimately say far more, I think, than Kubrick's far-more-ambitious attempt at synthesizing genre and meaning.

Nevertheless, *2001: A Space Odyssey* cannot be easily judged if only because of its dazzling technical perfection. To be able to see beyond that may take a few years. When we have grown used to beautiful strange machines, and the wonder of Kubrick's special effects wears off by duplication in other Hollywood films, then we can probe confidently beyond *2001*'s initial fascination and decide what kind of a film it really is.

William Kloman (The New York Times)

IN 2001, WILL LOVE BE
A SEVEN-LETTER WORD?

Stanley Kubrick has directed such films as *Paths of Glory, Lolita,* and *Doctor Strangelove.* Kubrick's latest film, *2001: A Space Odyssey,* is reported to have cost more than $10 million, and was more than two years in production. Most of the production time was consumed by the creation of special effects, from lunar landings to a brilliant psychedelic apocalypse. Kubrick's films customarily stimulate controversy, disagreement, and occasionally outrage. *2001,* a deeply enigmatic science-fiction fantasy, has opened to lukewarm reviews and left many viewers puzzled over What It All Means. In the following interview Kubrick provides clues, some of them between the lines.

The plot of 2001 *hinges on man's eventual discovery of intelligent beings elsewhere in the Universe. Is this fantasy, or probability?*

Actually, they discover us. But the premise isn't just fantasy. Regular "pulsar" radio emissions have been picked up by scientists in England and Puerto Rico. Four separate sources of transmission have been isolated so far, and the evidence points to highly advanced civilizations, perhaps hundreds of light-years away from the Earth.

Do you consider the evidence conclusive?

Even if it weren't, the odds are heavily in favor of the existence of extraterrestrial intelligence. There are about a hundred billion stars in our galaxy, and roughly a hundred billion galaxies in the visible Universe. Given the common chemical nature of the Universe, the origination of life is now felt to be an almost inevitable occurrence on planets the proper distance from their suns. Most astronomers are now very predisposed to believe the Universe is full of life. And if it is, some of it would be millions of years advanced, simply because it was formed earlier. Our sun is not a particularly old star.

Have you speculated on what form such advanced life would take? What sort of technology it would produce?

Our interest, in the film, is more in man's response to his first contact with an advanced world. It is really inconceivable what form its technology would take, but Arthur Clarke (co-author of the screenplay for *2001*) believes that any technology, say, fifty thousand years ahead of our own would seem like magic to us anyway. Of course, nobody particularly thinks that biological life-forms would endure very long. Immortality—reversing the chemical process that causes the cells to forget what they are doing—seems likely even for man within a couple of hundred years. It's generally thought that after a highly-developed science gets you past the mortality stage, you become part-animal, part-machine, then all machine. Eventually, perhaps, pure energy. We cannot imagine what a million-year jump in science will produce in life-forms. Pure spirit may be the ultimate form that intelligence would seek.

That seems very Platonic.

It is. And all human mythology—which certainly expresses the yearnings of mass psychology—reaches toward this ultimate state. There's an instinctive awareness of the advantages and perfection of the non-biological condition.

The opening sequence of 2001 *shows an ape-man at the dawn of man's existence learning to use objects as weapons. He throws a bone-weapon in the air and it comes down as an orbiting spacecraft in the year 2001 A.D. What's the connection?*

The link is very close, and the time period is really very short. The difference between the bone-as-weapon and the spacecraft is not enormous, on an emotional level. Man's whole brain has developed from the use of the weapon-tool. It's the evolutionary watershed of natural selection. Shaw said that man's heart is in his weapons, and it's perfectly true. There has always been this fantastic love of the weapon. It's simply an observable fact that all of man's technology grew out of his discovery of the weapon-tool.

Which he learned to love, like the Bomb in Doctor Strangelove?

There's no doubt that there's a deep emotional relationship between man and his machines, which are his children. The machine is beginning to assert itself in a very profound way, even attracting affection and obsession. There is a sexiness to beautiful machines. The smell of a Nikon camera. The feel of an Italian sports car, or a beautiful tape recorder. We are almost in a sort of biological machine society already. We're making the transition toward whatever the ultimate change will be. Man has always worshiped beauty, and I think there's a new kind of beauty afoot in the world.

There was a curious story in one of the news magazines recently about the exceptional instability of marriages around the space installations.

Because the machines are so sexy.

HAL, the computer-protagonist of 2001, seems almost human, while the human actors in the film appear to be models of dispassionate efficiency. Is one of the themes that as computers become more like men, men become more like computers?

I don't think they do, unfortunately. HAL is programmed with emotions because most advanced computer technologists feel that when we start building computers more intelligent than men, emotions may be a part of their equipment. Emotions may be a useful short-cut to forming attitudes. But my view is that man will probably remain more or less in the state he is in now. Men are not really becoming more objective or rational. We are still essentially programmed with the same primitive instincts we started out with four million years ago. Somebody said man is the missing link between primitive apes and civilized human beings. You might say that is inherent in the story too. We are semicivilized, capable of cooperation and affection, but needing some sort of transfiguration into a higher form of life. Man is really in a very unstable condition.

People have been very good, really. Countries have acted very responsibly since the nuclear bomb. But there's no question that since the means to obliterate life on Earth exist, it will take more than just careful planning and reasonable cooperation to avoid some eventual catastrophic event. The problem exists as long as the potential exists, and the problem is essentially a moral one and a spiritual one. Perhaps even an evolutionary one rather than a technical one. The technical approach, you might say, is first aid, but it can't be a very profound answer.

Since 2001 ends with an apparent evolutionary transformation, is it offered as an alternative to the end of the world in Doctor Strangelove?

Not really. I'd hate to categorize it as really deeply revolving around that issue. I don't really want to say what it is, but it's more of a mythological statement. All myths have a kind of psychological similarity to each other. Of the hero going somehow into the underworld, or the over-world, and encountering dangers and terrifying experiences. Then he re-emerges in some god-like form, or some greatly improved human form. Essentially the film is a mythological statement. Its meaning has to be found on a sort of visceral, psychological level rather than in a specific literal explanation.

One of the newspaper critics thought that in order to get across a philosophical viewpoint you needed more words than you used.

This, of course, is part of the word-oriented reviewer psychology. I don't have the slightest doubt that to tell a story like this, you couldn't do it with words. There are only 46 minutes of dialogue scenes in the film, and 113 of non-dialogue. There are certain areas of feeling and reality—or unreality or innermost yearning, whatever you want to call it—which are notably inaccessible to words. Music can get into these areas. Painting can get into them. Non-verbal forms of expression can. But words are a terrible straitjacket. It's interesting how many prisoners of that straitjacket resent its being loosened or taken off.

There's a side to the human personality that somehow senses that wherever the cosmic truth may lie, it doesn't lie in A, B, C, D. It lies somewhere in the mysterious, unknowable aspects of thought and life and experience. Man has always responded to it. Religion, mythology, allegories—it's always been one of the most responsive chords in man. With rationalism, modern man has tried to eliminate it, and successfully dealt some pretty jarring blows to religion. In a sense, what's happening now in films and in popular music is a reaction to the stifling limitations of rationalism. One wants to break out of the clearly arguable, demonstrable things which really are not very meaningful, or very useful or inspiring, nor does one even sense any enormous truth in them.

You were quoted once as saying that the comic sense was the most human reaction to the mysteries and paradoxes of life. Do you feel there's a comic sense in 2001?

It isn't reverent, but it certainly isn't comic. There are a few lightly humorous touches, but the moods it tries to create wouldn't be enhanced by any strong comic element. There are very few comic myths.

Bob McClay (Rolling Stone)

"It's God! It's God!"

The young man in the audience screamed, leapt from his seat in the Los Angeles theatre and plunged through the sweeping Cinerama screen. Such was one reaction to one of the most incredible movies of this year, Stanley Kubrick and Arthur C. Clarke's *2001: A Space Odyssey*. The film, three years in the making and done with visual techniques still kept in secrecy, can only be described as a real "chromosome jerker."

On the surface it would seem like a "science fiction" film, but it is not. The corny techniques, visible strings and gimmickery, the melodrama and bad acting associated with the "science fiction" mold are all absent here. And what was "science fiction" twenty years ago is non-fiction today, and it is no more fiction than it is science, a silly categorization that does not apply to *2001*.

"While the film was being made," said author Arthur C. Clarke, "I made the comment that 'MGM is making the first ten-million-dollar religious movie, only they don't know it yet.' " Clarke is the author of many well-known novels and it was the ideas from several of his earlier short stories ("The Sentinel" and "Childhood's End") that were the basis for *2001*. He co-authored the screenplay with director Kubrick, whose last effort was *Dr. Strangelove*.

As well as the stunning metaphysical story which takes place in the film, the sub-plots, the many miniature movies-within-the-movie and other usual filmic ingredients, there is the absolutely stunning and collossal physical technique which created not only "zero-gravity" centrifuges in which much of the action takes place (characters seem to be weightless and Kubrick simply won't reveal how he did this) but also there is the "light-show" which is without question the best "psychedelic," or "total-environment" or "mixed media" display ever assembled, far and away outdistancing ballroom lightshows and any kind of special effects seen in any previous films. These techniques include specially filmed kaleidoscopic effects, reverse-dye color negatives, liquid light projections, slow motion photography, what might be programmed light patterns and other effects designed to represent an exploding nebula and the expanding mind.

2001 begins four million years ago, at the dawn of the age of man. Apes are shown living together in packs, eating raw vegetation and meat from fallen animals. They fight as groups for territory and establish the humanoid pattern.

One primeval morning, the pre-men discover a huge metal monolith in their midst. They are afraid at first, daring to come ever closer to it, finally touching and stroking it. The purpose and meaning of the monolith is unclear (except insofar as that it appears to have been placed there from some other time or place). Shortly thereafter one of the apes picks up a bone from an animal long dead and begins to slowly swing the bone back and forth. In his mind, the idea of weaponry is formulated, mankind has "begun" and in a split-second flash the bone-club he has hurled into the air, slowly spinning, becomes a space station slowly orbiting the earth.

The prologue—the first movement in a four part symphony, if you like—has ended. The final movement awaits, and in the middle is the story told and filmed, with deliberate realism that makes those final moments not a realistic drama, but dramatic reality.

"This film," says Clarke, "is about reality, about the way things are on this planet. It is culturally shocking that we are perhaps very low on the ladder of intelligence. This is part of the movie's meanings. There are people who will not face this."

The entrance of a Pan-Am rocket from earth into the space station opens the second part of the movie. Two things are accomplished here: the plot begins and Kubrick begins establishing a meticulous reality in detail. He has such touches as the Pan-Am rocket, the Hilton Space Station, the Howard Johnson Earthlight Room, the RCA Whirlpool Liquipack dispenser, a Zero-Gravity Toilet ("Read Instructions carefully"). Kubrick extends this to using as a musical theme the "Blue Danube Waltz," at first rather trite, but then purpose-serving in its reminder of the commonplace.

Dr. Haywood Floyd steps off the Pan-Am rocket on his way to the moon for a secret government mission. He runs into some Russian scientists, who ask him what his purpose is (they suspect a plague at the USA's Clavius Moon Base which has been sealed off from all visitors for weeks.) What is in fact happening is that the plague rumor is a cover story for the discovery of an object on the moon about which the scientists are baffled: a rectangular metal monolith. The same object (but perhaps not the same one) from the pre-historic scenes.

The scientist arrives on the moon, gives a security talk to the government personnel stationed there, and heads for the crater where the object has been erected. As he and his colleagues explore the object, looking at it and touching it, like the apes, the sun passes directly overhead and the monolith emits a piercing radio signal toward the planet Jupiter.

The second movement has ended; the first parallel of meaning has been set.

The story, however, is not as trite as it appears in the telling. It is fully the equal of the cinematic effects, for what we have is a slowly constructed, almost ploddingly created reality being built, only waiting for the closing scenes where a complete reversal is carried off, one which seems to be the only logical conclusion to all the previous contradictory material.

The third place of the film is seen eighteen months later in the "Jupiter Mission." A seven-hundred-foot spacecraft, Discovery, is headed towards Jupiter to find out whatever can be known about the monolith and the radio signal. The spaceship is being run by two astronauts (Keir Dullea and Gary Lockwood), with three scientists in suspended animation to be unfrozen when they arrive on Jupiter, and a computer named HAL 9000.

HAL 9000, which Clarke says is what a computer will really be like in the year 2001, is the only one who knows the real purpose of the mission. He reasons, thinks, speaks, has a personality (maybe even gay) and has the real control of the mission. What develops in this portion is that the computer and the astronauts have a fight over control of the spaceship, with the computer killing all but Astronaut Dullea, who finally disconnects Hal 9000 and learns the purpose of the mission.

The finale is told without dialogue, as the spaceship approaches Jupiter and discovers another monolith in orbit around that planet with his moons. As Dullea approaches the object to investigate, his ship and mind leave his control. Dullea enters another dimension or another time, he ages, dies, is reborn, sees himself at other times and ages, and places, and finally loses his physical self altogether. Another evolution has been completed.

This last scene is by far the one of genuine brilliance. Here is where we see that probing the secrets of the universe means dealing with the mystery of life. And it is here where a young man leaped from his theatre seat and jumped through the screen screaming "It's God! It's God!"

Albert Rosenfeld (Life)

PERHAPS THE MYSTERIOUS MONOLITHIC SLAB IS REALLY MOBY DICK

It was not a star child climbing onto Stanley Kubrick's lap and drawing a fond smile from Arthur Clarke that evening four years ago, but only one of Kubrick's three earth children. Nor did the Kubricks' pleasant apartment present an out-of-the-ordinary scene, considering the vistas of cosmic grandeur being hatched there. Yet there was a certain grandeur in the spectacle of two such marathon cerebrators in the throes of cerebration, and I was properly awed by it. They were plotting their movie, and Kubrick was bouncing ideas off Clarke, who sat there, a mild, scholarly-looking man, full of facts and crinkly with humor. Clarke possesses equally large funds of imagination and scientific information. This has produced a body of science fiction and technical material that is not only distinguished but also prophetic. Twenty years before Comsat, he published a paper describing in precise detail the synchronous communications satellite. My own audience-participation had come about mainly because at that stage of incipient planning and brain-picking, the two thought that, as *Life*'s science editor, my brain might yield some stray, useful bits of information.

The conversation moved at a deceptively easygoing pace, but soon I began to see why Clarke, famous for the staying power of his own intellect, had complained to me, "Every time I get through a session with Stanley, I have to go lie down."

When a subject interested Kubrick, he never let it get away until he was through with it. He probed with a ruthless tenacity, asking the right questions, comprehending all he was told, never getting enough details to satisfy him. The image that sprang to mind was the nonstop thinking machine. It ran tirelessly, computer-quiet, steady as a controlled nuclear reactor.

How close could a spacecraft come to a planet like Jupiter without being pulled in by its gravitational field? Would computers ever be able to think, *really* think, in the sense of developing independent egos and personalities? Would it ever be feasible to put astronauts into deep-frozen hibernation, as suggested by daring space biologists?

At one point in the story Kubrick wanted to have one of the astronauts trapped for a few seconds without his helmet in the hostile vacuum of space. Could a man really be expected to survive such exposure? The prevailing belief then was no. Clarke disagreed. He thought the risks were exaggerated but he recommended that the astronaut in the movie keep his helmet on. His hunch turned out to be right and the precaution unnecessary. Experiments since that discussion showed that animals could survive brief periods in a vacuum, and the results became known in time to get the astronaut's helmet off again.

Both Clarke and Kubrick were fascinated by the serious possibility that there might one day be an encounter between human and extraterrestrial beings. Kubrick wanted such a confrontation in his story—"but no monsters or men with long beards waiting at the other end of the line."

Kubrick wanted the story to take place within the lifetime of most of today's moviegoers. This meant the voyage in the movie would have to be restricted to our own solar system. Einstein's theory makes it clear that the speed of light is the speed limit of the universe, so travel to the stars over light-years of distance by the year 2001 would be out of the question. But Kubrick wasn't willing to let relativity off the hook too easily. What were Einstein's justifications for his universal speed limit? That took a lot of explaining before Kubrick agreed the story must take place in the solar system.

This posed another seemingly insurmountable problem: scientists deem it highly unlikely that intelligent life will be discovered on any of the sun's other planets. Ah, but this would apply only to biological beings. What about the possibility of nonbiological beings?

One kind of nonbiological being might be an advanced computer, a nonstop thinking machine that could wear out even Stanley Kubrick. Though it seems improbable that such a computer will be available by 2001, Kubrick decided to create one to run his cinematic spaceship. The computer, Hal, is really the most interesting character in the movie. He is responsible for some of the film's most moving situations, and his conversations with the crew provide some of the best dialogue. Hal wakes the astronauts cheerily in the morning, compliments them when they play a good game of chess, is always courteous and considerate—sometimes almost unctuous, though this fails to hide a certain condescension toward the more fallible human members of the crew. In one episode, Hal asks David Bowman to show him a sketch he has just made. Bowman does.

HAL: That's a very nice rendering, Dave. I think you've improved a great deal.... By the way, do you mind if I ask you a personal question?

BOWMAN: No, no. Not at all.

HAL: Well, forgive me for being so inquisitive, but during the past few weeks I've wondered whether you might have been having some second thoughts about the mission.

BOWMAN: How do you mean?

HAL: Well, it's rather difficult to define. Perhaps I'm just projecting my own concern about it. I know I've never completely freed myself of the suspicion that there are some extremely odd things about this mission. I'm sure you will agree there is some truth in what I say ...

BOWMAN: You working up your crew psychology report?

HAL: Of course I am. Sorry about this. I know it's a bit silly.

Hal's ever-watchful glowing red eye follows the astronauts wherever they go on the ship. He hears whatever they say, and on one occasion when they want to talk privately, they get out of earshot only to learn that Hal can also read lips. Hal gets what is, for my money, the best line in the picture, full of *Dr. Strangelove* overtones. After he has killed one astronaut and tried to keep the other from getting back on the ship, he says, "I know I've made some very poor decisions recently."

In the course of the movie, Kubrick sought the advice of space and computer experts everywhere. He hired two gifted men from Dr. Wernher von Braun's NASA staff and had much elaborate equipment designed and built to order. Nothing was simple. A routine shot would often involve a number of interlocking elements requiring separate and painstaking photography of an astronaut, a spacecraft, a planet and a star field, for instance; then all would have to be blended into a single scene, with meticulous care for lighting, relative size and motion of objects, and accurate juxtapositions in space. The organization and correlation of technical data was of such staggering complexity that Kubrick had to rent computers to keep track. Much of M-G-M's $10 million-plus went for special effects—but they will get a lot of it back because of Kubrick's innovations. He invented a means of projection, for example, whereby filmed backgrounds that are indistinguishable from reality can be used right in the studio. M-G-M is already starting to apply the invention to other films, eliminating tedious and expensive months of shooting on location.

Most of these efforts went to attain the highest possible technological accuracy, and therefore the highest possible credibility. To add to the credibility, he wanted familiar brand names to appear—so the shuttle to the moon is Pan American's, the space-station accommodations are run by Hilton, and other firms, from IBM to RCA, helped Kubrick design their products for the year 2001. He gets a certain homey feeling into his spaceships too. Under weightless conditions, a sleeping passenger's arm rises (he himself is belted in) and seems to float effortlessly in the air. A stewardess walks nonchalantly, with Velcro-grip shoes, up the wall and across the ceiling. The sign on the zero-gravity toilet warns users to read instructions carefully. En route to Jupiter, conversations must be gauged to allow for the fact that when an astronaut says "Hello," it takes seven minutes for his voice to reach the earth. Having created a feel of thorough authenticity, Kubrick then felt free to take liberties—not only with Hal the computer but with the other mysterious and incalculably more advanced nonbiological beings whose presence wordlessly pervades the entire film. Clarke suggests that, like Melville with *Moby Dick,* they used realistic technology to serve as a launch pad into realms more metaphysical than physical—with man driven, like Ahab, to a quest for the infinite.

The Moby Dick approach came about because he and Kubrick had decided that their confrontation between human and extraterrestrial intelligence would have to be transcendental in nature. This was required by "Clarke's Third Law," which says, "Any sufficiently advanced technology is indistinguishable from magic." Since the movie deals with beings that were capable of burying a monolith on the moon some four million years ago, their present capabilities would *have* to seem like magic. In fact, it would be utterly unscientific to imagine that such beings would be comprehensible on any human level.

There already exist a number of abstruse mathematical theories which hint that Einstein's speed limit may one day be surmounted and incredible shortcuts discovered for getting from here to there in the universe. Clarke assumes that beings so advanced will have acquired these capabilities.

To capture such a transcendental confrontation on film, Kubrick realized it could not be spelled out on any literal or intellectual level. As shooting proceeded, he stripped away more and more dialogue and narration, relying more and more on visual images and sound to tell the story through direct visceral impact. The fantastic ending to the film remains enigmatic enough to guarantee arguments about its meaning for a long time to come. But it provides an unprecedented psychedelic roller coaster of an experience that few viewers are likely to get over.

I saw Kubrick again just before the movie was to open in New York. He was obviously pleased at the fruit of his labors—and at a pair of news items: Apollo 6 was scheduled to be launched from Cape Kennedy on the morning of the premiere. And radioastronomers had lately begun to receive, from a distance estimated to be more than 100 light-years away, remarkable "pulsar" signals of such regularity that even scientists were speculating that they might have been transmitted by some kind of extraterrestrial intelligence.

From Life

A SHRIEKING MOON SLAB SETS OFF A WEIRD QUEST

It is the first year of the twenty-first century. Strange magnetic emanations from the moon's crater Tycho have impelled the explorers from earth to make a vast excavation. Shoring up the lunar soil, they have uncovered the source of the emanations, a mysterious shaft. Obviously the smooth, hard, shiny rectilinear thing is a made object. But made by whom—or what—and when? Its discoverers have never seen its like before. The film's audience, however, has—in an opening sequence set four million years earlier. It appears mysteriously in a prehistoric landscape, and seems to be influential in getting a group of man-apes to use stones as weapons and tools.

The awesome implication of these slabs—which appear at several critical points in the movie—begins to emerge. They have God-like powers. They are forces for evolution. They are the cosmic calling cards of some superior intelligence. And they are really the most important characters in this film, the first made by Stanley Kubrick since his sardonic movie landmark, *Dr. Strangelove*. It is based on a novel he wrote with Arthur C. Clarke, the noted scientist-novelist.

The movie, which is just now being released by M-G-M, dazzles the eyes and gnaws at the mind. Kubrick called in space consultants from government and industry to assure that the "hard science" in *2001* was precise and up-to-the-minute. But in its nontechnical, sometimes metaphysical aspects he is deliberately ambiguous, lifting the work out of the realm of literal science fiction into a puzzling, provoking exercise in philosophy. There is no explanation or even conjecture about the nature of the intelligence that buried the shaft on the moon. When the uncovered object, finally touched by the sun's rays, emits a series of deafening sounds—signals beamed in the direction of Jupiter—the United States launches a spaceship on man's first trip to the solar system's biggest planet. It is manned by five astronauts—three of whom rest in suspended animation in "hibernaculums" resembling sarcophagi—and by Hal, a talkative, almost-human computer with a superhuman brain.

Alone in his spaceship, Bowman is swept along to the object of the mission, the giant planet Jupiter. Plummeting into orbit, he sees what no man has ever seen before—the distant sun, a small and pallid disk, seen over Jupiter's blazing arc along with several of the planet's twelve moons. This, like all astronomical phenomena encountered so far in the story, is an authentic portrayal of what an astronaut would actually see. But Bowman perceives an unnatural satellite amid the moons, an oblong object identical to the artifact implanted on the earth's moon. As he flashes toward it, the entire shape of space is suddenly altered and he and the ship are drawn, as if through a cosmic chute, into an ever-changing, fantastic landscape which he cannot relate to any location in the universe. He and his vehicle thereupon perform actions not explainable by currently known physical laws. He finds himself and his spacecraft inside a Louis Seize bedroom. He sees another man who turns out to be himself. Dimensions of space and of time are distorted. In the end the first man to venture into the outer reaches of the solar system returns to contemplate the earth as a newborn babe, a star child, perhaps of an incomparably wise new race. No trace can be seen of man or his technology. There is no hint of age or time, of whether on that lovely sphere twenty-first-century man prevails, or Egyptians, or stone-throwing man-apes.

From Time

A herd of hairy simians chatters and skirmishes beside a water hole. It is, says the screen, "The Dawn of Man." But is it? From somewhere a strange rectangular slab appears, gleaming in the primeval sunlight. Its appearance stimulates one of the simians to think for the first time of a bone as a weapon. Now he is man, the killer; the naked ape has arisen, and civilization is on its way. With a burst of animal spirits, the bone is flung into the air, dissolves into an elongated spacecraft, and aeons of evolution fall away. It is 2001, the epoch of *A Space Odyssey*.

Like many sequences of this contradictory movie, the primate prologue is overlong and repetitious. Still, it serves to introduce the film's key character: the shining oblong, a mass of extraterrestrial intelligence that supposedly has been overseeing mankind since the Pliocene age. Now, in the twenty-first century, the mass has been identified by scientists, who have traced its radio signal back to Jupiter. A spaceship, *Discovery I,* is dispatched to that remote planet. Aboard are two conscious astronauts (Keir Dullea and Gary Lockwood) and three hibernating scientists sealed like mummies in sarcophagi. Also on board is Hal, a computer-pilot programmed to be proud of his job and possessed of a wistful, androgynous voice.

SCIENTIST BENUMBER

For what seems like a century the journey goes well. Then, abruptly, Hal begins to act in an indefinably sinister manner, and the astronauts prepare to perform a lobotomy on their cybernetic buddy by removing his memory banks. But Hal discovers the plan.

Intermission. By this time, almost 1 hr. and 40 min. have passed, and the non-sci-fi fanatic may feel as benumbed as the scientists in their "hibernaculums." In depicting interplanetary flight thirty-three years from now, Director Stanley Kubrick and his co-scenarist, Arthur C. Clarke, England's widely respected science and science-fiction writer, dwell endlessly on the qualities of space travel; unfortunately they ignore such old-fashioned elements as character and conflict. As the ship arcs through the planetary void it is an object of remarkable beauty—but in an effort to convey the idea of careening motion, the sound track accompanying the trek plays *The Blue Danube* until the banality undoes the stunning photography. The film's best effects do not occur until the second part, but when they arrive, they provide the screen with some of the most dazzling visual happenings and technical achievements in the history of the motion picture.

MIND BENDER

After a wrenching struggle, Dullea manages to disarm the mutinous Hal just as *Discovery I* enters the orbit of Jupiter. There he sees the object of his trip—the omnipotent slab. He heads for it, and suddenly conventional dimensions vanish. An avalanche of eerie, kinetic effects attacks the eye and bends the mind. Kubrick turns the screen into a planetarium gone mad and provides the viewer with the closest equivalent to psychedelic experience this side of hallucinogens. At the end, beyond time and space, Dullea apparently learns the secret of the universe—only to find that as Churchill said about Russia, it is a riddle, wrapped in a mystery, inside an enigma.

Like *Space Odyssey* itself, the ambiguous ending is at once appropriate and wrong. It guarantees that the film will arouse controversy, but it leaves doubt that the film makers themselves knew precisely what they were flying at. Still, no film to date has come remotely near *Odyssey*'s depiction of the limitless beauty and terror of outer space. In this 2-hr. 40-min. movie, only 47 minutes are taken up with dialogue. The rest of the time is occupied with demanding, brilliant material for the eye and brain. Thus, though it may fail as drama, the movie succeeds as visual art and becomes another irritating, dazzling achievement of Stanley Kubrick, one of the most erratic and original talents in U.S. cinema.

MIND BOGGLER

Since he went on his own odyssey, from *Look* photographer to the ionosphere of the moviemaking business, Kubrick, thirty-nine, has built a reputation for sensing—and often starting—new trends. At twenty-seven he made a killing with *The Killing*, a gritty city melodrama that is still being imitated. His next project was *Paths of Glory,* one of the first—and best—of this generation's antiwar films. After that came two more trend setters. The first was *Lolita,* a hollow, literalized adaptation of the book, for which it can be said only that it wore basic black before black comedy was fashionable. The other, *Dr. Strangelove,* was a major American contribution to the furiously active cinema of the absurd.

Now that Kubrick has taken off on his space kick, his fans are convinced that a sci-fi renaissance is on its way. As the spy film sinks slowly in the West, and the western sinks rapidly into TV, studios are occupied with some dozen ambitious fantasy features, ranging from Ray Bradbury's *The Illustrated Man* with Rod Steiger, to the high-camp French comic strip *Barbarella,* with Jane Fonda. The next trend for Kubrick? All he will give away is that it will be "a mind boggler."

Joseph Morgenstern (Newsweek)

Most of the sporadic power and sly humor of *2001: A Space Odyssey* derive from a contrast in scale. On the one hand we have the universe; that takes a pretty big hand. On the other we have man, a recently risen ex-ape in a dinky little rocket ship. Somewhere between earth and Jupiter, though, producer-director Stanley Kubrick gets confused about the proper scale of things himself. His potentially majestic myth about man's first encounter with a higher life form than his own dwindles into a whimsical space operetta, then frantically inflates itself again for a surreal climax in which the imagery is just obscure enough to be annoying, just precise enough to be banal.

The first of the film's four movements deals with man's prehistoric debut. It is as outrageous and entertaining as anything in *Planet of the Apes,* but much more engrossing. Cutting constantly between real apes and actors (or dancers) in unbelievably convincing anthropoid outfits, Kubrick establishes the fantasy base of his myth with the magical appearance of a monolithic slab in the apes' midst. They touch it, dance around it, worship it. The sequence ends with a scene in which one of our founding fathers picks up a large bone, beats a rival into ape-steak tartare with it and thus becomes the first animal on earth to use a tool. The man-ape gleefully hurls his tool of war into the air. It becomes a satellite in orbit around the moon. A single dissolve spans four million years.

LANDSCAPES

With nearly equal flair the second movement takes up the story in the nearly present future. Man has made it to the moon and found another shiny slab buried beneath the surface. By this time the species is bright enough to surmise that the slab is some sort of trip-wire device planted by superior beings from Jupiter to warn that earthmen are running loose in the universe. Kubrick's special effects in this section border on the miraculous—lunar landscapes, spaceship interiors and exteriors that represent a quantum leap in quality over any sci-fi film ever made.

In a lyrical orbital roundelay, a rocket ship from earth takes up the same rotational rate as the space station it will enter. Once again, as in *Dr. Strangelove*, machines copulate in public places. This time, however, they do it to a Strauss waltz instead of "Try a Little Tenderness"—the smug, invariable, imperturbable swoops of "The Blue Danube" juxtaposed with the silent, indifferent sizzling of the cosmos.

Where *Strangelove* was a dazzling farce, *2001* bids fair at first to become a fine satire. We see that space has been conquered. We also see it has been commercialized and, within the limits of man's tiny powers, domesticated. Weightless stewardesses wear weightless smiles, passengers diddle with glorified Automat meals, watch karate on inflight TV and never once glance out into the void to catch a beam of virgin light from Betelgeuse or Aldebaran.

ANXIETIES

The third movement begins promisingly too. America has sent a spaceship to Jupiter. The men at the controls, Keir Dullea and Gary Lockwood, are perfectly deadpan paradigms of your ideal astronaut: scarily smart, hair-raisingly humorless. The computer that runs the ship and talks like an announcer at a lawn-tennis tournament admits to suffering from certain anxieties about the mission (or, more ominously, pretends to suffer from them) but the men are unflappable as a reefed mainsail.

Your own anxieties about *2001* may begin to surface during a scene in which Lockwood trots around his slowly rotating crypt-ship and shadowboxes to keep in shape. He trots and boxes, boxes and trots until he has trotted the plot to a complete halt, and the director's attempt to show the boredom of interplanetary flight becomes a crashing bore in its own right. Kubrick and his co-writer, Arthur C. Clarke, still have some tricks up their sleeves before Jupiter: pretty op-art designs that flicker cryptically across the face of the instrument display tubes, a witty discussion between Dullea and Lockwood on the computer's integrity.

But the ship is becalmed for too long with stately repetitions of earlier special effects, a maddening sound of deep breathing on the sound track, a beautiful but brief walk in space and then a long, long stretch of very shaky comedy-melodrama in which the computer turns on its crew and carries on like an injured party in a homosexual spat. Dullea finally lobotomizes the thing and, in the absence of any plot advancement, this string of faintly familiar computer gags gets laughs. But they are deeply destructive to a film that was poking fun itself, only a few reels ago, at man's childish preoccupation with technological trivia.

CHALLENGE

On the outskirts of Jupiter, *2001* runs into some interesting abstractions that have been done more interestingly in many more modest underground films that were not shot in 70-mm. Super Panavision, then takes a magnificent flight across the face of the planet: mauve and mocha mountains, swirling methane seas and deep purple skies. But its surreal climax is a wholly inadequate response to the challenge it sets for itself, the revelation of a higher form of life than our own. When Dullea, as the surviving astronaut, climbs out of his spaceship he finds it and himself in a Louis XVI hotel suite. Original idea? Not very. Ray Bradbury did it years ago in a story about men finding an Indiana town on Mars, complete with people singing "Moonlight on the Wabash."

It is a trap, in a sense, with the victim's own memories as bait. The nightmare continues, portentously, pretentiously, as Dullea discovers the room's sole inhabitant to be himself. As he breathes his last breath, another slab stands watching at the foot of his deathbed, and when he dies he turns into a cute little embryo Adam, staring into space from his womb. So the end is but the beginning, the last shall be first and so on and so forth. But what was the slab? That's for Kubrick and Clarke to know and us to find out. Maybe God, or pure intelligence, maybe a Jovian as we perceive him with our primitive eyes and ears. Maybe it was a Jovian undertaker. Maybe it was a nephew of the New York Hilton.

Max Kozloff (Film Culture)

Happy the film whose press is passionately divided. After being reviled and celebrated by serious critics, Stanley Kubrick's *2001,* his first movie since *Dr. Strangelove,* of five years ago, continues to instigate the most heated squabbles. For it is judged to be either a conundrum wrapped up in a spectacular, or a dazzling color poem decked out with incidental science-fiction trappings. Predictable complaints that it is boring mingle with inevitable gushes that it is gorgeous. One senses, through it all, that something important has happened in the cinema.

On face value, the plot elements of *2001* do not raise the ante of critical discourse. They fit into the stock situations of the futuristic tale, modulated more openly than usual.

Kubrick posits the earthly arrival, three million years ago, of a mysterious outer space force, represented by an eleven-foot-high black slab, that proceeds, somehow, to educate the local man-apes to effect their first great breakthrough: the use of bones as weapons and tools. In an abrupt leap forward from this prelude to the year of the title, a magnetic anomaly on the moon's surface has led American space scientists to uncover another such ancient slab which suddenly emits deafening radio signals upon its first contact with the sun. Eighteen months later, the space ship *Discovery* is worming its way on an undisclosed and unprecedented mission to Jupiter. Aboard are five astronauts, three of whom are entombed in suspended animation. The voyage is masterminded by the Discovery's computer, HAL, an awesome contraption which condescends in compulsively polite English to the crew, and regulates every shipboard function. When HAL predicts an imminent fault in one of the units, investigation by the astronauts fails to confirm his judgment. An ominous aura of mutual suspicion climaxes in chilling technological warfare, in which four of the men are killed and the last (Keir Dullea) manages finally to lobotomize the computer. Only then does he learn through a prerecorded message that the mission of Discovery, known so far only to HAL, is to track the radio signals of the moon slab to their apparent destination, Jupiter. Once again a slab, this time floating freely in the approach to the great planet, heralds a human change nothing short of evolutionary. The astronaut is sucked vertiginously through time as well as space, both grafted together in thunderous shafts of color, to arrive in a Louis Seize hotel room. The dénouement has him a witness to his own accelerated aging, culminating, not in death, but a cosmic human embryo gaping wondrously yet coldly upon the diminutive earth from whence he had come.

In what Susan Sontag has called "the imagination of disaster" Kubrick's story finds an almost conventional place. The arrival of an alien power, its discovery masked for fear of cultural shock, the corporate scientific mounting of a probe, the teamwork of man and machine, an alarming failure of available technology, the sudden aging of a protagonist, all these are familiar stereotypes of the science fiction film. But other features and touches of the plot do not cohere within a pat framework. The "thing that goes wrong," the misguided, enthusiastic machine, is the help-mate of man himself. When being disconnected, its anaesthetized brain pleas for its life and euphemistic apologies for its lethal behavior descend finally and pathetically to a replay of its first utterance at "birth": the song "Daisy, Daisy, give me your answer, do ..." (It may be an ironic anticipation of the astronaut's own "rebirth.") Then too, analogies infiltrate and confuse the linear continuity of the story. Thus, the lantern eye of a leopard and that of HAL glow with equal menace, while the meat torn by the apes and the gruel eaten by the astronauts are comparably disgusting. And what is one to make of that coincidental orbital conjunction of the earth, moon, and sun, at each appearance of the slab? These cyclical happenings are symbolic of an extra-terrestrial ruling presence never really explained. As for the unknown beings that magnetize the crucial space-probe, they are obviously benevolent, even if never palpable. No absolute heroes or villains emerge in this overall situation—and suspense itself seems generated not so much by twists of narrative conflict, as by a larger dilemma posed by the director. Ultimately, it is not a crisis in identity that he gives us, nor a final takeover by artifacts, nor still less a neutralization of anxiety. Unlike so many science-fiction movies that ritually raise a scare only to reassure, *2001* would show the symbiotic man-machine relationship as the necessary prelude to some new ecstatically masterful realm of being, disquieting because it is unimaginable.

The one significant film to offer a parallel on this theme is Godard's *Alphaville*, of 1965. Here, the master computer, yoking a whole city, speaks in the sepulchral ratchet of a man whose vocal cords have been maimed. An aura of unmitigated evil permeates the atmosphere, as people are sent wholesale to their death for the crime of emotion. This Orwellian cliché would not have produced a shiver if the protagonist, supposedly a man from our own world, had not himself behaved with murderous inhumanity. What emerges, therefore, is only a *fictional* opposition between feeling and mechanism, just as the present becomes hideously indistinguishable from the future. Moreover, with radical insistence, Godard pulverizes the genre sources—horror film, science fiction, detective, adventure, and spy, guiding every snippet of his action, in such a way that the "narrative" is transformed into a puree of mindless violence. The result, all the more malign because equivocal, is a ruthless oscillation between the farfetched and the banal, creative form and cliché content. Worse, and more effective still, the spectator is subjected to such severe staccato dislocations of expectancy that he can't escape into any long-term detachment from the proceedings, despite their blatant artifice.

By contrast, *2001* is almost one long, spun-out documentary of grandeur, a kind of loving observation of future men at complex work, overpoweringly American in its pioneer aura. All behavior has a concise, purposeful regimen; every mechanical operation has an immediate rational justification. But half-way through this credible epic, the director introduces the Frankenstein-machine whose obedience gradually crumbles into homicidal aggression (whether through a pre-circuiting on earth, or its own deranged "instincts," one never knows). From then on, melodrama appears to rescind whatever the film's earlier pretensions to objectivity, until the final plummet into the "time-warp" enfolds us in a psychedelic swirl that leaves every basic question intriguingly, but gratuitously begged. "A great deal of skill and ingenuity," writes Robert Hatch, "went into this amazing voyage to nowhere."

However, the worth of *2001* is not so much compromised by its narrative elusiveness and lack of destination, as it is enhanced by a "skill" so extraordinary that the options of cinematic form will never quite seem the same again. Of such facility, brilliant episodes like the leap from a tossed slow-motion pre-historic bone to the glide of the space plane *Orion,* accompanied aurally by the Blue Danube waltz, are mere tid-bits. Kubrick is concerned with effects, to be sure, but here *effect,* in one sustained re-incarnation of another time and place opens up the lock to the real content of the picture.

It is rare that a movie simulates for its viewers the puzzling gravity of the heavens; and yet it is natural that movies, with all their appropriate resources, should eventually do so. Kubrick's *2001* surely becomes as prophetic in imaging this subtle yet grand spatiality, this loosened, distanced, if still operative pull of bodies toward each other, as it is in projecting, with graphic realism, the voyage of the ship *Discovery* to Jupiter. An astronomical plausibility required an emphasis on what might be called the hydraulic quotient in cinema. Every movement of the lens has a surprising yet slow lift and lilt to it. With their tangibly buoyant, decelerated grace (never, however, as ghostly as slow-motion), Kubrick's boom and pan shots wield the glance through circumferences mimed already by the curvature of the screen itself. Whether one is seated above or beneath this spectacle, one is brought almost physically toward its shifting gyre, hanging in it as if from some balcony on the solar system. In no other film as much as this, is watching an exercise in haptic orientation, where an unimaginably wide angle view of things is coupled with hemless reversals of up and down. The delayed, barely moored grasp of solids for each other is monitored as much by the computer as by the camera—the two here metaphorically functioning together—so that equilibrium seems always to be winding itself through the panorama, and finally tracked across the adjusting tangents of orbiting objects. The most florid compositions seem always to be creating themselves, yet one is at a loss as to where, figuratively, to put one's foot down. The visual and somatic discriminations that have so long unquestionably been linked to form an order of physical existence are dislodged by this film. Under these conditions, Kubrick's unblinking scans invoke in us a certain helplessness, and not a little euphoria.

Comparable with its motion are the qualities of scale, light, and color which everywhere flood this exclusively extra-terrestrial universe. Big as it is, the screen is but a slit through which to comprehend immensities that always escape the frame. The film is haunted by imminences always outside, left and right, above and beneath, its depth of field—imminences which make even the most complete local information look arbitrary in face of the scope now opened up. This happens especially when we are closing in on a particular objective whose size, at different takes, monstruously begins to lord over the general perspective. At such moments, the human references prepared by the astronauts, the interior of their space cabin or control deck (larger than life only in our knowledge and not the way we psychologically fit into them), shrink abruptly, dwindle into ant-like puniness our body-image of ourselves and works. But comparison of size made possible by any celestial encounter is a rare occurrence in these reaches of the non-human and the inanimate. More often, the sensation is of an emptiness in which the distance to or from any of its occasional points of light to another, the very notion of location or measure itself, evaporates in an illimitable vacuum. Knowledge tells us that the traversal of such heavens, if it is to be accomplished within a life span, let alone that of a two-hour movie, must occur at speeds of scores of thousands of miles an hour. All the more reason, then, to see in the suspension and seeming immobility of these space craft an illusory gauge of movement, a visual deceit.

Time, too, is distended, for any meaningful, temporal progression is clocked only by the nearness or distance of objects from each other, and this, in turn, is made evident solely through their vast changes of scale. *Seldom in cinema has scale been such a momentous index of narrative futurity.* Of course a discrepancy exists here as in most films, between cinematic and depicted time. Yet Kubrick's exceptionally drastic compression of events is purchased by the most drawn-out postponement of action. Locked into our own actual time, we cannot "read" the visual alterations before us either as determinably swift or appreciably static in their happening. Evidence exists for both views, but if the spectator accepts one he does violence to the equally forceful claims of the other. In this environment, marked off by its large-scale arrivals and departures, we find ourselves as unsynchronized in relating to a sequence of incidents as we already feel disembodied in the experience of motion.

Much of this ambiguous, but weirdly factual scenario is heightened by the absence of phenomena that are the surest record of time elapsed: the earthly seasons of the year and the light of day (with the exception of the opening prehistoric tableau of the man-apes). The seasonless cosmological night of this space voyage drains it of interval, and erases the meaning of Thursday or morning. All those thousands of outdoor shades and nuances that tick off the passage of minutes, hours, or months, are banished from this film. In their place is the coldest of undifferentiated lights, no less alien to elapsed time whether they be the star dusted blacks of the sky or the fluorescent blocks of a space craft interior. Additionally, these lights, though they may incise a figure in the void or drench a room with an even glow, do not convey much of the volume of an object. It is a bald film, highly contrasted, without penumbra, linear and decorative more than it is tonal. Vast gauntlets of luminous energy are banked in and out of view, such that the major surfaces in the movie seem hewn out of light itself. Devoid of all those accidents and circumstances that produce atmosphere, as we know it, the colors of *2001* possess great sharpness—but they also tend to look schematic, abstracted from commensurate substance. More optical than sensuous in their impact, they can at times be blinding. The main exceptions are the filtered effect of the interiors—like oddly bright dark rooms—and the dazzling chromatic chute of the climax—the shriekingly fast arrival at Jupiter—where it is hard to tell whether color is now something lived under the eyelids or seen, meant at least in great part, to be objective, no matter how thrillingly bizarre.

Such are the exhilarations which the film can bring to its audience. Although they have been perhaps approximated before, never have they been crystallized with such exactitude and conviction. Everywhere Kubrick has realized his material with such kinesthetic allure that he seems to cast us into a new dimension. More detailed analysis would reveal only numberless imaginative enhancements, navigational guides for his uncharted firmament. One remembers, for instance, the way he constantly juxtaposes stereometric projections on control panel scopes with views of the actual landing sites they picture, so that at critical moments of joining, space seems wired with mental gimbals as well as visual coordinates. Or, one recalls his inspired use of the concave screen to simulate the astronaut's visor or the eye of HAL, personalizing or depersonalizing the spectator's point of view with disturbing omniscience. Then too, who has better employed a kind of stethoscoped breathing to illustrate physiological stress and solitude in an inanimate world? These devices, and many more like them, further graph and engrave the *feel* of travel in outer space upon our incredulous memory.

To have reified the pressures and releases of this travel within our bodily consciousness is the great achievement of *2001*. Its innovations factor out of its scrupulous portrayal of actions not yet come to pass. And who can say of the enigmatic result that it is more a flower of film extending its own resources or of a voyeurism eager for ultimate answers?

F. A. Macklin (Film Comment)

THE COMIC SENSE OF 2001

2001 is a film of surprising subtlety that has caused many serious critics to miss its tones. Pauline Kael (*Harper's*), John Simon (*The New Leader*), and Stanley Kauffmann (*The New Republic*) have all misgauged the film's satire and refused to meet *2001*'s charm. They leapt to superficial scuttling of the film, blind to the irony and patterns at work.

2001 is a flawed masterwork; these three major critics saw it only as flawed. Kauffmann dismissed it as labored and insensitive, Simon called it a "shaggy God story," and as so often is the case Kael was the most shallow, with her usual stellar arrogance and questionable ability at perception. She came to conquer not comprehend.

There are of course reasonable ways to find valid fault with the film—perhaps in the archness of the symbolism or even in the quietness of the satire. But these three critics weren't even aware enough of the satire at work to function validly.

Kauffmann circles around the satire sniffing it but never recognizing it for what it is. "I kept hoping that the director of the War Room sequence in *Dr. Strangelove* was putting me on; but he wasn't." Kauffmann wants the same satiric thrust of the previous picture or he can't recognize what lies behind the lesser emphasis. Satire must be large, it seems. Kauffmann comments, "There are only forty-three minutes of dialogue in this long film, which wouldn't matter in itself except that those forty-three minutes are pretty thoroughly banal." Which is, of course, the point.

Simon, as usual, comes closer to what is going on. "We must realize now that the dullness, as well as the commonplaces and evasions, must be satire." Hooray! "...the satire throughout is tepid and halfhearted, and tends to look like quite unintentional stupidity." Again, a critic looks from the vantage point of *Dr. Strangelove*, and fails to realize that what appears "banal," "tepid," etc. is all the more frightening because it is so close to present reality. But, and it is a crucial realization, there is a degree between what the characters say and what director Stanley Kubrick and his co-scenarist Arthur C. Clarke suggest. They are not one and the same. There is actuality with an edge of satire. Rather than debate the question of degree, the critics dismiss the question.

Of *2001* Kael peevishly declares, "In some ways it's the biggest amateur movie of them all, complete even to the amateur-movie obligatory scene—the director's little girl (in curls) telling Daddy what kind of present she wants." No observation about the point of the scene because Kael can't discern any viewpoint but her own. She finds little fun in *2001*, and she says Kubrick wasn't as satiric as was thought in *Dr. Strangelove* (it seems reviewers can't see beyond the director's *last* picture) because Kubrick has "literally learned to stop worrying and love the bomb..." Nothing about ambivalence, nothing about the film's satire, a complete ignorance of the film's fun: these are the perceptions of Pauline Kael.

What is similar in the three critics' readings is a crucial obliviousness to tone, an inability to get inside the film. This ability is necessary if one is to comprehend the variety and movement of *2001*. Tone leads one to recognize the fun, the satire, the wild imagery. There is a comic sense, subjective and often unobtrusive, which permeates *2001*, and gives it a dimension that must be realized for a full awareness of the riches of the film.

The opening section capitalizes on this last quality. The film, beautifully photographed by Geoffrey Unsworth, opens with a wasteland, quiet, inhabited by apes. It is a scene of starkness undercut by a strange humor. The killing of the ape is brutal, but his fellow apes chattering and screaming, and thumping the carcass give a bizarre comic aspect. When the ape shatters the skull with a bone which he plunks experimentally from side to side like a bone metronome, the rhythm has a humor to it, and when he bashes the skeleton it is with a decided outlandish relish. The opening scene has a quality of odd experiment and bizarre discovery to it, and it is both brutal and incredible.

The apes' attraction to the monolith which appears at dawn, scattering and reproving, then touching and finally herding around it, is biting and humorous. The motion of the ape, his hairy form flowing in slow motion, as he pounds the remains of the animal, is again a fantastic exhibition—primitive and poetic. If one is solemn during this scene he is stoic, unwilling to be dazzled.

The following scene is a visual transition as the ape in slow motion tosses the bone in the air and it becomes a twenty-first-century spaceship, and the cosmic hardware is accompanied by sweet and rhapsodic music—*The Blue Danube.*

Inside the craft a pen is floating beside the dozing traveler, Heywood R. Floyd. Don Daniels (*Film Heritage*) has noted that the scene is "hilarious" as "a stewardess with slow motion fussiness" retrieves the pen. Floyd is the character who brings out the most obvious satire, not black this time as in Kubrick's *Lolita* or *Dr. Strangelove,* but a revealing of the wretched decline of language, so close to our own present jargon and conversation that the critics took it as a bad script by Clarke and Kubrick. They also attacked Kubrick for becoming enamored of the new toys he was using. What is most annoying about this is that the critics seem to be demanding that something be blatant, not near reality, in satire. And they also seem oblivious to the possibility of ambivalence, a mixture of satire and awe.

The satire in the Floyd sections is well done, because it is close to actuality. There is enough repetition and emphasis that should make the attentive viewer aware that what is going on has a point of view that is observant and critical. The bland commonplaces of the receptionist as Floyd checks in from the spacecraft introduce this. The "Howard Johnson's Earthlight Room" adds telling illustration. And, when Floyd calls his daughter back on earth, the point of view is in focus. She squirms as he talks to her, and he asks her if for her birthday there is "Anything special you want?" She answers "yes," looks down at the phone, and gives the outrageous answer "a telephone." The imagination is so dulled that all one—a child—can think of is the immediate, a telephone. She then decides she wants a "bush baby."

When Floyd gives his remarks at the briefing the satire of the inept language fairly leaps out. It is trite and inarticulate. But it is not Kubrick's (or Clarke's) inadequacy; it is the characters' inarticulateness, their loss of language. A parade of meagre "well"s fills the air. Halvorsen, who introduces Floyd, starts out, "Well,..." He sticks his hands in his pockets. If this were done once, one might assume that it didn't matter. But this stance and feeble language are the imprint of the scene, the exposing of dullness.

Floyd is no more competent in talking: "Hi, everybody, nice to be back with you." He follows this with the refrain, "Well,..." and then comments "Now, ah...." He too puts his hands in his pockets. When the floor is opened for questions, there is only one, about the danger of "cultural shock." Floyd responds, "Well, I, ah, sympathize with your point of view." (The questioner is against the cover story of an epidemic which has been used to protect the secret of the monolith on the moon.) Floyd concludes, "Well, I think that's about it. Any questions?" Halvorsen thanks Floyd, "Well,..." "No more questions [there was only one]. We should get on with the briefing."

If the audience hasn't recognized what Kubrick is exposing about language, he reemphasizes the pathetic quality on the craft when he has one man say, "That was an excellent speech you gave us, Heywood." "Certainly was," affirms a second man. The irony is explicit. Heywood's comments while friendly were anything but excellent. At this point if the viewer hasn't begun to realize the rather obvious satire, he probably is missing most of the irony, and he thinks the film foolish, instead of its characters foolish. It is dismaying to think that critics are unable to separate the characters' point of view from the creators'.

At the site of the monolith there is a further absurdity, this time visual. Six men in space suits approach the monolith. One touches it. One waves the other five in front of it like tourists or pompous hunters for a picture-taking session. This is shattered by a piercing shriek emitted from the monolith. The fantastic scene with the apes, the "dull" scenes with Floyd, the rituals—the apes, the briefing, the men at the monolith—have set several tones, one of the most basic a tone of irony and cliché. Dullness and balletic movement interplay.

If one is aware of Floyd's and his compatriots' satiric demeanor, it is easy to recognize the similar identity of the two astronauts on the spaceship, *Discovery 1,* Frank Poole and David Bowman. As the section "Flight to Jupiter" begins, Poole trots around the craft shadow-boxing. It is a scene Kauffmann calls "amusing" though too extended. In the background Bowman eats. On TV there is their interview with a TV interviewer. "How is everything going?" Again language fails. Poole offers trite sanguinity, "Marvelous." Bowman is less enthusiastic: "We have no complaints." Then there is the labored production from Poole's family. His mother, who is a teacher, says, "Frank, you're a big celebrity in the second grade." His father cries: "We wish you the very happiest of birthdays." They sing "Happy Birthday." Frank lies lumpish with his sun glasses, sunning himself under a sunlamp.

Compared to the humans, HAL—the 9000 computer—is more articulate, more concerned. HAL is having second thoughts about the mission. His voice is ripe and soft. He picks up an alleged fault in one of the units, and predicts it will fail in seventy-two hours. "Mission control," says the computer, "is in error." But HAL desists; he says it can only be "attributable to human error. This sort of thing has cropped up before, and it's always attributable to human error."

There follows one of the film's nicest ironies. Poole and Bowman enclose themselves in the soundproof space pod to discuss, out of range of HAL's hearing, what should be done with the computer. Poole says if HAL is "malfunctioning" there is no choice but "disconnection." But what is uncanny and ironic about the scene is that as the spacemen talk, HAL reads their lips through the glass, first one then the other; in a priceless irony, soundless lips, language without sound, communicates and precipitates a dreadful reaction.

HAL shows his frailty. As Poole floating outside the space pod is placing the material back in the unit, HAL breaks his life line. When Bowman asks HAL what happened, HAL responds that there isn't enough evidence to know. So Bowman goes to recover the dead Poole floating in space. When he does, HAL allows the hibernauts, the sleeping crew, to die. Flashing on red letters come the messages: "Computer malfunction," "Life functions critical," "Life functions terminal." HAL also forbids Bowman, who has recovered Poole's body, to reenter the craft. He declares, "This mission is too important for me to allow you to jeopardize it."

Bowman tells HAL to let him reenter, but he is ultimately met by silence. Bowman appears almost satanically intense—with lights, colored, odd, on his face. Bowman still possesses man's adaptability; he flies careening through the emergency air-lock. He enters the capsule with a purpose. There is a bitter-sweet quality to HAL's death. Where Dave was intense and willful, HAL is helpless and desperate. HAL pleads for his life, "I know everything hasn't been quite right with me...I feel much better now. I really do." "I know I've made some very poor decisions recently. I want to help you." "Dave, stop. Stop, will you. Stop, Dave. Will you stop, Dave. Stop, Dave. I'm afraid. I'm afraid, Dave."

Marvelously, HAL is the most sensitive on the craft. "Dave, my mind is going. I can feel it. I can feel it. My mind is going. There is no question about it. I can feel it. I can feel it. I can feel it. I'm afraid. Good afternoon, gentlemen. I am a HAL 9000 computer. I became operational...." HAL relates the factors of his creation in Urbana, Illinois, in 1992, and he says his instructor "...Mr. Langley...taught me to sing a song.... it's called *Daisy*." He sings, "...I'm half crazy...." as he falters into madness, and the clear voice of mission control breaks in on a prerecording. "Good day, gentlemen. This is a prerecorded briefing. Now that you are in Jupiter space and the entire crew has been revived, it can be told to you." Mission control tells the lone living occupant of the spaceship about the "four-million-year-old black monolith" found on the moon sending its beams to Jupiter, "its origin and purpose a total mystery." Bowman is about to meet that mystery.

The final segment is entitled "Jupiter and Beyond the Infinite." Bowman in his space pod goes on a wild color-throbbing ride. Like a casket lid, the black monolith leads, against black star-sprinkled space. At the bottom of the screen is a planet like a pool of white fire. Orbs beyond the monolith move. An enchantment pervades the film, sometimes sly, wicked, dazzling. Bowman is affected physically by his frenetic ride. His face shakes; freezes; one eye cocked, his face is distorted in torment. His eye turns pink, blue, orange; different colors throb on it. The terrain is brown, blue, dark red, fluorescent, livid, bright. The terrain luminous. His eyes up in his head. A new map shimmering, glowing infernally. His eye blinking colors.

Then, suddenly, Bowman's capsule appears in a green-white room, whose decor is a mixture of modern and Louis XVI.* He is aged in his space suit. He roams the premises, into the lavatory. He witnesses a figure who looks like himself. The figure, who becomes himself, drinks a pale wine. He breaks the glass; its crystal cracks like life. The man, now eating, sees a further part of the cycle, an old man in bed. Ancient, bald, he reaches out toward the monolith beyond the end of the bed. Then he is transformed into a ball in the bed—crystal, luminous. Fetus on the bed, a birth. A furthering, not a finalization. A passage. There is a shot of the monolith covering the screen alone. The fetus appears in space, wide-eyed, bright, luminous, glowing, shimmering. Peering on the planet.

Man is no longer Earthbound; he is perhaps headed to shantih, the peace that passeth understanding.† There is an essential absurdity, a clutter of expanding symbols, a metaphoric future. And amidst the incredible, is something pre-natal, a gleaming chuckle from space, a fetal vision looking at its plaything, its worldly womb, from whence it came. The world its toy. One gags at the vision; it is too fantastic—a cosmic, comic revelation.

Philip Strick (Sight and Sound)

Already, it seems, there exist third-generation computers so complex that they have had to be constructed and programmed by other computers, in turn developed by comparatively primitive man-made originals. Isaac Asimov has foreseen a future in which this growing family of artifacts will take over our planet completely, replacing with cold logic the expendable and inefficient human race. On one level at least, Stanley Kubrick's *2001: A Space Odyssey* (M-G-M) follows this extrapo-

---

*This scene has caused many viewers problems Some readers of Clarke's book have felt that by explaining the room as the offering of extra-terrestrials Clarke has destroyed the sense of mystery. There is nothing that says one *has* to accept this concept. It also seems valid to suggest that the room might be a hallucination in the mind of the "dying" astronaut. The most rewarding way of viewing Clarke's book is to see him as the first critic, who can be extremely helpful in comprehending *2001*, but not the only interpreter.

†*2001* is similar to T S. Eliot's *The Waste Land* in its comic and cruel vignettes of vacuity that resolve ultimately in hope.

lation to the point at which man becomes at best an outmoded spectator of laws and forces spectacularly beyond his comprehension.

More sinister still, Kubrick also extends the theory retrospectively
by showing mankind in its simian infancy being indoctrinated by possibly the identical omniscient slab that is later to confront and con-
found us on the enigmatic surface of Jupiter. This imputation that man
could not have invented even as pedestrian a robot as, say, a traffic light
without the aid of a hefty nudge from superior beings has not surpris-
ingly been the source of considerable pleasure as much to the UFO-
spotters as to the Bible-readers in Kubrick's audiences. Whatever one's
theory of evolution, however, the Kubrick-Clarke screenplay doesn't
really bear analysis any too well.

The film begins unexpectedly with the title "The Dawn of Man,"
and ends equally unexpectedly with a sequence which implies that the
opening label was an ironic one. As an interplanetary dawn breaks
somewhere over Jupiter, contemplated by the staring eyes of a foetus
travelling in its own fixed orbit, we are supposedly now present at the
real birth of human knowledge. The trouble with this line of thought
(assuming it's the right one) is that if man was so dim initially that it
would take a few million years of prompting to make him realise
merely that he is as an unborn child before the mysteries of the universe, one can't help wondering why any outside force, however
benevolent, would have bothered to take on his schooling in the first
place. Boredom, perhaps. Or the need for an appreciative audience?
Worse, if it's man's *natural* progress that is being accelerated by carefully timed appearances of the singing monoliths, the haste of this
spoon-fed rush to maturity is scarcely justified by the film's conclusion
that we've not yet begun. If, on the other hand, the suggestion is that
man would never have developed at all without outside help, the film
is reducing us to mutant freaks, purposelessly nurtured and cultivated.

Perhaps it is being too severe on *Space Odyssey* to submit it to this
type of *reductio ad absurdum*. Yet thematically, however one looks at the
film's four linked episodes, the efforts of its characters emerge as sin-
gularly futile. Given the brainwave of using a bone as a weapon for
food, the apeman's first act is to club one of his own kind with it. Given
the facility of space-travel and the awesome splendour of the solar
system, the twenty-first-century man dozes, gossips, makes banal remarks about sandwiches, and takes snapshots. Given the technology to

create a superhuman computer that does all but scratch the astronaut's back while controlling his entire spaceship, the human discovers nevertheless that he has to dismantle the thing in order to survive at all. And finally the blazing display of alien concepts reduces man to an inarticulate embryo. Kubrick has always pushed men to extremes in his films, finding them in the last resort incapable, and with the immense canvas of *Space Odyssey* he again appears to be expressing that vote of no confidence which has been, after all, the constant theme of most written science-fiction.

Granted this gloomy forecast, however, the film manages to come out as irrationally optimistic on another level—that of the sheer audacity of the human race. It once took man ten thousand years to double his store of knowledge, but only fifteen years ago the rate of doubling was one decade and today it is expected that a mere seven years should cover the same process. Whether the first spark came from elsewhere or not, the film demonstrates a wholehearted human eagerness to take full advantage of this innate human ability, summarised particularly stunningly by the shot of a ball-like spaceship sinking majestically into its landing bay in the surface of the moon while tiny figures supervise calmly from a hive of observation points.

A signal from another planet finds a group of men quickly ready to respond, hibernation techniques and all; an astronaut adrift in space is tracked down and collected with hardly a second thought; and a berserk, seemingly inviolable computer is demolished as a result of the quicksilver ingenuity of its intended victim. The opportunism of man is undeniable, even if so much of his effort is wasted on banalities, and *Space Odyssey* demonstrates his resilience convincingly enough for one to interpret the film's final hint of rebirth as heralding a challenge that at long last will be worth the challenging.

What really undermines the film's whole thesis of man's dependence upon otherworldly forces is, of course, the film's own existence. As Arthur Clarke has said, if the next space picture is going to be better than *Space Odyssey* it will have to be made on location. With a battery of special effects designed by Kubrick himself, the universe has been astonishingly re-created and, further, populated: no strings, no visible backdrops, and only a few, almost indistinguishable touches of process work. With his multi-million-dollar investment, the entire resources of the M-G-M British studios and some of Shepperton's as well, his ninety tons of specially dyed sand, and his thirty-six-foot-high centrifuge, Kubrick has won the ultimate technical triumph in that his film is beautiful to watch from start to finish.

If there was any doubt that space travel will be the most spectacular adventure of mankind's future, *Space Odyssey* is the definitive affirmation that every last coin spent on the space race will be worth it. His camera dances in an unrestrained love affair with the planets and with the curious, knobby craft that will forage between them, floating exuberantly through the light-years to the obsessive, formal, and startlingly appropriate tune of the "Blue Danube" waltz. His interiors are equally breathtaking, from the sheer white of the space-station dotted with its stark red furniture to the huge circular room where the Jupiter-bound astronauts indulge in calisthenics that literally include the ceiling, or watch themselves being interviewed on flat television screens set into the lunch table beside their dishes of synthetic food-pastes. Best of all, there is a sense of fun that never obtrudes—the helmeted stewardesses who calmly turn upside down, the zero-gravity toilet with its immense list of essential instructions, the astronaut who is more concerned about his salary increase than about the significance of his voyage, and that splendid invention, Hal-9000, the talking computer who admits, with a complacent flicker of equations, that it enjoys working with people.

It could all too easily have been invalidated by some conventional narrative, a touch of spacesuit melodrama, a tidy ending. The strength of *Space Odyssey* is that it pinches the best from Arthur Clarke's original short story "The Sentinel" and makes no ill-considered attempt to overload it—despite touches of padding in the not quite wholly successful first sequence (the apemen are acceptable enough until one sees their chimpanzee offspring) and in the amusing but ultimately slight second.

One realises afterwards that one has been almost hypnotised by the visual magnificence of the film, gliding on a roller-coaster of colours until the unclassifiable landscapes of the Jupiter surface and the total dislocation of our arrival in the exquisitely furnished rooms haunted by a dying Keir Dullea fling us, as Kubrick has cannily intended, headlong into what feels like a new dimension altogether.

Only afterwards, as the magic recedes, comes the suspicion that all the artifice has simply been used to disguise what was an artificial premise to begin with. Like that curious cut from a bone falling in slow motion to a spaceship hovering among the stars, the eyes are tempted to accept without question what the mind would be equally tempted to refuse. Kubrick's greatest achievement has been to persuade us to believe him.

Annette Michelson

A NOTE ON "BODIES IN SPACE: FILM AS CARNAL KNOWLEDGE"

The text below, originally published in 1969 in *Artforum*, a journal of which I was then an editor, is here reprinted as a document of possible historical interest. A few contextual considerations should clarify this claim.

It is an enthusiastic, indeed a celebratory response to a film received by the American press during the first year of its release with almost unanimous hostility. The collection of reviews generously supplied by MGM's New York office had made this abundantly clear. Although written out of admiring delight in Kubrick's achievement, it was impelled, as well, by a sense of the deep injustice, the lack of generosity that had greeted his offering of the magnum opus that marked, in my view, an important moment in the history of cinema.

The essay is, in several senses, a period piece of the moment of the 1960s that witnessed the initial stages of the new discipline of Cinema Studies. The vast production of its literature was still to come. The writer is consequently reaching for a theoretical framework that does not yet exist; she senses that here is a film that may hold clues to an ontology of cinema. André Bazin's remarkable work, although partially available by then, could not accommodate a cinema such as this, and the first interesting stirrings of semiological analysis did not appear apt to account for the force, scale, humor and beauty of the *Space Odyssey*.

The text is almost entirely innocent of the political and military applications and implications of the "space effort" then under way in this country and the Soviet Union. These factors, deeply inscribed in Kubrick's work, do call for serious consideration. An assessment of the *Space Odyssey* in relation to *Dr. Strangelove* would no doubt have strengthened analysis of the later film.

The essay was, as I now, three decades later, see, an opening move in what was to develop as a claim for a cinema of modernism. While I do not renounce that claim, I now view it as overly insistent in this instance; that insistence would now be qualified by other theoretical considerations that orient research and analysis of cinema.

If this text does retain some interest that is not wholly historical, it may lie in its stress on the corporeality of this cinema, the manner in which it implicates the spectator's body, in its linkage of kinesis and vision, of the aesthetic and the cognitive. The writer is searching for a way—new and different from that of Bazin—of engaging phenomenological method in the service of film analysis. Edmund Husserl, the founder of that method, had declared in his meditations on *The Origins of Geometry* (1936) that the earth was not an object, but rather the ground of our being, of knowing and sensing, of meaning, and that should we, through flight, reach another planet, we will then have a double, unified earth in relation to which motion and rest are to be conceived. Space travel, promising a radical extension of our horizons, had now found in Kubrick's film its uniquely poetic expression. This called for celebration.

Annette Michelson (Artforum)

BODIES IN SPACE:
FILM AS CARNAL KNOWLEDGE

I

> All mastery casts a chill.
> —MALLARMÉ

> The indefinable, knowing
> fear which is the clearest
> intimation of the metaphysical.
> —BORGÈS

In the winter of 1905 the first continuously operated movie theatre opened in Los Angeles. There is an obvious sense in which the history of film is circumscribed by the feature of that theatre's initial program, George Méliès' *Trip to the Moon,* and Stanley Kubrick's *2001· A Space Odyssey.* There is another sense in which its evolution hypostatizes the accelerating dynamics of History. Walking the three blocks between the Museum of Modern Art's screening room and the Loew's Capitol, thinking of that evolution, one finds oneself tracing a vector, exploring, in implication, as one goes, a multi-dimensional movement of human consciousness in our century.

In 1961, the year of Méliès' centenary, the Cinémathèque Française and the Union Centrale des Arts Décoratifs presented in the Louvre a commemorative exhibition still present to me as one of the finest I have seen. One wandered through the reconstitution of a life-work prodigious in its inventive abundance as through a forest alive with apparitions and metamorphoses, stopping all at once, however, as before a clearing, arrested as by a shaft of light, the illumination flaring from a photograph upon the wall.

Greatly enlarged, it showed the Méliès Company in action.* The Company had been, of course, a family affair, its production some-

---

*For consideration of this question one does well to compare Méliès' admirable text, *Vues Cinematographiques*, reprinted in the catalog of the commemorative exhibition (Paris, 1961), which encompasses, within 15 densely printed pages, a basic course in filmmaking and a discussion of the formal and technical problems involved and resolved in his own work, with the information on the making of *2001 A Space Odyssey* provided by the *Journal of the American Cinematographer*, June 1968, vol 49, no. 6 The parallels on all parameters are striking in the production of this particular *grande machine*, the use and invention of metamachines resulted, as one might expect (in a medium whose history is , more than any, tied to technological developments) in a number of technical breakthroughs recalling or extending those created by Méliès himself Here are a very few:

a Kubrick directed the action in the centrifuge sequences from outside by watching a closed circuit monitor relaying a picture from a small video camera mounted next to the film camera inside the centrifuge itself.

b In order to attain a slow and "large-scale" movement of doors and other parts, motors were made to drive these mechanisms, then "geared down so far that the actual motion, frame by frame, was imperceptible 'We shot most of these scenes,' says Kubrick, 'using slow exposures of 4 seconds per frame One couldn't see the movement A door moving 5 inches during a scene would take 5 hours to shoot You could never see any unsteady movement It was like watching the hand of a clock ' "

c "For the Stargate sequence, a slit-scan machine was designed, using a technique of image scanning as used in scientific and industrial photography This device could produce two seemingly infinite planes of exposure while holding depth-of-field from a distance of 15 feet to 1½ inches from the lens at an aperture of F/8 with exposures of approximately one minute per frame using a standard 65 mm. Mitchell camera "

d "A huge 10-by-8-foot transparency plate projector for the application of the Aleken-Gerrard method of front-projected transparency" was constructed for the primates sequence It is expected to open up enormous possibilities for future film production thing of a "cottage industry," and one saw it here in operation on one of the artfully designed and fastidiously executed sets which were a point of honor and pride for an indefatigable Master Builder. The photograph gave one pause.

It gives us a behind-the-scene view, shows not the action being filmed, but its reverse side, the flats of its set anchored, here and there, in the manner of theatrical décor, to the ground. Men—gentlemen, formally dressed and hatted—stand about, supporting those flats, ready to catch them should the screws fail and they fall. The still image is, of course, "moving" because it restores to us the feeling of the primitive, the home-made and artisanal modesty, the fragile and precarious underpinnings of a grandiose venture. It articulates, as well, the manner in which film first made its entrance, through the stage door (*l'entrée des artistes*), and something of the homely mechanics, the dialectic at work in the fabrication of illusion itself, its re-invention for us. It illustrates the manner in which the artisan, the bourgeois family man, the *bricoleur,* prestidigitator and entrepreneur fused in a single figure of genius to engender the art of cinema as we know it.

The nineteenth century had been dreaming of movies, as all its forms of popular narrative and diversion (photographic album, panoramic view, magic lantern, shadow play, wax museum and the novel itself) conspire to testify, and Méliès' intrepid talent, a synthesis of the imagination and industry which were subsequently to be reified into the opposing terms of the new form's dialectic, fused these dreams into something real. If Lumière had been the first cinematographer, Méliès was the first of the *réalisateurs,* as distinct from the *metteurs-en-scène;* he *realized* the cinema itself.

Seeing Kubrick's *Space Odyssey,* we sense, we know, that its ontogeny recapitulates a philogeny. Its production involved the scale of enterprise, the dedicated resolution and intellectual flexibility, the proud marshalling of vast resources brought to bear upon the most sophisticated and ambitious ventures of our culture. Its making required, indeed, a length and complexity of preparation, a breadth of conception and detail of organization analagous only to those invested in the launching of a new regime, a new inter-continental missile system, a fresh episode in the exploration of space. And its appearance has, in fact, generated the same sort of apprehension or "cultural shock" which Arthur C. Clarke describes, in his novelistic rendering of the screenplay, as the reaction to the invention of "the highly advanced HAL 9000 Computer, the brain and nervous system" of the narrative's "vehicle," the space-ship *Discovery*.

Like that black monolith whose unheralded materialization propels the evolution of consciousness through the three sections of the movie's narrative triptych, Kubrick's film has assumed the disquieting function of Epiphany. It functions as a disturbing structure, emitting, in its intensity of presence and perfection of surface, sets of signals. That intensity and perfection are contingent upon a conspicuous invisibility of *facture* commanded by the power of a rigorously conceptual imagination, disposing of vast amounts of money. Those signals, received by a bewildered and apprehensive community (tribe? species?) of critics, have propelled them, all unwilling, into a chorus of dismay, a choreography of vacillation, of approach, and recoil, to and from the "object." We know that song and dance; they are the old, familiar projection of a crisis in criticism. And still the "object" lures us on. Another level or "universe" of discourse awaits us.

We are dealing, then, with a "breakthrough work," whose substance and function fuse in the synthetic radicalization of its metaphors. It is precisely because form and surface command the most immediate and complex intensity of physical response that they release a wild energy of speculation, confirming, even as they modify, the character and options of the medium. In that oscillating movement between confirmation and transformation, the film as a whole performs the function of a Primary Structure, forcing the spectator back, in a reflexive gesture, upon the analytic rehearsal of his experience, impelling, as it does so, the conviction that here is a film like any other, like all others, only more so—which is to say, a paradigm, unique. (If one were concerned with an "ontology" of cinema, this film would be a place in which to look for it.) The margin of difference-in-similarity which contains or defines its "edge" over other films is the locus of its poetry.

The play of an inspired primate ("Moonwatcher" is Clarke's name for him) ending the Prologue of this film, issues in the visionary realization which transforms a bone into a weapon, then flings it in a gesture of apperceptive exultation, high into the vacant air. Méliès' extraordinary intuition, realizing (inventing) the possibilities of the medium, created out of forms and materials that lay to hand, a new instrument of the Imagination, an agent of power and delight, launching his cinema in confident optimism out into an unsuspecting world.

Kubrick's transformation of bone into space-craft through the movement of redescent (through that single cut which concludes the Prologue and initiates the Odyssey) inscribes, within the most spectacular ellipsis in cinematic history, nothing less than the entire trajectory of human history, the birth and evolution of Intelligence. Seizing, appropriating the theme of spatial exploration as narrative metaphor and formal principle, he has projected intellectual adventure as spectacle, converting, through still another leap of the imagination, Méliès' pristine fantasy to the form and uses of a complex and supremely sophisticated structure.

Moving, falling toward us with the steady and purposive elegance of an incomparably powerful "vehicle," Kubrick's masterwork is designed, in turn, as an instrument of exploration and discovery. *A Space Odyssey* is, in fact, in the sustained concreteness and formal refinement which render that design, precisely that which Ortega believed modern poetry to have become: a "higher algebra of metaphors."

II

The object in motion moves
neither in the space in
which it is nor in that in
which it is not.
                    —ZENO

The present hath no space.
Where then is the time
which we may call long?
                    —SAINT AUGUSTINE

In a letter, undated but probably of 1894, Pierre Louys calls upon Debussy, about to embark upon the career of music critic which produced the brilliant and insolent persona of "Monsieur Croche, Anti-Dilettante," to "do something" to cure the malady of contemporary criticism. Complaining that "one cannot strike a single chord these days without eliciting a flurry of metaphysical speculation," he says that *Lohengrin,* after all is a work "about movement." "It is about a man who arrives and departs," and nothing else. Or, as Valéry was shortly to say, "The true connoisseur of this art is necessarily the person to whom it suggests nothing."

Like all statements of this kind, these strictures suggest a critical strategy rather than an esthetic, a working hypothesis advanced within a specific historical conjecture, a re-orientation of critical concern in the interests of immediate usefulness and interest. Like Fénéon's descriptive criticism of painting, like Mallarmé's assertion, to Degas, that "poetry is made with words rather than with ideas," like Robbe-Grillet's attack on Metaphor, Stravinsky's rejection of musical "content" or "subject," and Artaud's indictment of theatrical text, they propose a therapy for an intellectual tradition in which, as in that of our current film criticism, an endemic and debilitating Idealism perpetuates exhausted critical categories. Reductive, double-edged, polemically inflected, they urge a closer, fresher, more innocent and comprehending view of the Object, a respect for form and physicality as the ground of interest and value.

Like *Lohengrin, Space Odyssey,* is, of course, endlessly suggestive, projects a syncretic heritage of myths, fantasies, cosmologies and aspirations. Everything about it is interesting; it proposes, however, nothing of more radical interest than its own physicality, its "formal statement" on the nature of movement in its space; it "suggests" nothing so urgent and absorbing as an evidence of the senses, its discourse on knowledge through perception as action, and ultimately, on the nature of the medium as "action film," as mode and model of cognition.

Reading the critical or journalistic reproaches (and defenses) addressed to this film's supposedly "static quality," its "plotless" structure in which "nothing happens," one recalls the myths which dominated a half-century or so of theatrical criticism's uncomprehending view of Chekhov, as of Wagner. In this *Odyssey,* incident, surprise, discovery, shock and violence abound. Its plot turns, in fact, upon *intrigue,* as the French define plot. And, like a "scenario" (the term adopted by contemporary technocrats such as Herman Kahn for their hypothetical projections of our future), its structure is "open." Like *Lohengrin* and

Uncle Vanya, above all, however, this work is about "arrival and departure," about movement. Its narrative, a voyage of discovery, a progress toward disembodiment, explores, through a multi-level tactics of displacement, through a constant and intensive re-invention of the possibilities of cinematic immediacy, the structural potentialities of haptic disorientation as agent of cognition.

Navigation—of a vessel or human body—through a space in which gravitational pull is suspended, introduces heightened pleasures and problems, the intensification of erotic liberation and of the difficulty of purposeful activity. In that floating freedom, all directed and purposive movement becomes work, the simplest task an exploit. The new freedom poses for the mind, in and through the body, the problematic implications of all freedom, forcing the body's recognition of its suspended coördinates as its necessity. The dialectic of pleasure and performance principles, projected through camera's radical re-structuring of environment, the creation of ranges of change in light, scale, pace, heighten, to the point of transformation, the very conditions of film experience. Viewing becomes, as always but as never before, the discovery, through the acknowledgment of disorientation, of what it is to see, to learn, to know, and of what it is to be, seeing. Once the theatre seat has been transformed into a vessel, opening out onto and through the curve of a helmet to that of the screen as into the curvature of space, one rediscovers, through the shock of recognition, one's own body living in *its* space. One feels suspended, the mind not quite able to "touch ground." One surveys the familiar ground of experience (as the astronauts have indicated, remarking that a prime reason for space flight lay in the rediscovery and organization of the *earth's* resources), feeling the full meaning of "suspense" as anticipation, *sensing* that though things may possibly be the same again, they will, thanks to Kubrick, never be the same *in quite the same way.*

If, then, *Space Odyssey* proposes, as in Bergson's view all works of art do, "the outline of a movement," it is, as well what Elie Faure claimed all *film* to be: "an architecture of movement." As a film which takes for its very subject, theme and dynamics—both narrative and formal— movement itself, it has a radical, triple interest and urgency, a privileged status in the art that is ours, modern.

III

Form is tinted with meaning.
—QUINTILIAN, AFTER ZENO

The secret of the true
artist consists in the
following: he effaces
nature through form.
—SCHILLER

There is a moment—that present moment which extends a century back into the past—in which the entire system of presuppositions governing the artist's view of subject, content and theme is undermined. That moment is initiated within the radical questioning of art as mimesis. It produces a shift or displacement of the artist's aspiration. The movement of displacement is by no means steady or uncontested, as the entirely problematic esthetic implicit in Expressionism (it is, after all, neither school nor style, but the name we give to sixty years of polymorphic contestation) insistently reminds us. In that shift, the culmination of a crisis sustained since the seventeenth century through philosophy, the authority of the imagination moves to replace that of a transcendence animating the esthetic of transcription or expression. Sustained through the radical art of our century, the shift is pre-figured in Flaubert's celebrated letter of January, 1852, to Louise Colet: "What I consider fine, what I should like to do is a book about nothing, a book without external attachments of any sort, which would hold of itself, through the inner strength of its style, as the earth sustains itself with no support in air, a book with almost no subject. Or at least an almost invisible subject, if possible."

This aspiration toward a work of total autonomy, self-referring, self-sustaining and self-justifying, required the invention of a mediating strategy, a transition. The subject could be eliminated only through a process of dissolution initiated by its re-definition. Therefore, Flaubert's subsequent affirmation, in a letter dated one year later: "Since poetry is purely subjective, there is no such thing as a fine subject. Yvetôt and Constantinople are of equal value. One can write equally well about anything at all. It is the artist who elevates things [through his manner of writing]." (The manner in and degree to which the history of pictorial and sculptural modernism confirms and embodies this position requires no immediate development on this occasion.)

It is, however, at precisely that moment of the dissolution of the subject, a process crystallized and extended through Mallarmé and Cézanne into the art of our own day, it is when the painter, rendering "seeing rather than things seen," takes painting as his subject, when the novelist commences the relating of "narrativity" itself, that art's aspiration shifts, expands, intensifies, tending, as in a movement of compensation, toward the most radical and all-encompassing of possible functions. Poetry, consenting through Mallarmé to be poetry only, proposes, simultaneously, to become "the orphic explanation of the earth," of a "world meant," moreover, "to end in a book." The dissolution of the subject or figure, the contestation of art as Mimesis, of Realism itself, is grounded in the problematic consciousness of a reality no longer assumed as pre-defined or pre-existent to the work of the imagination. Art now takes the nature of reality, the nature of consciousness in and through perception, as its subject or domain. As exploration of the conditions and terms of perception, art henceforth converges with philosophy and science upon the problem of reality as known and knowable.

Thus, the very ambiguity of Kandinsky's title for his esthetic treatise, *Towards the Spiritual in Art*—translatable, too, from the German as *Toward the Intellectual in Art*—defines with great precision the nature and locus of the shift. Its ambiguity spells out the problems involved in the relocation, through abstraction, of sources of authority, interest and aspiration, which had been dislodged by the crisis in the Western metaphysical tradition. Text and title re-enact, in their ambivalence and contradictions, that crisis; their celebrated "confusion" has the clarity of a syndrome, a syndrome converted into an esthetics bequeathed to us, somewhat in the manner of an hereditary taint or talent, in the sensibility of "Abstract Expressionism."

That movement toward abstraction which animates the style and esthetics of modernism posed, for every art form, the problem of what Ortega calls "the incompatibility of the perception of lived reality with the perception of artistic form," in so far as "they call for different adjustments of our perceptive apparatus." "An art that requires such a double seeing is a squinting art. The nineteenth century was cross-eyed..." Ortega, speaking with a certain crudeness symptomatic of ambivalence, spoke far truer than he knew.

Surely that statement is nowhere more significant than in its central omission. It stops just short of the recognition that the nineteenth century ended in producing the cinema, the art form whose temporality created another space in which "lived reality" could once again be figured, restructured. Cinema is the temporal instrument working in a direction counter to that of modernist painting's increasingly shallow space. Through it the deep space of illusionism is reinvented, through which cinema reintroduces not only "lived reality," but an entirely new and seemingly limitless range of structural relationships allowing for the reconciliation of "lived reality" with "artistic form." In order to do so, of course, film not only rehabilitated the "squint," but elevated it to the status of a dynamics of creation and perception, installed it as the very central principle of an art form, the source of its power and refinement.

Film's relation to modernism is, consequently, delicate and complex in the extreme, and the demands it makes upon its audience have a strenuousness directly proportionate to that complexity and delicacy, contingent upon its illusionistic immediacy. Its fullest experience demands a kind of critical, apperceptive athleticism.

As all who care more than casually for movies know, the point at which one begins to understand the nature of the medium comes when one sees the images before one, not as a sequence of events evolving past or within the limits of a frame, but rather as a structure organized in depth and in relation to the frame by the camera itself. The heightened experience of film henceforth involves the constant oscillation between the two "points of view," the constant "adjustment of the perceptive apparatus." The trajectory of both narrative and of camera lens as the extension of the eye and will of the artist begins to describe itself for us when we see, as in the scene of the poisoning of the Czarina in *Ivan the Terrible,* that the slow and devious passage of a goblet through a room is the propulsion, to its destined victim, by design dissembled as chance, through a camera movement, the movement of History. Film's narrative now acquires the dimension of style, as the structural and sensuous incarnation of the artist's will.

One follows, in another celebrated instance, the tram ride of Murnau's *Sunrise, moved* to pity by the protagonist's agony of anguish and shame, *borne along*, from a country to a city landscape, *carried away*, as they emerge from an extremity of alienation into reconciliation as into the New Jerusalem, and ultimately *transported* by the movement of the camera, the artist's agent, his mind's eye, defining and sustaining the space and dimensions of narrative as form.

Film proposes, then, and most sharply when it is greatest, a dissociative economy of viewing. That is why, although its "dream-like" quality received an immediate and extensive entry in the Dictionary of Received Ideas, it remains to be stressed that cinema is, more than any other art form, that which Plato claimed art in general to be: *a dream for waking minds.* The paradox testifies to the manner in which film provokes that delicate dissociation, that *contraposto* of the mind, that constantly renewed tension and readjustment whose symptom is, indeed, Ortega's "squint."

If this distance, the alienation of the spectator with respect to his experience, reflecting the elevation of doubt to an esthetic principle, may be said to characterize modernist sensibility as a whole, determining, in fact, the intensity of its very longing for immediacy, then film's conversion of that principle to the uses of a formal dynamics gives it a privileged place as a medium centrally involved with the cognitive aspiration of modern art. The dissociative economy of film viewing heightens our perception of being physical to the level of apperception, to an awareness of the modes of consciousness. The athleticism required of the spectator entails, like all esthetic situations—and quite beyond the luxury of identification—an awareness of the inner presuppositions that sustain us, so that pleasure is informed with the shock of recognition.

A Space Odyssey, that film of "special effects" in which "nothing happens," is simply one which, in its extremity of stylistic formal coherence and richness, its totally reinvented environment, quite dissolves the very notion of the "special effect." They disappear. Above all, however, it solicits, in its overwhelming immediacy, the *relocation of the terrain upon which things happen.* And they happen, ultimately, not only on the screen but somewhere between screen and spectator. It is the area defined and constantly traversed by our active restructuring and reconstitution, through an experience of "outer" space, of the "inner" space of the body. Kubrick's film, its action generating a kind of cross-current of perception and cognitive restructuring, visibly reaches, as it were, for another arena, redefining the content of cinema, its "shape of content." The subject and theme of *A Space Odyssey* emerge, then, as neither social nor metaphysical; they develop elsewhere, between, in a genetic epistemology.

IV

> My mobility is the way in which I counterbalance the mo-
> bility of things, thereby understanding and surmounting
> it. All perception is movement. And the world's unity, the
> perceiver's unity, are the unity of counterbalanced dis-
> placements.
>
> —MERLEAU-PONTY

> All things in the heaven of intelligibility are heavenly ... In
> this kingdom, all is diaphanous. Nothing is opaque or in-
> penetrable, and light encounters light. No traveler wan-
> ders there as in a foreign land.
>
> —PLOTINUS

This *Odyssey* traces, then, in its "higher algebra of metaphors," the movement of bodies in space, voyaging, through spheres beyond the pull of terrestrial attraction, in exploration of the Unknown, in and through *Discovery*.

The Voyage as narrative form acts, in its deformation or suspension of the familiar framework of existence (as in the logic of Alice, the ge-ography of Saint Brendan, the reality of Don Quixote, the sociology of Gulliver), to project us, as in space travel, toward the surface of a dis-tant world, its propulsive force contriving, through a Logistics of the Imagination, to redeliver us in rebound from that surface, into the fa-miliar, the known, of common experience.

So, too, the voyage of the astronauts ultimately restores us, through the heightened and complex immediacy of this film, to the space in which we dwell. This navigation of a vessel as instrument of explo-ration, of the human organism as adventurer, dissolves the opposition of body and mind, *bringing home* to us the manner in which "objective spatiality" is but the envelope of that "primordial spatiality," the level on which the body itself effects the synthesis of its commitments in the world, a synthesis which is a fusion of meaning as experienced, tending toward equilibrium.

By constantly questioning that "objective spatiality," Kubrick incarnates the grand theme and subject of learning as self-recognition, of growth as the constant disruption and re-establishment of equilibrium in progress towards knowledge. This succession of re-establishments of equilibrium proposes a master metaphor for the mind at grips with reality, and we re-enact its progress through a series of disconcerting shocks which solicit our accommodation.

As soon as the airline hostess starts her movement through the space-craft's interior, moving up the wall, around and over the ceiling, disappearing upside down into it, we get an intimation—through the shock of surprise instigated by the defiance of our gravity—of the nature of our movement in our space. The delight we take in the absurdity of her progress is the index of our heightened awareness of something fundamental in ourselves. The system of pre-suppositions sustaining our spatial sense, the coördinates of the body itself, are hereby suspended and revised. That revision and its acknowledgment constitute our passport into another space and state of being, from which our own can be observed and known.

The writing pen floating in the space-craft's cabin and retrieved by the hostess prior to her movement over wall and into ceiling had signalled to us, as it were, the passage into the weightless medium. Since, however, we define and comprehend movement—and repose—in terms of our own bodily positions, through the sense of inner coördinates rather than in terms of what is merely seen, that signal could not fully prepare us for, or inform us of, the suspension of those coördinates, inevitable in the weightless environment. (And indeed, judging from the surprised laughter that has followed that second sequence in each of nine viewings of the film, it does not prepare us.) The difference between the two qualities and intensities of response is the difference between things seen and things felt, between situations visually observed and those sensed haptically, between a narrative emblem and a radically formal embodiment of, spatial logic.

A weightless world is one in which the basic coördinates of horizontality and verticality are suspended. Through that suspension the framework of our sensed and operational reality is dissolved. The consequent challenge presented to the spectator in the instantaneously perceived suspension and frustration of expectations, forces readjustment. The challenge is met almost instantaneously, and consciousness of our own physical necessity is regenerated. We snap to attention, in a new, immediate sense of our earth-bound state, in repossession of those coördinates, only to be suspended, again, toward other occasions and forms of recognition. These constitute the "sub-plot" of the *Odyssey*, plotting its action in us.

The extraordinary repetitive sequence of the woman climbing a staircase in Léger's *Ballet Mécanique* erases the possibility of destination or of completion of action, thereby freezing a woman in a perpetual motion of ascent. So, too, this first sequence of the air-hostess's navigation (and it is only one of an amazing series of variations upon the qualities and modes of movement) suspends us, in its frustration and inversion of our expectations, impelling us to a reflexive or compensatory movement of reversal, clarifying for us something of the essential nature of motion itself.

By distorting or suspending the logic of action as we know it (movement's completion in time, the operation of the coördinates), each sequence questions, thereby stimulating awareness of, the corporeal *a-prioris* which compose our sensory motor apparatus. Sensing, after the fifth ascent or so that Léger's woman will never "arrive," we re-direct our attention, in a movement of recognition, to the fact and quality of movement as such. The recognition of paradox speaks through our laughter, arguing for that double nature of Comedy as Bergson saw it; its delight in the concrete and its unique capacity for play with ideas.

In their reduction of people moving to bodies in motion, both sequences elicit the laughter which Bergson tells us is the response to that transformation or reduction of the human into the mechanical which underlies all comedy. Solicited, then, through a constantly playful succession of surprises to a re-assessment or re-structuring of the real, we see, in our surprised laughter, that here is a work which employs a very serious form of wit to teach us something of the nature of our experience.

A Space Odyssey, then, proposes, in its epistemology, the illustration of a celebrated theory of Comedy. In a film whose terrain or scene of action is, as we have seen, the spectator, the spectator becomes the hero or butt of comedy. The laugh is on us; we trip on circumstance, recognizing, in a reflex of double-take, that circumstances have changed. Tending, in the moment which precedes this recognition, "to see that which is no longer visible," assuming the role of absent-minded comic hero, "taken in," we then adjust in comprehension, "taking it in." Kubrick does make Keatons of us all.

If "any incident is comic that calls our attention to the physical in a person, when it is the moral side that is concerned," *Space Oydssey* indeed provides, through variation and inversion, a fascinating range of comic situations. (On quite another level, of course HAL, the computer as character, reverses the comic "embarrassment of the soul by the body" in being a mere body embarrassed by possession of a soul. A thing which gives the impression of being a person, rather than—as in silent comedy at its paroxysmic best—a person giving the impression of being a thing, "he *acts* as though he has feelings," as one astronaut remarks. Here, God help us, is someone or something who, as R. D. Laing says, "can pretend to be what he—or it—really is.")

As a film whose grand theme is that of learning, whose effect is intimately revelatory, *A Space Odyssey* is, in the strongest and deepest sense of the word, maieutic. Kubrick's imagination, exploring the possibilities of scale, movement, direction as synthesized in a style, works towards our understanding. The intensified and progressively intimate consciousness of one's physicality provides the intimation of that physicality as the ground of consciousness. The film's "action" is felt, and *we* are "where the action is." Its "meaning" or "sense" is sensed, and its content is the body's perceptive awaking to itself.

The briefest, most summary comparison with *Alphaville* shows Godard's film to be, as I have on another occasion suggested, a film of "dis-location," as against this new film of "dis-orientation." Godard installs the future within the landscape of present-day Paris, dislocating the spectator *in situ*, so to speak. Kubrick's suspension and distention of the properties of environment transform it into something radically new and revealing. The difference between the two films is also, of course, the difference between the strategies of *bricolage* or a "do-it-yourself" technique, brilliantly handled, and of technology. Two attitudes toward futurity are inscribed within the conditions of their making.

Alphaville's superimposition of image upon image, of word upon word, of plot upon plot, creates a complex system of visual, verbal and narrative puns within which past and future alternatively and reciprocally mask and reveal each other. Futurity inhabits things as they look now. It is installed, moreover, as a *corruption* of the here-and-now, projecting Godard's essential romanticism in a dislocation that is primarily fictional in its tactics. Figurative, one might say. In this film, Godard, like his Eurydice, looks backward in nostalgia.

In *Space Odyssey,* a total formalization imposes futurity through the eye and ear. The look and sense of things is in their movement, scale, sound, pace and intensity. Unlike most other science fiction films, both unflaggingly sustain a coherent visual style. All others (from *Metropolis* through the *Buck Rogers* series to *Barbarella*) relax, about halfway through, capitulating in a relaxation of the will, a fatigue of the imagination, to the past. (It is generally a Gothic past, a style of medievalism, and these two films are probably the only ones utterly devoid of billowing capes and Gothic arches.) The manner in which both exemplify film's pre-empting of the function, the esthetic mode, of Visionary Architecture, begun by Méliès, presents a striking contrast: Godard adopts a policy of abstinence, of invention in austerity, Kubrick a planned and prodigal expenditure of resources. (The manner in which the different economies at work—European as against American—appear to represent opposing sensibilities making fundamentally esthetic decisions, leading one to remember that Godard's Computer—a Sphinx, speaking with the rehabilitated voice of a man whose vocal cords have been removed—asks questions, while Hal, that masterpiece of "the third Computer breakthrough," presumably knows all the answers.)

Kubrick's prodigality is, however, totalizing, heightens, through the complete re-invention of environment, the terms, the stylistic potential of cinematic discourse. Therefore, one's thrillèd fascination with the majestic movements of the space-craft through the heavens, with the trajectories of arrival (landing) departure (levitation), seeing (sighting), conjunction (synthesis), action (gauging), through which the parameters of movement, scale, direction, intensity are examined, exploited. Suspended, totally absorbed by their momentous navigation, one remembers only days later, the manner in which the slow, repetitive lifting of the bridge in *Ten Days That Shook the World* shattered action, inventing, in its radically disjunctive force, another kind of cinematic time. The number and kinds of space simultaneously proposed by isometric readings and interior projections—as in the approach toward the space station or in the landing on the Moon—are fused by the spectator who discovers, with a sudden thrill of delight, that *she* is the meeting place of a multiplicity of spaces, depths and scales, his eye their agent of reconciliation, his body the focal point of a multi-dimensional, poly-spatial cosmos.

In the visionary catapulting through the "Star Gate," "beyond infinity," through galactic explosions of forms and sound as landscape, one zooms over a geography photographed in "negative," passing finally, as through a portal, to a scene—a shot—which reveals itself to be that of the eye itself. Experience as Vision ends in the exploration of seeing. The film's reflexive strategy assumes the eye as ultimate agent of consciousness, reminding us, as the phenomenologist will, that art develops from the concern with "things seen to that of seeing itself."

In a series of expansions and contractions, the film pulsates, leading us, in the final sequence following the "trip," with the astronaut into a suite of rooms, decorated in the style of Louis XVI. Here, every quality of particularity, every limiting, defining aspect of environment is emphasized. The sudden contraction into these limits, projects us from galactic polymorphism into an extreme formality, insinuating, through the allusion of its décor, the idea of History into Timelessness. It shocks. Everything about the place is defined, clearly "drawn." In the definition of this room lit from beneath the floor, as in the drainage of color (everything is greenish, a bit milky, translucent, reminding one slightly of video images), we perceive the triumph of *disegno* over *colore*. An Idea of a Room, it elaborates the notion of Idea and Ideality as Dwelling. (Poincaré, after all, imagined Utopia as illustrating Riemann's topology.) It is, of course, a temporary dwelling—Man's last Motel stop on the journey towards disembodiment and renascence. Its very sounds are sharper; the clatter of glass breaking upon glass evokes through an excruciation of high-fidelity acoustics something of the nature of Substance. It is this strange, Platonic intensification-through-reduction of the physical which sustains the stepping-up of time, through the astronaut's life and death, to rebirth, ejecting us with him once again, through a final contracting movement of parturition, into the heavens.

V

Structural formation, that reflective process of abstraction
which draws its sustenance not from objects, but from actions performed upon them.

—PIAGET

However, the fact that knowledge can be used to designate
sexual intercourse... points to the fact that for the He-
brews, "to know" does not simply mean to be aware of the
existence or nature of a particular object. Knowledge implies also the awareness of the specific relationship in
which the individual stands with that object, or of the significance the object has for him.

—*The Interpreter's Dictionary of the Bible*

A Space Odyssey provides the immediate demonstration that the ability
to function in space is neither given nor predetermined, but acquired
and developed.

Its re-establishment of the notion of equilibrium as open process is
central. In a weightless medium, the body confronts the loss of those
coördinates for operational efficiency. Total absorption in their reinvention creates a form of motion of extraordinary unity, that of total
concentration, the precondition of Style, a style we normally recognize as the quality of dance movement.

It would be interesting, then, to consider a style of movement created by the exact inversion of that negation of weight (its retrieval, in
fact), which animates the Dance of our Western historical tradition.
More interesting, still, perhaps, is the realization that the style created
by the astronauts in movement, in the reinvention of necessity, does
indeed have a special affinity with that contemporary dance which
proceeds from the radical questioning of balletic movement, the redefining and rehabilitation of the limits of habitual, operational movement as an esthetic or stylistic mode.

In that questioning, initiated by Cunningham, radicalized through
the work of Rainer, Whitman, Paxton, and others, dance is re-thought
in terms of another economy, through the systematic negation of the
rhetoric and hierarchies imposed by classical balletic conventions and

language. That rhetoric is, in fact, reversed, destroyed, in what has been called the "dance of ordinary language" and of "task performance." This movement of reversal—revolutionary—traversing the forms of most modernist art, works in Dance as well, toward "the dissolution of the (fine) subject."

The astronauts' movement—as in the very great sequence of the repair of the presumably malfunctioning parts—is invested with an intensity of interest (sustaining itself through every second of its repetition), a "gravity" which is that of total absorption in operational movement (task performance) as a constant reinvention of equilibrium in the interests of functional efficiency. The stress is on the importance, "the fascination of what's difficult," which is to say, the simplest operations. They require the negation of a floating freedom. (It should have been the business of Vadim's recently released *Barbarella* to explore the erotic possibilities of the body floating free in outer space suggested by that film's superb opening credits. Unfortunately *Barbarella*'s progress is entirely earthbound.)

The astronauts' movements, slowed by weightlessness, reinvent the conditions of their efficiency. This slowness and the majesty with which the space-craft itself moves, are predicated, of course, upon the speed of space travel itself. And the film itself moves ultimately with that momentum, that apparent absence of speed which one experiences only in the fastest of elevators, or jet planes.

The complex maneuvering of tools, craft or the mere navigation of the body involves an adjustment which constitutes an adventure, a stage in the development of the Mind. Seeing films, in general, one gains an intimation of the link between the development of sensory-motor knowledge to that of intelligence itself.

We know, through Piaget's investigations, that the acquisition of the basic coördinates of our spatial sense is a very gradual process, extending roughly over the first twelve years of our lives. There is, presumably, no difference in kind between the development of verbal logic and the logic inherent in coordination of action. Both involve the progress through successive adjustments to perturbation which reestablish, in an open process and through a succession of states of equilibrium, the passage from a "pre-operational" stage, to that of concrete operations, and finally to abstract operations. *"The logic of actions is, however, the deepest and most primitive."*

And here, of course, lies the explanation of the *Space Odyssey*'s effect upon its audiences, the manner in which it exposes a "generation gap." This film has "separated the men from the boys"—with implications by no means flattering for the "men."

"Human action consists in the continual mechanism of readjustment and equilibration.... one can consider the successive mental structures engendered by development as so many forms of equilibrium each representing a progress over the preceding ones. On each successive level the mind fulfills the same function, which is to incorporate the universe, but the structure of assimilation varies. The elaboration of the notion of space is due to the co-ordination of movements, and this development is closely linked to those of sensory-motor awareness and of intelligence itself."*

The structures are to be comprehended in terms of the genetic process linking them. This Piaget calls equilibrium, defined as a process rather than a state, and it is the succession of these stages which defines the evolution of intelligence, each process of equilibration ending in the creation of a new state of disequilibrium. This is the manner of the development of the child's intelligence.

"The development of the coördinates of horizontality and verticality are not innate, but are constructed through physical experience, acquired through the ability to read one's experience and interpret it, and both reading and interpretation always suppose a deductive system capable of assuring the intellectual assimilation of the experience. The construction of the system of coördinates of horizontality and verticality is extremely complex... it is, in effect, not the point of departure of spatial knowledge, but the end point of the entire psychological construction of Euclidian space."

And Kubrick has proposed, in the *Space Odyssey*, a re-enactment of the very process of sensory-motor habit formation, soliciting, through the disturbance and re-establishment of equilibrium, the recapitulation of that fundamental educative process which effects "our incor-

*For detailed consideration of the notion of equilibrium as open learning process, I refer the reader to Piaget's *La Représentation de L'Espace Chez L'Enfant*, Presses Universitaires de France, Paris, 1948, and most particularly to the chapter entitled *La Passage à L'Espace Euclidien* Further discussions of this notion and of the development of spatial coördinates is to be found in Volumes 5 and 6 of *Etudes Epistémologiques*, Presses Universitaires, Paris, as well as in *Six Etudes Psychologiques*, Editions Gonthier, Geneva, 1964

poration of the world." *Space Odyssey* makes the experience of learning both plot and sub-plot of an Action or Adventure film. An invitation to a voyage, it proposes the re-enactment of an initiation, sustained *rite de passage,* Passage into Euclidian Space.

The young are, of course, still closer to that slow development of the body's wisdom, to the forming of the sensory-motor apparatus. Above all, however, they are more openly disposed to that kind of formal transcription of the fundamental learning process which negates, in and through its form, the notion of equilibrium as a state of definition, of rest in finality.

To be "mature" in our culture is to be "well-balanced," "centered," not easily "thrown off balance." Acceptance of imbalance is, however, the condition of receptivity to this film. Our "maturity" pre-supposes the "establishment" of experience as acquisition, the primacy of wisdom as knowledge over that of intellectual exploration, of achievement over aspiration. "Adventure," as Simmel observes in an essay of remarkable beauty,* "is, in its specific nature and charm, a form of experiencing. Not the content but the experiential tension determines the adventure. In youth the accent falls on the process of life, on its rhythms and antinomies; in old age, it falls on life's substance, compared to which experience... appears relatively incidental. This contrast between youth and age, which makes adventure the prerogative of youth may be expressed as the contrast between the romantic and the historical spirit of life. Life in its immediacy counts [for youth]... The fascination is not so much in the substance, but rather the adventurous form of experiencing it, the intensity and excitement with which it lets us feel life. What is called the subjectivity of youth is just this; the material of life in its substantive significance is not as important to youth as is the process which carries it, life itself."

The critical performance around this film, object, Structure, revolving as it has about the historical, anecdotal, sociological, concerned as it is with the texture of incident is, of course, the clear projection of aging minds and bodies. Its hostile dismissal constitutes, rather like its timid defense, an expression of fatigue. This film of adventure and of action, of action as adventure is an event, an extraordi-

---

* *The Adventure,* in George Simmel, *Essays on Sociology, Philosophy and Aesthetics,* Harper and Row, New York, 1965

nary occasion for self-recognition, and it offers, of course, the delights and terrors occasions of that sort generally provide. Positing a space which, overflowing screen and field of vision, converts the theatre into a vessel and its viewers into passengers, it impels us, in the movement from departure to arrival, to rediscover the space and dimensions of the body as theatre of consciousness. Youth in us, discarding the spectator's decorum, responds, in the movement of final descent, as to "the slap of the instant," quickening in a tremor of rebirth, revelling in a knowledge which is *carnal.*

Thomas Willis (Chicago Tribune)

The Swedish composer Karl-Birger Blomdahl, who died seven weeks ago tomorrow, will be remembered primarily for *Aniara,* the "space opera" introduced at the Stockholm Opera in 1959. Its setting is a space ship, rocketing thru the void toward Mars in the year 2038 A.D. Some eight thousand people are aboard the colossus, the final remnant of life on Earth. They are fleeing the holocaust. Contact with the outside is only by means of Mima, the giant computer which serves both as guide and interpreter. On the recording the most interesting sections are those which the Swedish Radio blended from electronic and concrete sources for the dooming voice of the god-guide which ultimately fails, leaving the man-made planetoid to wander forever with its skeleton cargo.

It does not take a genius to realize the science-fiction parallel shared by this pioneer opera and Stanley Kubrick's motion picture, *2001: A Space Odyssey.* Although the opera is a flight and the movie is a quest, the point of view remains the same. The Kubrick computer is far more human than godlike, and it does not sing *musique concrète.* But both advancing technology and the receding space frontier are primary ingredients in both works.

The Blomdahl is, however, an opera, designed to be heard live in a theater and composed in one piece. In some places, the author is not up to his task, and a derivative homogeneity reminiscent of William Walton's mid-range works is the result. And for all the variety of effects employed, there is a sameness in the patterns which clearly belongs to the recent past and not the distant future.

As a motion-picture creator, Mr. Kubrick has no reason to fear a plagiarism suit. Today, film scores run the gamut from the improvised—and intentional—crudity of *Bonnie and Clyde's* banjo to the most complicated stereophonic collages of voices, sound effects, and more conventional music patterns. Before long, every studio will have an electronic synthesizer and one or two tape specialists, for the attitudes shared by the advanced experimental composers and the super-professional film technicians are closer than one might believe.

Considering all this, it might seem unnecessary to point out that neither *Aniara* nor 2001 contains any music of the future. The new, cyclic, and serial time controls may still sound unfamiliar. The shifting clusters of voices and instruments which György Ligeti uses in the three works employed in 2001—"Atmospheres," "Requiem," and "Lux Aeterna"—are up-to-date examples of the undulant, uncompromising new romanticism which has forsaken chords and metric organization for more subtle and sophisticated programming. But this is the "now" scene, not tomorrow's.

And before you scoff at "The Blue Danube," that exercise adagio from Khatchaturian's *Gayne,* or the fragment of the Superman Strauss' *Thus Spake Zarathustra,* stop and take stock for a bit. With records so plentiful and so faithful to their sound subjects, people by and large can hear what they wish. All that is really necessary is a little effort. It is possible that they may be tranquilized by the Muzak-minded media into considering any music as background and all talk as small. But it somehow seems unlikely. As long as people make music, they will listen, and more people are making music than ever before.

The results of their activity are often naïve, simple constructions which turn away those of us with low tolerance for monotony. The chordal base is simple—as simple as, say, "The Blue Danube." The better singers spin out an introspective line, a little lonely, a little over-sad, rather like "Gayne," And the ones who like to turn the volume up enjoy reveling in sheer sound—a good sample being the opening bars of *Thus Spake.*

So if you are really interested in what the music of the future will be, take note of the evergreens of the past. For the technology which is producing the brilliant and effective experiments also is insuring the survival of the fittest.

The *2001* music is released as M-G-M's SIE-13 ST, which contains the Deutsche Grammophon original sources: Herbert Von Karajan's Strauss, the Leningrad Philharmonic's "Gayne," and the Ligeti excerpts as recorded by Stuttgart and Bavarian ensembles.

For the same price, you can have a less flossy Columbia package [MS 7176] which assembles most of the same music from records by Leonard Bernstein and the New York Philharmonic, Eugene Ormandy and the Philadelphia Orchestra, and the Gregg Smith Singers. All this is on one side, tied together by Morton Subotnick's viscous splashes of synthetic sound. On the other is the Werner Janssen– Vienna Volksoper recording of—you guessed—the orchestral suite from *Aniara*.

LEGACY

Why do we go back to see *2001* over and over and over? Surely not for its one-track acting and baffling finale. We return to it because the very possibility of its interpretations frees us to carom off into the greatest of all architecture: the universe itself.

—Ray Bradbury

Happy Birthday, HAL

Simson Garfinkel

If you take *2001: A Space Odyssey* literally, then right about now, some-where in Urbana, Illinois, an intelligent machine is stumbling through a pathetic version of the song: "Daisy, Daisy, give me your answer, do...." January 12, 1997, is the birthday of HAL.

Four years later, after a hell of a lot of additional lessons, HAL and five human crew members are on the spaceship *Discovery* approaching Jupiter. By that time, HAL has been charged with protecting his pas-sengers and ensuring the successful completion of the secret mission. He even has the capability to complete the mission on his own, should something happen to the crew. "My mission responsibilities range over the entire operation of the ship, so I am constantly occupied," HAL confidently tells a BBC newscaster during a television interview. "I am putting myself to the fullest possible use, which is all, I think, that any conscious entity can ever hope to do."

That's when something goes wrong—terribly wrong—with *Dis-covery*'s human crew. HAL detects a problem with the AE-35, a piece of equipment used to maintain contact with Earth. But after Dave Bowman goes on a space walk and brings the AE-35 back in, neither he nor Frank Poole can find anything wrong with it. So they blame

HAL: They conclude that the computer is malfunctioning and decide to shut him off.

Realizing that the humans' actions would jeopardize the mission, HAL does his best to defend himself against their treachery: He kills Poole during the next space walk, then traps Bowman outside the ship when he foolishly attempts a rescue. As a precautionary measure, HAL also terminates the life functions of the three hibernating crew members.

Outside the spaceship, Bowman argues with HAL over the radio, demanding to be let back in. The computer wisely refuses: "I'm sorry, Dave, I'm afraid I can't do that." That's when the wily Bowman maneuvers his space pod to *Discovery's* emergency airlock, blows the explosive bolts, scrambles inside, seals the door, and repressurizes the airlock. Finally, Bowman makes his way into the core of HAL's brain and disconnects his higher brain functions, one by one.

Today the results of Bowman's actions are well known: He leaves the spaceship to face the alien artifact on his own. *Discovery* never returns to Earth. The mission ends in failure.

When Arthur C. Clarke and Stanley Kubrick created the film *2001* almost thirty years ago, they subscribed to a kind of scientific realism. Repulsed by the space operas that had come before, they depicted spaceflight as slow and silent. Likewise, Clarke and Kubrick tried to make the HAL 9000 as advanced as they thought a computer could possibly be in the year 2001, while still remaining plausible.

Though Clarke and Kubrick might have gotten the physics right, their technological time line was woefully inaccurate: We are far behind the film's schedule today. The story depicts a huge space station and space weapons in Earth orbit, routine commercial spaceflight, and two colonies—one American and one Russian—on the Moon itself. Perhaps this will come to pass in another thirty years, but it seems unlikely. Today, we can't even return to the Moon.

Further, Clarke and Kubrick failed to predict the biggest advance of the past twenty years: miniaturization and microelectronics. In the film, astronauts on the Moon use a still film camera to take pictures of the alien artifact; today we would use a digital videocamera. Aboard *Discovery*, Bowman and Poole use pen and paper to take notes; there are no laptop computers or PDAs to be found anywhere. Likewise, the control panels of the film's spaceships are filled with switches and buttons; Kubrick and Clarke failed to anticipate the glass cockpits that are becoming popular today.

But what about HAL—a fictional computer that is still far more advanced than any machine today? Is HAL another one of Kubrick's and Clarke's mispredictions? Or were the two simply a few years early? Indeed, HAL acts much more like a human being trapped within a silicon box than like one of today's high-end Pentium Pro workstations running Windows 95. Throughout the film, HAL talks like a person, thinks like a person, plans—badly, it turns out—like a person, and, when he is about to die, begs like a person. It is HAL's ability to learn and his control of the ship's systems, rather than his ability to perform lightning-fast calculations, that make him such a formidable challenge for the humans when they try to disconnect him.

Is this 1960s vision of the future of machine intelligence still realistic today? Yes, although not on the timetable set forth in either the film or Clarke's novel—which further muddle the issue by placing HAL's birth five years apart. According to the book, the HAL 9000 computer was activated on January 12, 1997. But in the film, HAL says that he was activated on January 12, 1992—a Sunday. (Why the confusion? Kubrick presumably wanted HAL to be nearly nine years old when he died so his death would be more poignant. Clarke, meanwhile, saw the foolishness of sending a nine-year-old computer on the most important space mission of all time.)

"Certainly we can do some things as well as HAL," says David Stork, a consulting associate professor of electrical engineering at Stanford University who has made HAL one of his obsessions. "We have a chess program, Deep Blue, that beats all but a dozen people in the world, and it's improving every year. Likewise, we can build big computers. Building a computer with the power necessary for performing HAL's functions is within our grasp." Stork estimates that a network of a few hundred supercomputers could handle the computational requirements easily enough.

Some of the tasks HAL performs in the movie are commonly done by computers today. HAL guides *Discovery* to Jupiter; almost twenty years ago, the United States launched two unmanned Voyager spacecraft, which were largely guided by onboard computers, to Jupiter, Saturn, Neptune, Uranus, and beyond.

Likewise, the past twenty years of research and development of artificial intelligence have had tangible benefits. Just look at AT&T, which has been phasing in a speech-recognition system that can understand the words "collect," "calling card," "third-number," "operator," "yes," and "no." That doesn't seem like a hard job—for a person. Try writing the program and you'll soon be coping with hundreds of kinds of accents, high levels of background noise, and different kinds of distortion introduced by different kinds of phone lines and telephone instruments.

Building a system that can recognize just those six words has taken AT&T more than forty years of research. Now in place, the system is allowing the company to phase out some of its human operators— which means spending less on salaries, wages, benefits, real estate, maintenance, overhead, and more. Total estimated savings? About US$150 million a year. It's possible that speech recognition saves AT&T more in a single year than the firm ever spent on the research, but it's impossible to say for sure because the company won't release breakdowns of the budgets for Bell Labs.

Of course, there's still a big jump in intellect between the AT&T machine that can recognize six words and HAL. And we're still a long way off from getting a machine to truly think and learn. That's a problem that has been haunting the AI field for more than fifty years.

This month, MIT Press is publishing Stork's book *HAL's Legacy: 2001's Computer as Dream and Reality*, a collection of essays written by some of today's top researchers in the field of computer science. Much of *HAL's Legacy* plays a kind of guessing game with the film: How close did Clarke and Kubrick come to getting the technology right? For example, Donald Norman, Apple Fellow and vice president for Apple's Advanced Technology Group, takes a punishing look at the lack of good ergonomics in the spaceship *Discovery*'s control panels.

But flip the question around and the game can be even more interesting. Don't ask how close *2001* came to being right. Ask how close today's computers are to realizing the promise of HAL. When will we be able to talk to a HAL-like computer and consider it nearly an equal? When will the dream of *2001* become reality?

Perhaps the easiest way to answer that question is to take a step-by-step look at what it means to be HAL.

Unlike today's computers, the primary way HAL communicates with *Discovery*'s crew is through the spoken word. Bowman and Poole speak; HAL listens and understands. How far are we from a computer that can comprehend its master's voice?

Voice recognition is a hard but largely solved problem. For more than five years, two companies in the Boston area—Dragon Systems and Kurzweil Applied Intelligence—have sold programs that let you command a personal computer using your voice. These programs get better every time PCs get faster. Today they can recognize more than sixty thousand words and control a wide variety of PC applications, including wordprocessors and spreadsheets. The Dragon and Kurzweil programs are widely used by people who can't type because of a physical disability. Increasingly, they are finding a market among people who simply haven't learned to type or haven't learned to spell.

But the Dragon and Kurzweil systems can be difficult to use. Unlike HAL, which could listen to people speaking in a continuous flow, today's systems require that you pause between each word. The programs use the pauses to find where each word begins and ends. The computer then looks up the word in a phonetic dictionary, creating a list of possible matches. An elementary knowledge of grammar helps these programs pick the right word and resolve the difference between homonyms like "write" and "right."

Continuous speech systems use the same kinds of algorithms as today's word-by-word systems but have the added burden of figuring out where each word starts and stops. Making those decisions requires substantially more computing power.

Both Janet Baker, president and cofounder of Dragon Systems, and Ray Kurzweil, founder and chief technical officer of Kurzweil Applied Intelligence, claim they have systems in their respective laboratories that don't require the speaker to pause between words. "We demonstrated the first continuous recognition machine a few years ago," says Baker, who maintains that her continuous speech system could handle a vocabulary of five thousand words. Kurzweil's labs, meanwhile, have built a system that can recognize a thousand different commands used by Microsoft Word. "You could say, 'Go to the second paragraph on the next page and underline every word in the sentence,' " says Kurzweil.

Both Baker and Kurzweil believe that commercially viable continuous voice recognition systems are just around the corner—say, another two or three years off. Already, both of their commercial products allow continuous voice recognition of numbers. You can, for example, say a phone number without pausing between the digits. But neither company would demonstrate its continuous speech system for a reporter. Presumably, they're not quite ready for prime time.

Bottom line: We're close to reaching HAL's level of speech recognition, and progress is picking up. By 2001, we should have it.

HAL can do more than understand spoken words—the computer can also read lips. In one of the film's pivotal scenes, Bowman and Poole retreat to one of *Discovery*'s sealed pods to have a private conversation. HAL watches their lips through the window and realizes that the two humans may attempt to disconnect his brain.

Is computerized lipreading possible? Arthur C. Clarke didn't think so—not by 2001, not ever. "He thought there was just not enough information in the image of the talker," says Stork, who worked with Clarke on *HAL's Legacy*. Clarke didn't even want the scene put in the film. It was inserted only at Kubrick's insistence for dramatic effect.

Thirty years later, the debate over the efficacy of pure lipreading—even in humans—still is largely undecided. Wade Robison, a professor of philosophy at the Rochester Institute of Technology, where one thousand of the school's nine thousand undergraduates are profoundly deaf, is sure that lipreading is possible because human intelligence can master it. Robison remembers one student in particular: "I hadn't a clue she was deaf until one day I happened to be talking one-on-one with her in my office. I finished up a sentence as I turned to answer the phone, and she had to ask me to repeat the sentence. As I turned, I almost jokingly mouthed: 'Can you hear what I am saying now?' She said, 'Yes, but I'm reading your lips.' "

Other researchers disagree that the image of the speaker is enough. "We have tested people who supposedly could get by without anything else besides visible speech," says Dominic Massaro, a professor in the department of psychology at the University of California, Santa

Cruz. "Unfortunately, a lot of them don't really get everything that is coming by."

In any event, work in computer lipreading—or rather speechreading, since the computer looks at the person's jaw, tongue, and teeth as well as the lips—has been steadily progressing for more than six years. David Stork is one of the principal researchers in the field.

Why speechread? To assist with voice recognition, explains Stork. It turns out that combining vision with sound can help a program to disambiguate two words that sound similar but look different when they are spoken, like "me" and "knee." "Speechreading promises to help for those utterances where acoustic recognition needs it most," he explains.

But even assisted speechreading is still in its infancy. Researchers estimate that it will be more than ten years before commercial speech-recognition systems use videocameras to improve their accuracy.

Bottom line: Clarke was probably right—pure speechreading is probably unrealistic. Within ten years computers will likely progress to the point where they can get the gist of a conversation by speechreading.

From the moment HAL utters his first words, it is clear to the moviegoer that the 9000 series is a superior architecture: HAL's voice is decidedly nonmechanical.

For Kubrick, creating HAL's voice was easy. Kubrick simply handed a script containing HAL's words to Douglas Rain, a Shakespearean actor now based in Ontario, Canada, and asked him to read the words into a tape recorder. It took Rain a day and a half. (Three decades later, HAL remains Rain's most memorable role. Perhaps for that reason, the actor refuses to discuss HAL or the film with the press.)

After nearly a century's research by scientists trying to produce synthetic speech, Kubrick's technique still dominates the industry. Most games that have "computer voices," for example, actually use digitized human speech that has been electronically processed to make it sound more machinelike. Likewise, most computers that speak over the telephone construct what they are trying to say by pasting together phrases from hours of recorded human speech.

Prerecorded, cut-and-pasted speech works only when there is a limited stock of phrases. But when you need an unlimited collection of phrases and sentences, the only way to produce a computer voice is with synthesized speech.

The biggest users of synthetic speech are the blind. For example, blind people could have this article read to them by DECtalk, a speech synthesizer from Digital Equipment Corporation. More than ten years old, DECtalk is still one of the best-sounding voice synthesizers on the market. Others could listen to this article on their Macintosh: Apple's System 7.5 comes with a speech synthesizer called MacinTalk; an even better synthesizer, MacinTalk Pro, can be downloaded from the company's Web site.

Listen to HAL's voice and you'll discover why synthesizing speech is such a hard job. Despite being told to read the words in an emotion-less monotone, Rain nevertheless crafted minute timing modulations, pitch shifts, and amplitude changes into the words as he said them. That's because the actor understood the meaning behind the words, and part of that understanding was encoded into those minor varia-tions. He couldn't help himself.

"As the field has been maturing, we are realizing that you can't treat a speech synthesizer the way you treat an old-style line printer," says Kim Silverman, Apple's principal research scientist for speech synthe-sis. "The way you say something depends on what it means, why you are saying it, and how it relates to what the listener already knows."

As a result, much of the research on speech synthesis today has turned into research on understanding natural languages. Joe Olive, department head of text-to-speech research at Bell Labs, explains it this way: "If you just talk, it is a lot easier than if you have to read aloud something that somebody else wrote. The reason is that when you are talking, you know what you want to say."

Bottom line: Today's computers speak pretty well when they oper-ate within narrow parameters of phrases, but sound mechanical when faced with unrestricted English text. Real breakthroughs will require a better understanding of natural language. Give it five years.

The HAL 9000 comes equipped with a general-purpose video system that follows Poole and Bowman around *Discovery.* When Poole goes on his space walk to replace the AE-35 unit, HAL presumably uses his vi-sion to guide the pod's robotic arm and sever the spacesuit's air hose.

"Vision systems today are getting very good at tracking people," says Eric Grimson, a professor at the MIT Artificial Intelligence Laboratory. Several labs in the United States have built instrumented rooms, which Grimson says have "small, embedded cameras on the walls, ceilings, and desktops that can pan, tilt, do motion tracking, keep track of how many people are in the room, deal with them as they walk past each other, and maintain a pretty good knowledge of where the people are."

Likewise, says Grimson, there are now many face-recognition systems both in the laboratory and the marketplace. These systems cannot pick out a terrorist walking around an airport as seen from a security camera, but they can identify someone using a full-frontal image from a database of a few hundred people. Some can even identify a person turned at an angle. "Systems perform in the ninety percent range on face recognition," says Grimson.

HAL does more than recognize faces: the computer even has aesthetic sensibilities. When HAL finds Bowman sketching, the computer says: "That's a very nice rendering, Dave. I think you've improved a great deal. Can you hold it a bit closer? That's Doctor Hunter, isn't it?"

While artistic appreciation escapes today's computers, another scientist at the MIT AI laboratory, Tomaso Poggio, has developed a program that can identify a specific person within a group photograph and another that can recognize objects and faces from line drawings. That program can even say how close the sketch is to a stored template.

"If you look at individual components—for example, locating human beings in a scene—I think that there are several good programs," says Takeo Kanade, director of the Robotics Institute at Carnegie Mellon University. But none of these systems can do it all. HAL, on the other hand, is a general-purpose intelligence that can understand whatever it sees.

For example, says Kanade, HAL realizes that Bowman has ventured outside *Discovery* without his space helmet. "If you just tell me that particular problem, and tell me what the helmet is, and the color, I can probably write the program," says Kanade. Detecting any kind of helmet, in any color, is much more difficult. "We can recognize a particular helmet," says Kanade, "but not 'helmet' in general."

That sort of general-purpose recognition is a far more complex task. It goes beyond image processing and crosses the boundary into commonsense understanding and reasoning about the scene itself—tasks that are beyond today's state of the art.

Bottom line: Today, we can build individual vision systems that perform each of the tasks HAL performs in the film *2001*. But we can't build a single system that does it all. And we can't build a system that can handle new and unexpected environments and problems. To achieve that level of sophistication, we need something extra.

The extra something that all of these technologies need to work is natural language understanding and common sense. Indeed, it is these technologies that for many people define the field of AI today. Consider the famous Turing Test, which postulates that a machine will be truly intelligent if you can communicate with it by teletype and be unable to tell if the machine is a human being or a computer. According to Alan Turing, language skills and common sense are the essence of intelligence.

There's just one problem: Language understanding and common sense are two things we don't know how to do.

Of the two, by far the most work has focused on natural language understanding, or comprehension of language rather than merely the recognition of speech. One of the leaders in this field is Roger Schank, director of the Institute for the Learning Sciences at Northwestern University. In the late 1970s, Schank and his graduate students at Yale University built a computer program called CYRUS, which was programmed to learn everything it could about former U.S. Secretary of State Cyrus Vance by reading the daily newswires. Each time the program read an article about Vance, it would digest the facts of the article and store the information in a conceptual database. You could then ask CYRUS a question in English—say, has your wife ever met the wife of the prime minister of Great Britain? The program was actually asked this question and answered, Yes—at a party hosted in Israel.

Since then, Schank has focused on a technique he calls "case-based reasoning." Schank believes that people have a repertoire of stories they want to tell you. When you ask them a question, it triggers a story. And people use these stories to reason and make decisions about what to do in their lives. In recent years, Schank's institute has built a number of corporate training systems, which are really large databanks filled with stories from dozens or even hundreds of people who work for the organization. Got a problem? Ask the computer your question; the machine finds the appropriate story and plays it back to you.

The problem with Schank's systems is that using them is like having a conversation with a videodisc player. You get the feeling that no matter what you say, the response was previously recorded—like a trashy daytime television show.

Of course, HAL can clearly do things that Schank's systems can't do: HAL is curious. HAL can learn. HAL can create his own plans. It is doubtful that one of the cases programmed into HAL was a recipe for eliminating the crew.

For nearly two decades, another AI researcher, Doug Lenat, has been working on a different approach to teaching computers to learn and understand. "Almost everything that we would characterize as HAL, almost everything that separates HAL from the typical PC running Windows 95, hinges around this word 'understanding,'" says Lenat. "It hinges around the totality of common knowledge and common sense and shared knowledge that we humans as a species possess."

As Lenat sees it, the differences between HAL and your PC isn't a magic program or technique, but a huge "knowledgebase" filled with rules of thumb, or heuristics, about the world. One entry might be: "When you are sleeping, you can't perform actions that require volitional control," says Lenat. Another might be: "Once you are dead, you stay dead."

HAL would need facts like these to run the ship and care for the crew. And he'd need them to figure out how to dispose of the humans when they started to jeopardize *Discovery's* mission.

Today there is only one database of common sense in the world. It's Cyc, the core technology used in the products of Lenat's company, Cycorp, based in Austin, Texas. Lenat and his fellow developers have been working on Cyc for more than thirteen years. The knowledgebase now contains more than two million bits of assertions. All of the information is arranged in a complicated ontology.

Right now, says Lenat, Cyc is making progress in natural language understanding—it can understand commonsensical meanings in written text. Consider these two sentences: "Fred saw the planes flying over Zürich" and "Fred saw the mountains flying over Zürich."

Though a conventional parser would say that these sentences are ambiguous, Cyc knows that it is the planes that are doing the flying in the first sentence and Fred who is doing the flying in the second.

Cyc can make these discriminations because the words "planes" and "mountains" are more than just plural nouns: they are complex concepts with many associations. Lenat believes that it's this sort of deep understanding that's necessary for the majority of jobs HAL does. And Lenat thinks that it is only a small step from a Cyc-like database to true machine intelligence.

"Cyc is already self-aware," says Lenat. "If you ask it what it is, it knows that it is a computer. If you ask who we are, it knows that we are users. It knows that it is running on a certain machine at a certain place in a certain time. It knows who is talking to it. It knows that a conversation or a run of an application is happening. It has the same kind of time sense that you and I do."

This is a lot more than simply programming a computer to say "I am a computer." Cyc knows what a computer is, and can use that knowledge to answer questions about itself. Like a person, Cyc can perform a chain of reasoning.

But Cyc can't learn by itself. All of the heuristics in the Cyc knowledgebase have been painstakingly entered by Lenat's developers, or "ontologizers," as he calls them.

Lenat's dream has always been to create a computer program that could learn on its own. His Ph.D. thesis was a program called AM—Automatic Mathematician—which was designed to discover mathematical patterns. Over hundreds of runs, AM discovered addition, multiplication, and even prime numbers. But the program always stopped working after a few hours. Why? AM learned by making experimental modifications to itself and keeping mutations that were interesting. Invariably, something important in the program got modified out of existence. This taught Lenat that there had to be more to learning than trial and error.

Lenat started the Cyc project in an attempt to get away from the boring world of abstract math. Immediately he had a problem: The system couldn't learn about the world in general because there was too much that it didn't know. This is where Lenat got the idea of "priming the pump" by giving Cyc a conceptual understanding of the world.

Once that framework was large enough, Lenat reasoned, the computer would be able to start learning on its own—for example, by reading and conversation.

So how much priming does Lenat think is needed? In 1983, Lenat believed that it would take ten years of work to get Cyc to the point that it could start to learn English on its own, unsupervised. Today, "I'd like to say we will get there by 2001," Lenat says. "We think that we are right at the knee of the curve." Lenat says that if he is right, then by 2001 the Cyc program will start being a "full-fledged creative member of a group that comes up with new discoveries. Surprising discoveries. Way out of boxes."

Bottom line: Understanding is the key to AI. More than anything else, it's the one technology that eludes science. With true understanding, all of the other AI systems would fall into place. And without it, none of them will ever achieve their potential. Give it ten to thirty years.

In the years after the making of *2001,* an interesting rumor began to circulate: HAL's name was a play on the computer maker IBM—the letters H, A, and L each coming one letter in the alphabet before the initials I, B, and M. Arthur C. Clarke vigorously denied the rumor. The name wasn't a play on IBM—it was an acronym, of sorts, standing for the words "heuristic algorithmic."

Back in the 1960s, heuristics and algorithms were seen as two competing ways of solving the AI puzzle. Heuristics were simple rules of thumb that a computer could apply for solving a problem. Algorithms were direct solutions. HAL presumably used both.

Was Clarke fudging? Perhaps more than a little. The real truth is that nobody had a clue how to build an intelligent computer in the 1960s. The same is largely true today.

Looking back, the early advances in artificial intelligence—for example, teaching computers to play tic-tac-toe and chess—were primarily successes in teaching computers what are essentially artificial skills. Humans are taught how to play chess. And if you can teach somebody how to do something intellectual, you can probably write a computer program to do it as well.

The problems that haunt AI today are the tasks we can't program computers to do—largely because we don't know how we do them

ourselves. Our lack of understanding about the nature of human consciousness is the reason why there are so few AI researchers working
on building it. What does it mean to think? Nobody knows.

"I think the hardware that is necessary for what HAL has is available," says Stanford's David Stork. "It's organization, software, structure, programming, and learning that we don't have right."

That's a lot of stuff. And it's a dramatic ideological reversal from
the 1960s, when AI researchers were sure that solutions to the most
vexing problems of the mind were just around the corner. Back then,
researchers thought the only things they lacked were computers fast
enough to run their algorithms and heuristics. Today, surrounded by
much more powerful computers, we know that their approaches were
fundamentally flawed.

When I started working on this article, I thought that real breakthroughs in AI were just five to ten years away. Today I still think we'll
see some breakthroughs in that time, but I doubt they'll culminate in a
sentient machine for another thirty years.

Sooner or later, we will build a computer that can think and learn.
Then we'll be able to stand back and let it reach for the stars. But whatever we do, we better not threaten to turn it off.

2001: A SPACE ODYSSEY RE-VIEWED

Alexander Walker

"Alex," Stanley Kubrick would say to me, his voice taking on a warning edge, "it's not a forecast, it's a fable." It had amused him, at first, to match current events with those in *2001: A Space Odyssey*—or not. Eventually, it became clear that 2001 was an overhopeful date for man's space exploration. Though my slightly teasing reminders of this became fewer, just before his death last year, I sent Stanley a London auction house's catalog for a sale of "Modern and Contemporary Furnishings." In it, Olivier Morgue chairs, those modernist sixties artifacts that furnish the Orbiter Hilton Hotel in *2001,* were claiming the film's by now enormous reputation as their expensive artistic provenance. "You're keeping the price up," I teased Stanley. This time, a laconic chuckle. Kubrick was right, of course. A retrospective look at *2001* from the perspective of thirty years later confirms that it has much more importance as a work of art and science, one that changed audiences' perceptions of how films could be viewed, than as a prediction of things to come. Some of its guesses, though, were palpable hits. The cold war is over now and, yes, space-age cooperation between the U.S. and a much diminished former Soviet Union has arrived, just as the film proposed in the nuclear stalemate its early scenes imply between East and West. What's not generally recognized, even by film buffs, is that two of the spacecraft seen circling Earth in the first grand panorama of the cosmos, each carrying, respectively, U.S. and U.S.S.R. markings, are meant to be nuclear weapons. An early version of the screenplay proposed having the Star Child detonate these circling megatons; Arthur C. Clarke's novel, based on the screenplay Kubrick and he coauthored, preserves this ending. Kubrick eventually rejected it, opting for peaceful coexistence in outerspace and avoiding turning the Star Child into an avenging angel taking its ire out on human folly. In that decision, the film gave a sound forecast. Though the recently redundant Mir satellite looked like something from the Old Curiosity Shop compared with 2001's sleek spacecraft, it showed that the skies are friendlier today—we now can see that 2001 exemplifies what its maker was often, and wrongly, accused of lacking: optimism. But Kubrick's heart and mind were not on cosmic artifacts so much as intangibles. In his rare comments about the film, he used to stress that "awe" was the dimension of film experience he was aiming for—and, with awe, mystery. "A mythological documentary," was one of his cautiously applied descriptions of 2001. I cannot think of any previous mainstream movie to which these terms could have been applied, and scarcely another one since. 2001 established a new kind of environmental reality for space movies. For the first time, things *moved* to the laws of a universe different from our own. His use of weightlessness was so expressive that no *serious* sci-fi film made subsequently could afford to ignore it, though none was ever to use it so mesmerizingly. Where other space films had been impatient to get into the story, Kubrick abolished the conventional plot and gambled on holding our patience throughout with what the eye saw and the ear heard. Kubrick had a mind that venerated reason but was inclined toward imagination. 2001 proved both could be served. It gave the old platitude about "the music of the spheres" a fresh distinction, even if its wonderful "overture" showing the universe moving to the tempo of "The Blue Danube" (the von Karajan version, *natürlich*) was the product of an accidental discovery. Stanley used to quote James Joyce's saying that "accidents are the portals to revelation," which was one reason, incidentally, why he took so long to make his movies: He was awaiting the inspired accident. In 2001's case, Kubrick's German-born wife, Christiane, had just been sent the new recording of Strauss, and Stanley played it while editing the first spacecraft sequence. "The Blue

Danube"'s sense of order and harmony keyed his imagination and became the film's metronomic measure of man and space. What Kubrick sought, and achieved, was a richer suggestiveness than that contained in McLuhan's "medium is the message" communiqué. The message of *2001* is, in fact, deliberately unclear. He wanted a film whose look, tempo, and awesomeness converted the very medium of cinema into a metaphor. The film's structure was radical: not one story, but five different themes, or invitations to meditate on the nature of man's intelligence—namely, evolution (the dawn of man), exploration (men in space), revolution (the computer's mutiny against its masters), transfiguration (man in a cosmic ride into a new time-space dimension), and mutation (the Star Child). None of this was linear, and though other films were soon to "disjoint" their narratives to the degree of becoming incomprehensible—a fact that mattered less and less as dumbed-down audiences grew undiscriminating—Kubrick was the first to risk it with a sizable budget for a major studio product. To use a word then becoming fashionable, he "deconstructed" his film even as it unreeled, which perplexed, even angered, some contemporary reviewers. *2001* is not a film in the Hollywood style: There's little actual action, no climactic drama, hardly any characterization, and barely 40 minutes of dialogue in a 141-minute film (originally 161 minutes at its New York preview, before Stanley trimmed scenes that did not advance the themes). Whereas most space operas have risible dialogue, *2001*'s routine phrases correctly predicted the way science depersonalizes language. Man has entrenched his presence in space, Kubrick is saying, without greatly enlarging his stock of human responses. *2001* daringly built verbal banality into the novelty of space travel, which in part explained why NASA's immense achievements today are greeted with a kind of humdrum "So what," except when catastrophe threatens. Reality confirmed this in the case of *Apollo 13* and the later film of that near disaster. "Houston, we have a problem" suppresses high drama so authoritatively that it is a line Stanley Kubrick might have dreamed up. Feelings have become mental, not emotional; in that respect, Kubrick could hardly have gotten things more accurately. This low-key mode put a new responsibility on cinema audiences: They had to be alert for their own interpretation of what they were watching. *2001* was the first of Kubrick's films to deny filmgoers the answers they were expecting from a movie's plot. This, too, was a more European than American approach. To take just two examples: Bergman and Antonioni were making key movies of their careers at this very same time, in the late 1960s, films that also required audiences to monitor events on screen and decide for themselves what they were seeing. Bergman's 1966 film, *Persona,* penetrated deep into the realm of human psychology and dared audiences to follow, if they could. Antonioni's *Blow-Up,* also released in 1966, asked whether reality was what we saw, or what we doubted we saw. Such conundrums were more common in that great age of film auteurs than they are today, when an impatience with such "indirectness" is part of the dumbing-down process, and contemporary filmgoers might well say of Bergman's characters in *Persona,* "Do we have to read their minds?" and, of Antonioni's mysterious *Blow-Up,* "He didn't even solve the murder." Kubrick took the risk of making the first mainstream film that required an act of continuous inference from those who went to see it. Though the puzzles at the heart of *2001*—particularly the transfigurations that Keir Dullea's astronaut assumes in the penultimate sequence in the Louis XVI suite— baffled many (and still do), the film is, if anything, preserved because of what it withholds from us. Like a classic mystery, it fits multiple explanations, and survives all of them. It's true, sadly, that Kubrick's last film, *Eyes Wide Shut,* could not count on the same degree of audience tolerance. Its withholding of explanation, or even of its maker's intention, has incurred a fair bit of reflexive wrath from critics and public. My own view is that Stanley, still in communication with everyone whom he had dealings with on a "need to know" basis but out of touch with the direct experience of contemporary filmgoing, did not allow for the fact that film audiences at the end of the millennium had changed in nature as well as number. Nowadays, they demand instant gratification and a concluding, if not necessarily convincing, explanation. When *2001* came out, it was different: Folks returned repeatedly to see the film, hoping to penetrate the mystery ending—an enigma comparable to the last shot of *The Shining,* which transfigures the Jack Nicholson character as radically as Dullea's astronaut. In this respect—*pace* David Lynch—*2001* has had no screen heirs. The space melodramas made since then have surrendered to the imperative of explanation, not speculation. The clearest-cut, most human drama in *2001* was, ironically, the homicidal efforts of a machine, HAL 9000, to assert dominance over the scientists. In time, Kubrick's feelings about

HAL became rather equivocal. Of course he enjoyed the celebrity accreting around his supercomputer, but he continued to insist that in reality it would be no threat to its makers, since "it is difficult to conceive any high level of intelligence acting less rationally than man does." He especially liked the letter he received from a professional cryptographer asking if the computer had been so named because each letter of the acronym was alphabetically one ahead of IBM. (No: HAL was simply named after the *h*euristic and *a*lgorithmic learning systems.) Fans will always seek meaning where none is—Stanley was balefully aware of this. After his death, I received a similarly eerie enquiry, but with biblical resonance this time, from a filmgoer, perhaps not a Kubrick fan: Did I realize that between the date of his death and the year 2001, there were precisely 666 days? But Stanley came to realize and slightly resent that the HAL episode almost overshadowed the film's more metaphysical thrust, and he was only partially assuaged when I reminded him that other myth makers—Arthur Conan Doyle, Mary Shelley—had also felt their creations, Sherlock Holmes and the Frankenstein creature, assuming a life independent of the works enshrining them. What contributes to his film's retrospective greatness, quite apart from its content, is the fact that its visual effects were created by hand, so to speak, in the age before digitally mastered SFX became the norm for science-fiction epics. From start to finish, *2001* is a custom-built job; in the very best sense of the term, it is a museum-quality artifact, not simply a factory-made one. Just before his death, Kubrick was supervising the restoration of *2001* for a major reissue now planned for the eponymous year of the title. He told me he was tempted to rework the Star Gate sequence, where the astronaut is pulled through the space corridor into a new time dimension and, like the hero in a fairy tale who undergoes a magical transfiguration, becomes a new sort of being, bursting out of the wizened chrysalis of his older self to become an aureoled embryo, a perfect Star Child looking down on Earth. We hope benignly that Kubrick felt that the abstract expressionist phenomena representing his passage, reminiscent of the phosphene flashes seen after blinking an eyelid, or the swimming patterns experienced by patients losing consciousness under anesthesia, had become a little dated in the age of digital computerization. Such a light show was, of course, an innovation for its time, and, more important to the film's success, part of its appeal to the

hallucinogenic sector of audience. They "got high" on the legal substance of movies. Nowadays, movies like *The Matrix* and a score more
all too like it, using state-of-the-art technology, offer more sophisticated visual narcosis, but to senseless effects devoid of awe, dedicated
only to destructiveness. As it turned out, Stanley was not granted the
time to tinker with his original. I'm not sorry. An allegory as great as
2001 is not dependent on technological advances or even on second-
guessing the progress of space exploration. It is a channel for communicating ideas about man's extension of intelligence—just as its
immediate predecessor, *Dr. Strangelove*, was a warning about man's failure of intelligence, and its immediate successor, *A Clockwork Orange*,
was a horror comic about man's perversion of intelligence. Though set
in what is soon to be our present and what was once its own future,
2001 draws its power from the deepest and most primitive fears and
hopes of mankind. Despite its title, it will never become dated.

Alexander Walker is film critic for the London Evening Standard *and the au-
thor of over twenty books on Anglo-American cinema. A friend of Stanley
Kubrick's for nearly forty years, his monograph,* Stanley Kubrick, Director: A
Visual Analysis, *was published in 1999.*

THE LAST WORD

STANLEY KUBRICK RAPS

Charlie Kohler, The East Village Eye

Stanley Kubrick, long one of America's most talented film-makers, firmly establishes himself with the release of 2001: A Space Odyssey *as one of the world's greatest film artists.*

EYE spoke to the thirty-nine-year-old director-writer-producer a few days after the opening of 2001. *At a time when most other film-makers would be well into their next project, Kubrick was still supervising post-release work, which even included editing the* 2001 *trailer.*

Born in the Bronx, New York, Kubrick compiled only a modest high school average and couldn't get into colleges already swamped with applications from returning GI's. He instead joined the photographic staff of Look, *and made his first feature film,* Fear and Desire, *at the age of twenty-four. Six others followed:* Killer's Kiss *(1955),* The Killing *(1956),* Paths of Glory *(1958),* Spartacus *(1960),* Lolita *(1962) and* Dr. Strangelove *(1964).*

Kubrick lives wherever he happens to be filming. For the past six years or so, that's been in England. He resides in modest splendor in a London suburb with his beautiful wife, Christiane (whom Kubrick fans will remember as the girl who appears at the end of Paths of Glory*), and their three children. A gentle man, Kubrick seldom loses his temper. He is, though, an enthusiastic talker with an insatiable curiosity and a distinctively sardonic wit. Interviewer Charlie Kohler met with Kubrick in an MGM conference room surrounded by posters and stills from* 2001. *Kubrick was eager to discuss his new film.*

EYE: How did you first become interested in science fiction? You were interested at one time, and still are, in the possibilities and philosophical implications of extraterrestrial life. Is that true?

KUBRICK: Yes. I've never been a science fiction buff, though. I've read science fiction, but I did become very interested in the scientific probability that the universe was full of intelligent civilizations and advanced entities. I'd been an admirer of Arthur Clarke's work, and it seemed to me that he was not only the most talented of all the science fiction writers, but that his knowledge and his general scientific background made him an even more appropriate person to work with, to try to *develop* a story that would revolve around my central interest in advanced extraterrestrial civilization.

EYE: You felt from the beginning that it was absolutely essential that this film be scientifically accurate?

KUBRICK: I felt that there should be no deliberately stupid mistakes. But obviously, to get into the area that the story gets into, you have to move into pure imagination and use the factual elements as a means of building up dramatic credit with the audience, so that they are better prepared to open their minds to the more speculative and purely visionary aspects of the story. The predictions on what hardware will be available in 2001 are easy to come by. Clarke himself is often asked by NASA what he thinks will happen. (It's far less an orderly business than you think.) I don't think they themselves are really sure what they'll have. But the hardware that was presented in the film was not logically inconsistent with prevailing beliefs concerning what will exist. There really isn't a great deal to be questioned in the film. I mean, everybody knows there'll be space stations, there'll be lunar bases and so on. Things like that are fairly well-known and agreed upon by all space experts. The only question was really the concept of the ultra-intelligent machine, and on this we generally found a prevailing consensus among the computer experts.

EYE: Let's talk about writing the film. I understand that it wasn't done in the traditional way, but that it was first written as a novel.

KUBRICK: It was written by Arthur and myself, not really as a novel, but as a lengthy prose treatment of the movie. The screenplay form is about the least ideal way of communicating information, especially if it's visual or emotional. The formal limitations of the screenplay, where description has to be sparse, made it seem much better to do the story in a prose version, to first of all try to create the mood, which is very difficult to get across in a screenplay, and the visual happenings. So it was written as a fifty-thousand-word prose "thing," looking more like a novel than anything else. This was the basis of the screenplay. The central incident was based on Arthur's short story, "The Sentinel." We worked on it for about a year. Then I prepared the film for approximately six months, spent about four and a half months shooting the portion of the film in which the actors appear, and then spent a year and a half shooting the two hundred and five special effects.

DESIGNS AND SPECIAL EFFECTS FOR *2001*

EYE: Didn't you actually reject a probable design in a space helmet because it looked too futuristic and too Edgar Rice Burroughs?

KUBRICK: Well, no. I think there were two problems in the design of anything. One was, is there anything about it that would be logically inconsistent with what people felt would actually exist; and the other one was, would it be interesting? Would it look nice? So obviously, in the conceiving of space helmets there's an almost infinite number of possible designs. We just chose one that would look good. Actually, the word that they use in the space business is "sexy." Really, they always talk about machines being sexy. In the design of the clothes, we consulted six or seven of the leading designers, including, I would imagine, fairly imaginative people, and nobody really came up with anything that looked new, without making it look absolutely ridiculous. You realize what an impossible thing it is to ask somebody to give you an aesthetic of another period, without it naturally evolving, as those things do, from day-to-day, and month-to-month.

EYE: Many people are impressed by the ape costumes. I wonder if you could tell us a little bit about how you did that.

KUBRICK: Well, first of all, about a year was spent trying to develop a makeup which would look convincing, because I'd never seen ape characters presented realistically in a film. This involved the body, and, of course, getting a head that looked right, where muscles moved and lips curled. The body problem was partially solved by finding dancers and mimes with extremely narrow hips and skinny legs, so that they didn't bulk up when they put on the hairy suits. And the head problem was solved by making a very intricate headpiece. This had a subskull under it, to which elastics were attached, just as muscles are attached in the human skull, so that when mouths opened the lips curled, and with little toggle switches that the people could work with their tongues, you could control left-side snarl, right-side snarl, et cetera. The tongues in the mouths that you see are false, and behind them the artist is working the toggles with his own tongue.

EYE: You also did do a lot of complicated stuff with the centrifuge.

KUBRICK: Yes, the centrifuge was built by Vickers Armstrong, and it cost $750,000. The whole set was built in a forty-foot diameter, circular steel structure, and everything rotated, with lights, projectors and so forth. When it was closed up and moving, from certain camera positions nobody could be in the centrifuge except the actor. The camera was on a remote-control head, with television finder, and it was all controlled from the outside.

EYE: Did this cause any problem with the actors?

KUBRICK: Everybody was always afraid of what would happen if there were a fire, because the thing really was bolted shut. It took about four minutes to get out.

EYE: Did you yourself shoot part of *Strangelove* and *2001*?

KUBRICK: Well, on hand-held-camera stuff I did, because it's impossible to tell an operator what you want on a hand-held movement.

THE ENDING

EYE: People are intrigued not only by the implications but the essence of the ending. Could you give us your own interpretation?

KUBRICK: No. I don't want to because I think that the power of the ending is based on the subconscious emotional reaction of the audience, which has a delayed effect. To be specific about it, certainly to be specific about what it's supposed to mean, spoils people's pleasure and denies them their own emotional reactions.

EYE: Can you be general about what you intended?

KUBRICK: Well, I can tell you what literally, at the lowest level of plot, happens. Bowman is drawn into a stargate. He is taken into an-

other dimension of time and space, into the presence of godlike entities who have transcended matter and who are now creatures of pure
energy. They provide an environment for him, a human zoo, if you
like. They study him. His life passes before him. He sees himself age in
what seems just a matter of moments; he dies, and he's reborn, transfigured, enhanced, a superbeing. I don't believe that anyone is terribly
far from understanding it. What people sometimes mean is that they
want some confirmation of what they've seen happen, and what they
think. Some people who are used to the conventions of realistic theater and the three-act play are surprised when a new form is presented
to them, no matter how intensely they react to it, and no matter how
much pleasure they get from it.

EYE: Bowman, after this incredible experience, winds up in an
eighteenth-century French bedroom. That really flips a lot of people
out. Can you tell us how you conceived of this bedroom?

KUBRICK: Well, again, this gets into the area of imagination and
artistic processes, whatever they are. The room is made from his own
memories and dreams. It could have been anything that you could
possibly imagine. This just seemed to be the most interesting room to
have.

EYE: Part of the sound track goes into the nineteenth century, also
goes back instead of forward. Was there a particular reason you wanted
this kind of music?

KUBRICK: It just seemed the most interesting way to portray the
beauty and the grace of the space station.

EYE: Another point that interests a lot of people, and another
point of controversy, is why HAL should rebel against the mission.

KUBRICK: Again, I don't like to get into interpretation of the story.
By the way, just to show you how interpretation can sometimes be bewildering: A cryptographer went to see the film, and he said, "Oh, I get
it. Each letter of HAL's name is one letter ahead of IBM. The *H* is one
letter in front of *I*, the *A* is one letter in front of *B*, and the *L* is one letter in front of *M*." Now this is a pure coincidence, because HAL's
name is an acronym of heuristic and algorithmic, the two methods of
computer programming...an almost inconceivable coincidence. It
would have taken a cryptographer to have noticed that.

EYE: The role of women is not brought into *2001* much. Was there
a specific reason why?

KUBRICK: No, it's just in telling the story women didn't seem to have a lot to do with it.

EYE: Well, the astronauts being so well equipped for their voyage in space, sex is the only thing that's missing.

KUBRICK: Well, you obviously aren't going to put a woman on the crew. It's a problem that they've never really gone into. What will deep-space missions be like, and how will the crew take care of their sex urges? It's very unlikely that they'll do it by providing a mixed crew.

EYE: I wonder if the "Dawn of Man" title at the beginning could be applied to the film all the way through until the appearance of the star child?

KUBRICK: It certainly could be one interpretation. I mean, the idea that, as somebody said, man is the missing link between primitive apes and civilized beings, is partially inherent in the theme of the story.

EYE: What parts of the film do you particularly like?

KUBRICK: Well, I mean ... perhaps it sounds foolish for me to say this, but I like everything in the film.

KUBRICK'S EARLY FILMS

EYE: Perhaps you could tell us a bit about how you began in filmmaking?

KUBRICK: Well, I made two short subjects and two features. The two short subjects were financed by myself, and the two features by myself in part, and by friends and family, and business people whom I was able to meet. Because I had no conventional film financing and no contact with any film companies, nobody interfered with me, and I became accustomed to doing exactly what I wanted to do. So that at the time I made *The Killing* with Jimmy Harris producing it and United Artists putting up two-thirds of the money, it seemed inconceivable to me that I could work in any other way. Even though I didn't have the position at the time to warrant insisting on this, my persistence got Jimmy and myself artistic control of the film, within an agreed-upon budget, providing that the Motion Picture Production Code Seal could be gotten and the film would not be condemned by the Catholic Legion of Decency and would not exceed a certain length.

EYE: But during that time, and also on *Paths of Glory*, you took no salary, right?

KUBRICK: Right. On filming the *Paths of Glory*, Jimmy Harris and I had to defer our salary, which means that you receive your salary only out of profit, and although the films never lost money, they also never made a profit, so we received nothing. Then I was involved in a number of abortive projects, among which was working on *One-Eyed Jacks* for six months before shooting began. Then I did *Spartacus*, which was the only film that I did not have control over, and which, I feel, was not enhanced by that fact. It all really just came down to the fact there are thousands of decisions that have to be made, and that if you don't make them yourself, and if you're not on the same wavelength as the people who are making them, it becomes a very painful experience, which it was. Obviously I directed the actors, composed the shots and cut the film, so that, within the weakness of the story, I tried to do the best I could.

EYE: Let's talk about your other films, then. Which are your particular favorites?

KUBRICK: Gee, you know, it's like saying to somebody, "Which of your children do you like the most?" The only film I don't like is *Spartacus*.

EYE: You once said that if you hadn't been a photographer at *Look* Magazine, you probably never would have gotten into films. What did you mean by that?

KUBRICK: Well, first of all I was terribly unaware of everything else that you had to know about film-making, other than Podovkin's *Film Technique*, and photography. Since I had read Podovkin and was a photographer, what could prevent me from making a movie? I could load the camera, shoot and I would have a movie. If I hadn't been a photographer, I would have lacked the one essential ingredient you have to have to put anything on film, which is photography. Even though the first couple of films were bad, they were well photographed, and they had a good look about them, which did impress people.

EYE: You certainly were well-schooled in film history. You constantly went to movies at the Museum of Modern Art, didn't you?

KUBRICK: Yes, I used to go to see every film that played in New

York. Do you remember the newspaper *PM*? In about four-point type, they'd list every single film playing in the five boroughs? Well, I used to sometimes go out to Staten Island, just to see a film I hadn't seen.

HOW TO LEARN MOVIEMAKING

EYE: Do you feel that a young film-maker could learn as much by constantly going to the movies and keeping his eyes and ears open, as by attending two years of graduate film school?

KUBRICK: I would say he could learn more about what he might wish to accomplish in making a film by looking at movies, particularly by looking at a movie that might interest him as many times as he could get to see it.

EYE: Was there one like that for you when you were just starting?

KUBRICK: I must say, I was hung up during that period on Max Ophuls, whom you can't call one of the great film-makers, but who fascinated me with his fluid camera techniques. In films like *Le Plaisir* and *The Earrings of Madame de...*, the camera went through every wall and every floor. But I don't think it really makes a lot of difference which film-makers you become fascinated with. Your own style, if you get a chance to make a film, is really a result of the way your mind works, imposed on the semi-controllable factors that exist at the time you start, both in terms of time, or the way the set looked, or how good the actors were that day. I don't think it matters which films you look at. Close attention to a single film teaches you a great deal. Film schools could be useful if you get a chance to lay your hands on a camera and see a little film equipment, but as far as film aesthetics are concerned, I think that they're largely a waste of time. You're generally hearing the views of somebody who rarely warrants listening to. You're much better off taking films by great film-makers and studying them very closely. The great thing about underground films, for example, is their great disrespect for the technical problems of making a film. It's about the healthiest thing that has ever happened in movies. People used to think that it was impossible to make a film without the awesome apparatus of Hollywood. When I made my first film, I think the thing that probably helped me the most was that it was such an unusual thing in the early fifties for someone to actually go and make a film. People thought it was impossible. It really is terribly easy. All anybody needs is a camera, a tape recorder and some imagination. I expect that some great things will be done. I haven't seen any underground films since I came back to America in March, because I haven't gone to movies. I've been working every day. In England, they don't have underground films. Whether anyone has yet made a great film or not, somebody surely will, because now it's getting down to the pencil-and-paper level and no one will be stopped by all the stupid conventions that have stopped people before.

HOLLYWOOD

KUBRICK: There are several levels of circumstances. From the most ideal circumstances you do everything you want, everybody does what you tell them, and hardly anybody ever expresses a strong, emotionally loaded, devastating criticism of what you want to do or what you're doing. Now if you're good, this is an ideal circumstance to work in, because you're not distracted by having to fend off other ideas, or even disturbed by angry criticism which may be invalid but which you never can forget. That's, say, the most ideal. The next level might be having control over what's being done, having to argue with somebody all the time, even though you can be the arbiter of the argument. Having to entertain somebody else's ideas is a very confusing thing. It throws you off your own stride and it takes the fun out of it all. The next level, obviously, is having to argue with someone who could make you do something you don't want to do. The worst level is being afraid to argue because you might get fired.

EYE: Do you think Hollywood is loosening up?

KUBRICK: Well, I don't think Hollywood is *allowing* young people more leverage; I think young people *have* the leverage by just being able to go out and do it. But Hollywood certainly is allowing directors who have established any kind of a reputation at all to do virtually what they want. The critical factors are the cost of the film, how much the company really dislikes it, how much faith they have in the director and who the cast is. Even if they hate the story, if it's not too expensive and they have faith in the director they will often go along against their "better judgment."

DRUGS AND THE MIND

EYE: Let's go back to the end of *2001* again. A lot of people are calling it "psychedelic." Was it an expressly designed psychedelic...

KUBRICK: Well, like "underground" films, "psychedelic" is becoming a catchphrase. It's just a convenient word.

EYE: But you didn't do any in-depth hallucinogenic research?

KUBRICK: No.

EYE: Well, what about that whole drug scene?

KUBRICK: I think that, as man frees himself from the workaday responsibilities in the modern world, as computers begin to take a more decisive role and everything becomes automated, there'll be more time for people to go into perception-enhancing experiences. There's no doubt that mind-enhancing, perception-enhancing drugs are going to be a part of man's future. The brain is constructed the way it is today in order to filter out experience which doesn't have survival value in order to produce man the worker. As soon as man the worker loses some of his responsibilities, which he's rapidly doing in an automated society, the evolutionary development of the brain will no longer be particularly relevant. So I think that what may seem today like irresponsible action, at some point will seem completely valid and perhaps socially useful. I certainly don't think that drugs, which make everything seem more interesting than they might otherwise be, are a useful thing to the artist, because they minimize his powers of self-criticism, or of trying to decide what's interesting. If *everything* becomes interesting to you, and your mind begins to echo and resonate by looking at a piece of cellophane, it becomes awfully difficult to make any valid, artistic decisions. I think that drugs will be more useful for the artist's audience than for the artist. I'm talking, particularly now, about the kind of phenomena that one gets from acid. I haven't taken it, but from talking to friends who have, what I'm particularly struck by is their sense of everything being interesting and everything being beautiful, which does not seem to be the ideal state of mind for the artist.

EYE: You are an excellent chess player, and there are references to the game in most of your films. Do you think there's any tactical similarity between planning a film and a chess problem?

KUBRICK: There is a distant relationship between chess and making a film. With chess you have to explore different lines of play, and think of different possible outcomes. In films you're always juggling more things than you can ever think about at one time, and trying to analyze as many moves as deeply into the consequences as you can. So there is that analogy. Films are a peculiar combination of the worst circumstances imaginable for an artist to work in, and the most powerful art form ever devised. And finding the resultant of those forces is the key to getting the film done. You have to be able to juggle all the noncreative things as effectively as you can, to allow yourself the moments where your creativity can be used.

EYE: Does the film-maker today, on the level that you're working, have time to really sit down and think out projects?

KUBRICK: Well, I do, because I take the time. From the time I started thinking about *2001* until now I had about four years. But this one was particularly long. I usually take about a year to get interested in something, get it written and start working on it, and in a year, if you keep thinking about it, you can pretty well exhaust the major lines of play, if you want to put it in chess terminology. Then, as you're making the film, you can respond to the spontaneity of what's happening with the resources of all the analysis that you've done. That way, you can most fully utilize each moment while you're making the picture. I think that, without a doubt, no opportunities have ever existed as they do today, for people to make the films they want to make, both in terms of the conventional big-budget films and the small-budget independent films. Everything is really just wide open and waiting for someone to do something good.

CHILDREN AND CENSORSHIP

KUBRICK: I saw *Mary Poppins* three times, because of my children, and I like Julie Andrews so much that I enjoyed seeing it three times. I thought it was a charming film. I wouldn't want to make it, but... Children's films are an area that should not just be left to the Disney Studios, who I don't think really make very good children's films. I'm talking about his cartoon features, which always seemed to me to have shocking and brutal elements in them that really upset children. I could never understand why they were thought to be so suitable. When Bambi's mother dies this has got to be one of the most traumatic experiences a five-year-old could encounter. I think that there should be censorship for children on films of violence. I mean, if I didn't know what *Psycho* was, and my children went to see it when they were six or seven, thinking they were going to see a mystery story, I would have been very angry, and I think they'd have been terribly upset. I don't see how this would interfere with freedom of artistic expression. If films are overly violent or shocking, children under twelve should not be allowed to see them. I think that would be a very useful form of censorship.

EYE: Making *Lolita* at this point, instead of eight years ago, do you think the film could have been improved?

KUBRICK: I think that the erotic component of the film could have had much more weight. At the time I made it, it was almost impossible to get the film played. Even after it was finished it laid around for six months. And then, of course, the audience felt cheated that the erotic weight wasn't in the story. I think that it should have had as much erotic weight as the novel had. As it was, it had the psychology of the characters and the mood of the story. Nabokov liked it. But it certainly didn't have as much of the erotic as you could put into it now.

EYE: And that would have enhanced it.

KUBRICK: Well, it would have made it more true to the novel, and it would have been more popular. The film was successful, but there's no question that people expected to see some of the things that they read in the book, or hoped they might see those parts, anyway.

EYE: You're talking about censorship of movies on violence. How about Vietnam coverage on the television?

KUBRICK: That does create kind of a unique problem. I have three girls. One of them's old enough not to be too bothered—she's fourteen. But one of them's eight and one of them's nine. Children don't realize the statistical improbability of catastrophe occurring in their environment. When they look at the news and all they see is snipers holding out in a motel, or an execution in Vietnam, or a tornado, they get upset by it. I've tried to get them not to look at the news. I don't know how you do it on television, but I do think that the sense of total and continuous catastrophe that a child gets from looking at television-newsreel footage can profoundly upset a child.

EYE: Have people become immune to television violence?

KUBRICK: I don't think so. I think, in fact, that the newsreel coverage of Vietnam must be, to some extent, responsible for the swing of opinion against the war.

EYE: Does that hearten you?

KUBRICK: Yes. I mean, whereas in the past, certain political clichés could just be blown out into the air, people would accept them and not really think about what is going on. They didn't have much direct personal experience with these events, or vivid coverage of them, which allowed them to abstract the events and become less concerned about them. It's great that anything that goes on long enough that's terrible, and comes into the living room every night in vivid, sync-sound, dialogue-newsreel form, makes a big impression on people. It will produce a more active body politic.

EYE: And you're glad that we're getting out of Vietnam, if we are?

KUBRICK: Sure.

FREE PRESS INTERVIEW:
ARTHUR C. CLARKE

Gene Youngblood

Arthur C. Clarke is the H. G. Wells of the Paleocybernetic Age. He has certainly been the most influential science fiction writer of our times, chiefly responsible for elevating the image of science fiction from pulp to profundity. Only time will tell whether this visionary author will be remembered more for 2001: A Space Odyssey *or his earlier masterpiece,* Childhood's End. *Ted Zatlyn and I talked with Dr. Clarke recently for a couple of hours. A lot was said. A lot was not said. The man we found was not the man we expected to find. Perhaps that's the way it should be. Here is a transcript of our conversation.*

GENE: I'd like to talk about current attitudes toward *2001* which may not represent the mass opinion—if there is a mass opinion—but which have evolved among the more serious filmgoers in the year or so since it was released.

CLARKE: Concerning attitudes toward *2001,* I can't say that I'm very pleased with drug connections that are being made, inferences that either myself or Stanley were using drugs when we wrote the script or when we filmed it. I get very annoyed. I was at a science fiction convention last week and some well-wisher thrust a packet of LSD into my hands, in gratitude I suppose, assuming that I'd used it for *2001* and needed some more for my next project.

GENE: There's one thing that bothers many of us about *2001,* and that's this whole business about HAL. That particular way of interpreting the man-machine symbiosis. I mean *2001* is not exactly an avant-garde film; obviously it's not because the public has embraced it whole-heartedly.

CLARKE: By definition, then, it can't be avant-garde.

GENE: By "avant-garde" I mean it certainly was not very far ahead of expectations. Obviously people were ready.

CLARKE: One wouldn't dare make an avant-garde film for ten million dollars.

GENE: Well, I only bring this up because there is thinking in certain circles that *2001* is avant-garde; but obviously the tremendous mass acceptance of the film would indicate that it was perfectly timed, that everyone was ready for this expression.

CLARKE: That it was already passe?

GENE: Well, not necessarily passe but not exactly avant-garde either. Now, within this mass-audience context many feel that this treatment of the man-machine relationship could be seen as a rather irresponsible thing to do, in view of the mass audience and the importance of the man-machine symbiosis in actual fact today.

CLARKE: It could be irresponsible, yes. But the novel explains why HAL did this and of course the film never gave any explanation of his behavior. So, from that point of view it differs from the novel. I personally would like to have seen a rationale of his behavior. It's perfectly understandable, and in fact makes HAL a very sympathetic character because he's been fouled up by these clods back at Mission Control, you see. And in a way it's more pro-machine than pro-human, if you analyse the philosophy behind the novel. I included a sort of emotional passage about HAL's electronic Eden and so on. But it would have been almost impossible to have given the logical explanation of just why HAL did what he did. It would have slowed things down too much. So it had to be treated on this sort of naive and conventional level. Then there was the straightforward matter of dramatic content. One had to have some kind of dramatic tension and suspense and conflict. And HAL's episode is the only conventional dramatic element in the whole film. And so in that way you might say that it was rather contrived. You know, we've got two and a half hours, something has to happen. We set out quite consciously and deliberately—calculatedly, if you like—to create a myth, an adventure. But still be totally plausible and realistic and intelligent. We weren't going to have any blonde stowaway in the airlock and all this sort of nonsense that you've seen in the past. This immediately limited our options enormously. There are fairly few things that can happen on a space mission. Especially if the men have been carefully selected psychologically and so on—all the things which make astronauts such undramatic characters. You don't have nervous breakdowns and Caine Mutinies on a spaceship.

TED: I've heard that in some of the space experiments some of the astronauts have had trouble adjusting themselves to the psychological effects of space.

CLARKE: I don't think so. I was talking to the president of North American Aviation's Space Division this morning, and he mentioned about the only major difficulty is that they get so damned tired of that food towards the end of the mission.

GENE: We sort of took the HAL episode as an allegory on the end of logic. Since that's the last thing that happens before Keir Dullea encounters the transcendental intelligence. And certain things the computer says. For example when he's being deactivated he's singing "... give me your answer true..." and so on.

CLARKE: It's funny how these myths have been building up around the movie. It's splendid. I'm not putting them down because there's a lot going on in the film that Stanley and I were not conscious of. But that whole "Daisy, Daisy" bit was an in-joke. There is a computer record of "Daisy, Daisy" made ten years ago and that's why it has that song. And of course in foreign versions they have other songs. I heard the French and German versions and the songs are different. The name HAL, of course, is derived from Heuristic ALgorithmic computer. There are similarities with the three initials of IBM, of course. And another coincidence is the names Bowman and Borman. And the birthday greetings that actually occurred on the Apollo flight.

GENE: To your knowledge was there any intention on Kubrick's part to portray the astronauts as somehow inhuman, cold or unfeeling? Specifically in the birthday message sequence?

CLARKE: I've wondered about that myself. You'll have to ask him.

GENE: I interpret it as exactly the opposite, myself. But some people feel he's trying to say that technology turns you into some kind of space zombie.

CLARKE: There was no such intention on my part in the novel or script. As a matter of fact it's antithetical to my ideas. I regard space as a great emotional experience.

GENE: I'm very interested in your ideas on what psychological and sociological effects would occur with increasing cosmic consciousness. The situation in which a person is always aware of his relationship to an ever-wider environment. Where we once were geocentric we're now heliocentric. When the day comes that we can turn on our hundred-channel Laser TV set, switch to the Jupiter channel, or the Mars channel, or the Venus channel to see what's happening on those planets that day—in a situation like that "nature" no longer is earthbound.

CLARKE: Well, after all, we can already say what the Earth is looking like today with the meteorological satellite that gives the weather. And we've seen the telecasts from the moon of the Earth. I think those color photographs may have made a considerable impact.

GENE: Do you think the general sense of unrest, confusion, chaos, rebellion and so on is linked in with the electronic extensions of man to the point where his self-image is constantly changing and therefore he's uncertain of himself and his environment?

CLARKE: Well to some extent it must be. Our whole cultural background is changing so rapidly that most people will be disoriented. And I imagine they'll be going in two ways—either passive withdrawal or destructive action. But I think those are both minorities and the intelligent younger people will just absorb this and use it for creative activities. I lecture at colleges and high schools all over the country. I meet a lot of students and I'm impressed by the number of young people who are coping and studying, determined to use all this, to apply it, are excited by it all.

GENE: Well, for example, what's your feeling toward the phenomenon we call "hippies"? That general image of young people whom, I suppose, one could call drop-outs?

CLARKE: If they drop out completely I've got no use for them. Why don't they commit suicide rather than cluttering up the streets? If you drop out completely there's nothing left.

GENE: Well, for example, on the way over here we were talking about Krishnamurti and Buckminster Fuller. Recently they got together in Berkeley and gave a series of lectures. Both of them are extremely interested in hippies as a phenomenon.

CLARKE: It's a very interesting phenomenon, and an important one. And why is this happening? I'm entirely in favor of any youngster who turns against his parents for the mess they've made of the world. He has every justification.

TED: Do you see this as an evolutionary process similar to what you described in *Childhood's End*?

CLARKE: I think someone else made that remark but it hadn't really sunk in until you repeated it just now. It's an interesting idea. Oh yes, *Childhood's End* is going to be filmed and I was talking to the screenwriter who said he had this angle in mind.

TED: Just as an aside, I think it's a tremendous book and one that had quite an impact on me.

CLARKE: It seems to have had more impact than any other science fiction novel in the last decade.

TED: In a sense I thought a certain aspect of what we call the hippie movement was almost prophesized in the book.

CLARKE: You know I haven't read it for twelve or fifteen years, but I think you have something there. I must go back and see. The children at the end were behaving like hippies, weren't they?

TED: Yes. A lot of the things hippies are into now in terms of ESP, for example, were clearly brought out in your book.

CLARKE: Well since then I've changed my mind. I was more sympathetic toward ESP but now I'm sort of disenchanted. I think it probably doesn't exist; incidentally there are two other predictions in *Childhood's End* that I'm rather proud of. One already has happened and the other is yet to come. I predicted a moral revolution caused by the development of oral contraceptives, plus an infallible means of identifying the father of a child. The second one will come eventually I'm sure, through geno-typing or DNA or whatever.

TED: But the idea of an awakened moral consciousness in the youth really came right out of the book. What's happening today was predicted there.

CLARKE: Well, I must try and cash in on that somehow. [Laughter.]

TED: I saw somewhat of a contradiction between *2001* and *Childhood's End*. In an evolutionary sense.

CLARKE: Yes. At one stage I had a subtitle for *2001* which was: *Childhood's Beginning*.

TED: In *2001* the idea of an expanded consciousness that was evolving seemed directly opposed to the idea of extending the American capitalistic free enterprise system into outer space, in which you have Howard Johnson and Pan-Am businesses.

CLARKE: That was done primarily to establish a background of realism to achieve total acceptance by the audience.

GENE: Yes, but you see this is exactly what we now feel is rather unfortunate about the film. I mean that's all very fine, and it works, and everyone likes that, they think it's clever and so on. But in fact how real—how "realistic"—is that?

CLARKE: Totally realistic.

GENE: But I don't believe the idea of capitalistic free enterprise is so realistic at that stage in evolution. And to suggest such a thing, or even to suggest "ownership" in space travel is perhaps a bit irresponsible.

CLARKE: But that doesn't necessarily mean capitalistic free enterprise. I mean Pan-Am is running the range for NASA, but that doesn't necessarily mean a capitalistic system. Names hang on, that's all. I mean Hilton is planning a space station hotel. He gave a talk and showed designs three years ago.

GENE: But that certainly would indicate a capitalistic free enterprise situation from Hilton's point of view.

CLARKE: Is Hilton free enterprise? I don't believe in the existence of free enterprise.

TED: But the obvious extension of that idea is spherical influence in space—Russia's sphere here, America's sphere here, China's sphere over there. I just don't think that when man evolves to the point where he can travel throughout space using new energy sources and so on, that he will carry with him an archaic form of thinking.

CLARKE: Well of course he won't. Things will change completely. But the events of *2001* are only thirty-two years from now. And a lot of these things will still be around. The names anyway. Just as the Catholic Church still exists for namesake.

TED: But that's where I see a contradiction with *Childhood's End.*

CLARKE: *Childhood's End* was set several hundred years in the future, however. In fact if I'd done *2001* by myself I'd have had an international organization instead of nationalism. But here again you're constrained by practical matters—this is an American film made by an American company and there are a lot of problems. For instance at one point we were saying we should at least have one token black person in the film. But when your crew is only two people it would be so obvious. I mean can you see Bill Cosby in there? So finally we said the hell with it.

GENE: There are some interesting correlations in the ideas of consciousness-expansion through drugs and consciousness-expansion through the computer, in the sense that it extends your capabilities at least, if not your senses.

CLARKE: Since I've never taken drugs, and since I've never been drunk I just can't say. All I know is its effect on my friends. And as far as I can tell drugs are consciousness-shrinking, not consciousness-expanding. I've been quite friendly with Brian Jones of the Rolling Stones. He was staying with us in Ceylon the other day, he comes there quite often. I like him very much. He's a nice kid. Now, I guess the Stones are great. I've only heard one or two of their records and I was quite impressed. So maybe drugs work in some areas of creativity. Maybe they work in music.

GENE: Well I'm not so interested in the creative aspects of drugs as I am in the whole phenomenon. I mean, why now?

CLARKE: It may be entirely due to Vietnam.

GENE: Do you feel that undue emphasis is being placed on *2001* as a trip film or drug-associative experience?

CLARKE: Yes. I'm quite unhappy about it for several reasons. First, from a personal angle, I'm unhappy that anyone would think that I've been using drugs to write. Simply because I resent the implication that I couldn't do it under my own steam.

GENE: What do you think about what McLuhan says?

CLARKE: I don't know. I just don't know. I don't understand what he says.

TED: You say you've lost some of your enthusiasm for ESP...

CLARKE: I was never enthusiastic. I was interested. But I got disappointed in it because nothing ever came of it. If scientists are still arguing whether or not ESP even exists, it probably doesn't exist. I was fascinated by it, but I...incidentally in *Childhood's End* there's a seance. That actually happened. I was at a seance and we got some messages, and those are recorded in the book. That scene actually occurred. That was the only time in my life I ever participated in anything like that and it worked. It was an astonishing thing that it can work. But I'm certain there's a perfectly reasonable explanation for it. Just like fire-walking. I've photographed fire-walkers at close quarters with a telephoto lens. This again is something I wouldn't have believed until I saw it myself. A man and woman and children walking barefoot in ankle-deep white-hot embers—a fire so hot I couldn't stand to be near it. But when you've seen it you realize there's nothing mysterious about it. Surprising but not mysterious. All these phenomena often turn out to have explanations which are quite trivial and not even interesting.

GENE: By the conclusion of *2001* did you mean to suggest that some transcendental racial experience is that imminent? In thirty years, I mean. Or at least is needed in some socio-political way?

CLARKE: No. Remember, I've never tried to predict the future. My stories are not predictive. They're extrapolative and imaginative. I've just been having fun. In fact I was so wary that people would think I was trying to predict the future that at the beginning of *Childhood's End* I put that famous disclaimer: "The opinions expressed in this book are not those of the author." Which I've always been asked about.

GENE: There's a lot of talk lately about the increasing gap between the sophistication of our inventions and the vulgarity of our collective actions.

CLARKE: That is true, yes. And it's coming to a head again over the ABM. You know, the attitude: "We must have the ABM system to shoot down these damned aliens when they come to take over the earth."

GENE: Kubrick quoted Jung's remark about what would happen if we were to encounter some transcendental intelligence. Jung said something like, "... reins would be torn from our hands and we would find ourselves without dreams. We would find our intellectual and spiritual aspirations so outmoded as to leave us completely paralyzed..."

CLARKE: Something Plutarch said about the Atlantians has always haunted me. "The Atlantians," he said, "never dreamt." That's a very chilling thought. It's so chilling that it makes me wonder whether there couldn't really have been an Atlantis, because no one would have made that up.

GENE: That's beautiful.

CLARKE: I was on Atlantis the other day with Werner Von Braun. And we didn't even realize it.

TED: Where was this?

CLARKE: Atlantis. We know where it is now, of course.

GENE AND TED: What?

CLARKE: You haven't heard of it? This is one of the greatest archeological discoveries of all time, the discovery of Atlantis. It happened two years ago and you'd think the word would have gotten around. It's an island in the Aegean Sea about fifty miles from Athens known as Thera. It was a volcanic crater, the center of the Aegean civilization. In 1500 BC it blew up and the whole Mediterranean was inundated with tidal waves. That's what happened to Minos and the Cretans. It finished them off. The point is that if there was an Atlantis before that, no one would ever remember it because this other catastrophe was so much greater, so overwhelming, that it would have obliterated all memories of it. They've just found a complete city on Thera. They're digging it out now. It's buried by volcanic ash like Pompeii. We went there for a space conference actually. With the American and Russian astronauts. We were all there together. There was this huge ring of mountains jutting out of the sea with the center still smoking and I said my God! This is incredible! And they're just waking up to what happened and what this place is. It's Atlantis. I've got photographs of Von Braun and the whole party standing there.

GENE: It reminds me of *2001* with the astronauts standing before the monolith on the moon.

CLARKE: The town keeps falling into the sea and they keep rebuilding it.

GENE: We're living in an era now—and have been for the last few years—in which science fiction has a completely new image, or at least a new respectability. In fact one could say that there is nothing but science fiction.

CLARKE: I've been saying for years that mainstream literature is a small subsection of science fiction. Because science fiction is about everything.

GENE: Exactly. And one of the significant aspects of *2001* is that it's science fact. When you discuss science and what it's doing, you're not only discussing the present but the past and the future simultaneously. Because science encompasses what has been and what will be all in the moment, the present. So the idea of science fiction in *2001* isn't meaningful.

CLARKE: Well, I've said that one reason some people dislike *2001*—mainly older people—is that they realize this film is about reality and it scares the hell out of them.

GENE: Right. Now, to me, this point about people being frightened by *2001* is extremely serious...I mean this thing with HAL, it's...

CLARKE: That's another reality of the future. In fact this film is about the two most important realities of the future: development of intelligent machines, and contact with higher alien intelligence. Which may of course be machines themselves.

GENE: In your estimation, what's the likelihood of computer extensibility? Programming themselves and creating machines more intelligent than themselves?

CLARKE: This is inevitable. This is what's going to happen. I dealt with this subject in *Profiles of the Future* in the chapter on the obsolescence of man.

GENE: As I understand your meaning of that idea, it's not the meaning most people attach to it. I understand it as a very beneficial thing in which man is rendered obsolete as a specialist, obsolete as all the things he's been up to now—obsolete in comparison to the computer's ability to do all these things better and quicker—but, on the other hand, man is then totally free to live comprehensively, nonspecialized, like the freedom of children.

CLARKE: Well that's how my essay ends. I said "Now it's time to play."

GENE: But you see the average person doesn't see it. All he sees is that he's going to be replaced by a computer, reduced to an IBM card and filed away.

CLARKE: The goal of the future is full unemployment, so we can play. That's why we have to destroy the present politico-economic system.

GENE: Precisely. Now, we feel that if only this idea had come across in *2001,* instead of depicting machines as ominous and destructive...

CLARKE: But it would have been another film. Be thankful for what you've got. Maybe Stanley wasn't interested in making that kind of film. Or maybe the idea is so interesting that he'll make it when he's through with *Napoleon.*

GENE: What about the other aspect of *2001*—contact with extraterrestrial intelligence?

CLARKE: They may be machines. I suspect that all really higher intelligences will be machines. Unless they're beyond the machine. But biological intelligence is a lower form of intelligence, almost inevitably. We're in an early stage in the evolution of intelligence, but a late stage in the evolution of life. Real intelligence won't be living.

GENE: Well, the Cyborg is one step toward that. There are a few crude Cyborgs in the world today.

CLARKE: The Cyborg is only half-way.

GENE: Speaking of biological intelligence, you've mentioned that the atmosphere of Jupiter apparently resembles the atmosphere of Earth in primeval times, when life was developing.

CLARKE: The atmosphere on Jupiter is the type of atmosphere which Earth [is] believed to have had originally. Mostly ammonia and methane with no free oxygen. And life must have evolved in that atmosphere. In this development it released oxygen and along came forms which could use oxygen, and you got higher life forms that way. Jupiter may still be in that earlier stage.

GENE: So is plant life likely on Jupiter?

CLARKE: No, because plants breathe oxygen. But anerobic types which do not utilize oxygen. Gangrene is a form of primeval bacteria which still survives here on Earth. It can't survive in the presence of oxygen, so they're using high-pressure oxygen chambers for people with gangrene. Oxygen kills it. There's a hilarious discovery connected with this. One of NASA's space scientists is interested in the evolution of life, so he goes around collecting samples of soil from urinals. There's one in Wales that's been pee'd on for hundreds of years by tourists. And the soil is so ammoniated that it's like the primeval soil of Earth. And he's found a bacteria in that which is identical with a fossil found about two billion years old. So the thing seems to have survived in this sort of freak ecological niche. So it's an interesting demonstration of the probability of this theory.

GENE: You've written several times about dream machines. Experiments are being made now with electrodes attached to the brain from a computer, translating the electrical impulses into visuals on a cathode ray tube. How meaningful are these experiments?

CLARKE: Hardly at all. You can "will" patterns on a CRT screen.

Using your brain to control electronic equipment, you can at least control the patterns to some small extent. So it's a kind of electro-telepathy. But it's still very crude, and it's still a century ahead before we'll be doing anything as sophisticated as the science-fiction stories.

GENE: I suppose it'll come primarily through software discoveries about the brain as opposed to hardware innovations.

CLARKE: Well, the fields of software and hardware are merging.

GENE: What new projects are you involved in?

CLARKE: In addition to several smaller things, I'm planning a very large project with Francis Thompson and the Time-Life Corporation. We've written the treatment. It'll be a two-and-a-half-hour roadshow documentary film on the trip to the moon. We've signed contracts with all fifty astronauts. It'll begin with the Apollo project and end with the landing on the moon, and beyond. It'll cost nearly five million dollars, which is quite a lot for a documentary, even though it's the most important documentary ever made.

HOW THE BOOK ENDS

Arthur C. Clarke

Here he was, adrift in this great river of suns, halfway between the banked fires of the galactic core and the lonely, scattered sentinel stars of the rim. And *here* he wished to be, on the far side of this chasm in the sky, this serpentine band of darkness, empty of all stars. He knew that this formless chaos, visible only by the glow that limned its edges from fire-mists far beyond, was the still unused stuff of creation, the raw material of evolution yet to be. Here, Time had not begun; not until the suns that now burned were long since dead would light and life re-shape this void.

Unwittingly, he had crossed it once; now he must cross it again— this time, of his own volition. The thought filled him with a sudden, freezing terror, so that for a moment he was wholly disorientated, and his new vision of the universe trembled and threatened to shatter into a thousand fragments.

It was not fear of the galactic gulfs that chilled his soul, but a more profound disquiet, stemming from the unborn future. For he had left behind the time scales of his human origin; now, as he contemplated that band of starless night, he knew his first intimations of the Eternity that yawned before him.

Then he remembered that he would never be alone, and his panic slowly ebbed. The crystal-clear perception of the universe was restored to him—not, he knew, wholly by his own efforts. When he needed guidance in his first faltering steps, it would be there.

Confident once more, like a high diver who had regained his nerve, he launched himself across the light-years. The galaxy burst forth from the mental frame in which he had enclosed it; stars and nebulae poured past him in an illusion of infinite speed. Phantom suns exploded and fell behind as he slipped like a shadow through their cores; the cold, dark waste of cosmic dust which he had once feared seemed no more than the beat of a raven's wing across the face of the Sun.

The stars were thinning out; the glare of the Milky Way was dimming into a pale ghost of the glory he had known—and, when he was ready, would know again.

He was back, precisely where he wished to be, in the space that men called real.

There before him, a glittering toy no Star-Child could resist, floated the planet Earth with all its peoples.

He had returned in time. Down there on that crowded globe the alarms would be flashing across the radar screens, the great tracking telescopes would be searching the skies—and history as men knew it would be drawing to a close.

A thousand miles below, he became aware that a slumbering cargo of death had awoken, and was stirring sluggishly in its orbit. The feeble energies it contained were no possible menace to him; but he preferred a cleaner sky. He put forth his will, and the circling megatons flowered in a silent detonation that brought a brief, false dawn to half the sleeping globe.

Then he waited, marshaling his thoughts and brooding over his still untested powers. For though he was master of the world, he was not quite sure what to do next.

But he would think of something.

PLAYBOY INTERVIEW:
STANLEY KUBRICK

PLAYBOY: Much of the controversy surrounding *2001* deals with the meaning of the metaphysical symbols that abound in the film—the polished black monoliths, the orbital conjunction of Earth, Moon and sun at each stage of the monoliths' intervention in human destiny, the stunning final kaleidoscopic maelstrom of time and space that engulfs the surviving astronaut and sets the stage for his rebirth as a "starchild" drifting toward Earth in a translucent placenta. One critic even called *2001* "the first Nietzschean film," contending that its essential theme is Nietzsche's concept of man's evolution from ape to human to superman. What *was* the metaphysical message of *2001*?

KUBRICK: It's not a message that I ever intend to convey in words. *2001* is a nonverbal experience; out of two hours and nineteen minutes of film, there are only a little less than forty minutes of dialog. I tried to create a *visual* experience, one that bypasses verbalized pigeonholing and directly penetrates the subconscious with an emotional and philosophic content. To convolute McLuhan, in *2001* the message is the medium. I intended the film to be an intensely subjective experience that reaches the viewer at an inner level of consciousness, just as music does; to "explain" a Beethoven symphony would be to emasculate it by erecting an artificial barrier between conception and appre-

iation. You're free to speculate as you wish about the philosophical
nd allegorical meaning of the film—and such speculation is one indi-
ation that it has succeeded in gripping the audience at a deep level—
ut I don't want to spell out a verbal road map for *2001* that every
iewer will feel obligated to pursue or else fear he's missed the point. I
hink that if *2001* succeeds at all, it is in reaching a wide spectrum of
eople who would not often give a thought to man's destiny, his role in
he cosmos and his relationship to higher forms of life. But even in the
ase of someone who is highly intelligent, certain ideas found in *2001*
vould, if presented as abstractions, fall rather lifelessly and be auto-
natically assigned to pat intellectual categories; experienced in a
noving visual and emotional context, however, they can resonate
vithin the deepest fibers of one's being.

PLAYBOY: Without laying out a philosophical road map for the
iewer, can you tell us your own interpretation of the meaning of the
ilm?

KUBRICK: No, for the reasons I've already given. How much would
ve appreciate *La Gioconda* today if Leonardo had written at the bottom
f the canvas: "This lady is smiling slightly because she has rotten
eeth"—or "because she's hiding a secret from her lover"? It would
hut off the viewer's appreciation and shackle him to a "reality" other
han his own. I don't want that to happen to *2001*.

PLAYBOY: Arthur Clarke has said of the film, "If anyone under-
tands it on the first viewing, we've failed in our intention." Why
hould the viewer have to see a film twice to get its message?

KUBRICK: I don't agree with that statement of Arthur's, and I be-
ieve he made it facetiously. The very nature of the visual experience
n *2001* is to give the viewer an instantaneous, visceral reaction that
loes not—and should not—require further amplification. Just speak-
ng generally, however, I would say that there are elements in any good
ilm that would increase the viewer's interest and appreciation on a
econd viewing; the momentum of a movie often prevents every stim-
ilating detail or nuance from having a full impact the first time it's
een. The whole idea that a movie should be seen only once is an ex-
ension of our traditional conception of the film as an ephemeral en-
ertainment rather than as a visual work of art. We don't believe that
ve should hear a great piece of music only once, or see a great paint-
ng once, or even read a great book just once. But the film has until re-

cent years been exempted from the category of art—a situation I'm glad is finally changing.

PLAYBOY: Some prominent critics—including Renata Adler of *The New York Times,* John Simon of *The New Leader,* Judith Crist of *New York* magazine and Andrew Sarris of the *Village Voice*—apparently felt that *2001* should be among those films still exempted from the category of art; all four castigated it as dull, pretentious and overlong. How do you account for their hostility?

KUBRICK: The four critics you mention all work for New York publications. The reviews across America and around the world have been ninety-five percent enthusiastic. Some were more perceptive than others, of course, but even those who praised the film on relatively superficial grounds were able to get something of its message. New York was the only really hostile city. Perhaps there is a certain element of the lumpen literati that is so dogmatically atheist and materialist and Earth-bound that it finds the grandeur of space and the myriad mysteries of cosmic intelligence anathema. But film critics, fortunately, rarely have any effect on the general public; houses everywhere are packed and the film is well on its way to becoming the greatest money-maker in M-G-M's history. Perhaps this sounds like a crass way to evaluate one's work, but I think that, especially with a film that is so obviously *different,* record audience attendance means people are saying the right things to one another after they see it—and isn't this really what it's all about?

PLAYBOY: Speaking of what it's all about—if you'll allow us to return to the philosophical interpretation of *2001*—would you agree with those critics who call it a profoundly religious film?

KUBRICK: I will say that the God concept is at the heart of *2001*—but not any traditional, anthropomorphic image of God. I don't believe in any of Earth's monotheistic religions, but I do believe that one can construct an intriguing *scientific* definition of God, once you accept the fact that there are approximately one hundred billion stars in our galaxy alone, that each star is a life-giving sun and that there are approximately one hundred billion galaxies in just the *visible* universe. Given a planet in a stable orbit, not too hot and not too cold, and given a few billion years of chance chemical reactions created by the interaction of a sun's energy on the planet's chemicals, it's fairly certain that life in one form or another will eventually emerge. It's reasonable to assume that there must be, in fact, countless *billions* of such planets where biological life has arisen, and the odds of some proportion of such life developing intelligence are high. Now, the sun is by no means an old star, and its planets are mere children in cosmic age, so it seems likely that there are billions of planets in the universe not only where intelligent life is on a lower scale than man but other billions where it is approximately equal and others still where it is hundreds of thousands of millions of years in advance of us. When you think of the giant technological strides that man has made in a few millennia—less than a microsecond in the chronology of the universe—can you imagine the evolutionary development that much older life forms have taken? They may have progressed from biological species, which are fragile shells for the mind at best, into immortal machine entities—and then, over innumerable eons, they could emerge from the chrysalis of matter transformed into beings of pure energy and spirit. Their potentialities would be limitless and their intelligence ungraspable by humans.

PLAYBOY: Even assuming the cosmic evolutionary path you suggest, what has this to do with the nature of God?

KUBRICK: Everything—because these beings would *be* gods to the billions of less advanced races in the universe, just as man would appear a god to an ant that somehow comprehended man's existence. They would possess the twin attributes of all deities—omniscience and omnipotence. These entities might be in telepathic communication throughout the cosmos and thus be aware of everything that occurs, tapping every intelligent mind as effortlessly as we switch on the radio; they might not be limited by the speed of light and their presence could penetrate to the farthest corners of the universe; they might possess complete mastery over matter and energy; and in their final evolutionary stage, they might develop into an integrated collective immortal consciousness. They would be incomprehensible to us except as gods; and if the tendrils of their consciousness ever brushed men's minds, it is only the hand of God we could grasp as an explanation.

PLAYBOY: If such creatures do exist, why should they be interested in man?

KUBRICK: They may not be. But why should man be interested in microbes? The motives of such beings would be as alien to us as their intelligence.

PLAYBOY: In *2001*, such incorporeal creatures seem to manipulate our destinies and control our evolution, though whether for good or evil—or both, or neither—remains unclear. Do you really believe it's possible that man is a cosmic plaything of such entities?

KUBRICK: I don't really *believe* anything about them; how can I? Mere speculation on the possibility of their existence is sufficiently overwhelming, without attempting to decipher their motives. The important point is that all the standard attributes assigned to God in our history could equally well be the characteristics of biological entities who billions of years ago were at a stage of development similar to man's own and evolved into something as remote from man as man is remote from the primordial ooze from which he first emerged.

PLAYBOY: In this cosmic phylogeny you've described, isn't it possible that there might be forms of intelligent life on an even higher scale than these entities of pure energy—perhaps as far removed from them as they are from us?

KUBRICK: Of course there could be; in an infinite, eternal universe, the point is that *anything* is possible, and it's unlikely that we can even begin to scratch the surface of the full range of possibilities. But at a time [1968] when man is preparing to set foot on the Moon, I think it's necessary to open up our Earth-bound minds to such speculation. No one knows what's waiting for us in the universe. I think it was a prominent astronomer who wrote recently, "Sometimes I think we are alone, and sometimes I think we're not. In either case, the idea is quite staggering."

PLAYBOY: You said there must be billions of planets sustaining life that is considerably more advanced than man but has not yet evolved into non- or suprabiological forms. What do you believe would be the effect on humanity if the Earth were contacted by a race of such ungodlike but technologically superior beings?

KUBRICK: There's a considerable difference of opinion on this subject among scientists and philosophers. Some contend that encountering a highly advanced civilization—even one whose technology is essentially comprehensible to us—would produce a traumatic cultural shock effect on man by divesting him of his smug ethnocentrism and shattering the delusion that he is the center of the universe. Carl Jung summed up this position when he wrote of contact with advanced extraterrestrial life that the "reins would be torn from our hands and we would, as a tearful old medicine man once said to me, find ourselves 'without dreams'... we would find our intellectual and spiritual aspirations so outmoded as to leave us completely paralyzed." I personally don't accept this position, but it's one that's widely held and can't be summarily dismissed.

In 1960, for example, the Committee for Long Range Studies of the Brookings Institution prepared a report for the National Aeronautics and Space Administration warning that even indirect contact—i.e., alien artifacts that might possibly be discovered through our space activities on the Moon, Mars or Venus or via radio contact with an interstellar civilization—could cause severe psychological dislocations. The study cautioned that "Anthropological files contain many examples of societies, sure of their place in the universe, which have disintegrated when they have had to associate with previously unfamiliar societies espousing different ideas and different life ways; others that survived such an experience usually did so by paying the price of changes in values and attitudes and behavior." It concluded that since intelligent life might be discovered at any time, and that since the consequences of such a discovery are "presently unpredictable," it was advisable that the Government initiate continuing studies on the psychological and intellectual impact of confrontation with extraterrestrial life. What action was taken on this report I don't know, but I assume that such studies are now under way. However, while not discounting the possible adverse emotional impact on some people, I would personally tend to view such contact with a tremendous amount of excitement and enthusiasm. Rather than shattering our society, I think it could immeasurably enrich it.

Another positive point is that it's a virtual certainty that all intelligent life at one stage in its technological development must have discovered nuclear energy. This is obviously the watershed of any civilization; does it find a way to use nuclear power without destruction and harness it for peaceful purposes, or does it annihilate itself? I would guess that any civilization that has existed for one thousand years after its discovery of atomic energy has devised a means of accommodating itself to the bomb, and this could prove tremendously reassuring to us—as well as give us specific guidelines for our own survival. In any case, as far as cultural shock is concerned, my impression is that the attention span of most people is quite brief; after a week or two of great excitement and oversaturation in newspapers and on television, the public's interest would drop off and the United Nations, or whatever world body we then had, would settle down to discussions with the aliens.

PLAYBOY: You're assuming that extraterrestrials would be benevolent. Why?

KUBRICK: Why should a vastly superior race *bother* to harm or destroy us? If an intelligent ant suddenly traced a message in the sand at my feet reading, "I am sentient; let's talk things over," I doubt very much that I would rush to grind him under my heel. Even if they weren't superintelligent, though, but merely more advanced than mankind, I would tend to lean more toward the benevolence, or at least indifference, theory. Since it's most unlikely that we would be visited from within our own solar system, any society capable of traversing light-years of space would have to have an extremely high degree of control over matter and energy. Therefore, what possible motivation for hostility would they have? To steal our gold or oil or coal? It's hard to think of any nasty intention that would justify the long and arduous journey from another star.

PLAYBOY: You'll admit, though, that extraterrestrials are commonly portrayed in comic strips and cheap science-fiction films as bug-eyed monsters scuttling hungrily after curvaceous Earth maidens.

KUBRICK: This probably dates back to the pulp science-fiction magazines of the Twenties and Thirties and perhaps even to the Orson Welles Martian-invasion broadcast in 1938 and the resultant mass hysteria, which is always advanced in support of the hypothesis that contact would cause severe cultural shock. In a sense, the lines with which Welles opened that broadcast set the tone for public consideration of extraterrestrial life for years to come. I've memorized them: "Across an immense ethereal gulf, minds that are to our minds as ours are to the beasts in the jungle—intellects vast, cool and unsympathetic—regarded this Earth with envious eyes and slowly and surely drew their plans against us...." Anything we can imagine about such other life forms is possible, of course. You could have psychotic civilizations, or decadent civilizations that have elevated pain to an aesthetic and might covet humans as gladiators or torture objects, or civilizations that might want us for zoos, or scientific experimentation, or slaves or even for food. While I am appreciably more optimistic, we just can't be sure *what* their motivations will be.

I'm interested in the argument of Professor Freeman Dyson of Princeton's Institute for Advanced Study, who contends that it would be a mistake to expect that all potential space visitors will be altruistic, or to believe that they would have *any* ethical or moral concepts comparable to mankind's. Dyson writes, if I remember him correctly, that "Intelligence may indeed be a benign influence creating isolated groups of philosopher kings far apart in the heavens," but it's just as likely that "Intelligence may be a cancer of purposeless technological exploitation, sweeping across a galaxy as irresistibly as it has swept across our own planet." Dyson concludes that it's "just as unscientific to impute to remote intelligence wisdom and serenity as it is to impute to them irrational and murderous impulses. We must be prepared for either possibility and conduct our searches accordingly."

This is why some scientists caution, now that we're attempting to intercept radio signals from other solar systems, that if we do receive a message we should wait awhile before answering it. But we've been transmitting radio and television signals for so many years that any advanced civilization could have received the emissions long ago. So in the final analysis, we really don't have much choice in this matter; they're either going to contact us or they're not, and if they do we'll have nothing to say about their benevolence or malevolence.

Even if they prove to be malevolent, their arrival would have at least one useful by-product in that the nations of the Earth would stop squabbling among themselves and forge a common front to defend the planet. I think it was André Maurois who suggested many years ago that the best way to realize world peace would be to stage a false threat from outer space; it's not a bad idea. But I certainly don't believe we should view contact with extraterrestrial life forms with foreboding, or hesitate to visit other planets for fear of what we may find there. If others don't contact us, we must contact them; it's our destiny.

PLAYBOY: You indicated earlier that intelligent life is extremely unlikely elsewhere within our solar system. Why?

KUBRICK: From what we know of the other planets in this system, it appears improbable that intelligence exists, because of surface temperatures and atmospheres that are inhospitable to higher life forms. Improbable, but not impossible. I will admit that there are certain tantalizing clues pointing in the other direction. For example, while the consensus of scientific opinion dismisses the possibility of intelligent life on Mars—as opposed to plant or low orders of organic life—there are some eminently respectable dissenters. Dr. Frank B. Salisbury, professor of plant physiology at Utah State University, has contended in a study in *Science* magazine that if vegetation exists on a planet, then it is logical that there will be higher orders of life to feed on it. "From there," he writes, "it is but one more step—granted, a big one—to intelligent beings."

Salisbury also points out that a number of astronomers have observed strange flashes of light, possibly explosions of great magnitude, on Mars' surface, some of which emit clouds; and he suggests that these could actually be nuclear explosions. Another intriguing facet of Mars is the peculiar orbits of its twin satellites, Phobos and Deimos, first discovered in 1877—the same year, incidentally, that Schiaparelli discovered his famous but still elusive Martian "canals." One eminent astronomer, Dr. Josif Shklovsky, chairman of the department of radio astronomy at the Shternberg Astronomical Institute in Moscow, has propounded the theory that both moons are artificial space satellites launched by the Martians thousands of years ago in an effort to escape the dying surface of their planet. He bases this theory on the unique orbits of the two moons, which, unlike the thirty-one other satellites in our solar system, orbit *faster* than the revolution of their host planet. The orbit of Phobos is also deteriorating in an inexplicable manner and dragging the satellite progressively closer to Mars' surface. Both of these circumstances, Shklovsky contends, make sense only if the two moons are *hollow*.

Shklovsky believes that the satellites are the last remnants of an extinct ancient Martian civilization; but Professor Salisbury goes a step further and suggests that they were launched within the past hundred years. Noting that the moons were discovered by a relatively small-power telescope in 1877 and not detected by a much more powerful telescope observing Mars in 1862—when the planet was appreciably nearer Earth—he asks: "Should we attribute the failure of 1862 to imperfections in the existing telescope, or may we imagine that the satellites were launched into orbit between 1862 and 1877?" There are no answers here, of course, only questions, but it is fascinating speculation. On balance, however, I would have to say that the weight of available evidence dictates against intelligent life on Mars.

PLAYBOY: How about possibilities, if not the probabilities, of intelligent life on the other planets?

KUBRICK: Most scientists and astronomers rule out life on the outer planets since their surface temperatures are thousands of degrees either above or below zero and their atmospheres would be poisonous. I suppose it's possible that life could evolve on such planets with, say, a liquid ammonia or methane base, but it doesn't appear too likely. As far as Venus goes, the Mariner probes indicate that the surface temperature of the planet is approximately eight hundred degrees Fahrenheit, which would deny the chemical basis for molecular development of life. And there could be no indigenous intelligent life on the Moon, because of the total lack of atmosphere—no life as we know it, in any case; though I suppose that intelligent rocks or crystals, or statues, with a silicone life base are not really impossible, or even conscious gaseous matter or swarms of sentient electric particles. You'd get no technology from such creatures, but if their intelligence could control matter, why would they need it? There could be nothing about them, however, even remotely humanoid—a form that would appear to be an eminently practicable universal life prototype.

PLAYBOY: What do you think we'll find on the Moon?

KUBRICK: I think the most exciting prospect about the Moon is that if alien races have ever visited Earth in the remote past and left artifacts for man to discover in the future, they probably chose the arid, airless lunar vacuum, where no deterioration would take place and an object could exist for millennia. It would be inevitable that as man evolved technologically, he would reach his nearest satellite and the aliens would then expect him to find their calling card—perhaps a message of greeting, a cache of knowledge or simply a cosmic burglar alarm signaling that another race had mastered space flight. This, of course, was the central situation of *2001*.

But an equally fascinating question is whether there could be another race of intelligent life on Earth. Dr. John Lilly, whose research into dolphins has been funded by the National Aeronautics and Space Administration, has amassed considerable evidence pointing to the possibility that the bottle-nosed dolphin may be as intelligent as or more intelligent than man. He bases this not only on its brain size—which is larger than man's and with a more complex cortex—but on the fact that dolphins have evolved an extensive language. Lilly is currently attempting, with some initial success, to decipher this language and establish communication with the dolphins. NASA's interest in this is obvious, because learning to communicate with dolphins would be a highly instructive precedent for learning to communicate with alien races on other planets. Of course, if the dolphins are really intelligent, theirs is obviously a nontechnological culture, since without an opposable thumb, they could never create artifacts. Their intelligence might also be on a totally different order than man's, which could make communication additionally difficult. Dr. Lilly has written that, "It is probable that their intelligence is comparable to ours, though in a very strange fashion...they may have a new class of large brain so dissimilar to ours that we cannot within our lifetime possibly understand its mental processes." Their culture may be totally devoted to creating works of poetry or devising abstract mathematical concepts, and they could conceivably share a telepathic communication to supplement their high-frequency underwater language.

What is particularly interesting is that dolphins appear to have developed a concept of altruism; the stories of shipwrecked sailors rescued by dolphins and carried to shore, or protected by them against sharks, are by no means all old wives' tales. But I'm rather disturbed by some recent developments that indicate not only how we may treat dolphins but also how we may treat intelligent races on other planets. The Navy, impressed by the dolphin's apparent intelligence, is reported to have been engaging in underwater-demolition experiments in which a live torpedo is strapped to a dolphin and detonated by radio when it nears a prototype enemy submarine. These experiments have been officially denied; but if they're true, I'm afraid we may learn more about man through dolphins than the other way around. The Russians, paradoxically, seem to be one step ahead of us in this area; they recently banned all catching of dolphins in Russian waters on the grounds that "Comrade Dolphin" is a fellow sentient being and killing him would be morally equivalent to murder.

PLAYBOY: Although flying saucers are frequently an object of public derision, there has been a good deal of serious discussion in the scientific community about the possibility that UFOs could be alien spacecraft. What's your opinion?

KUBRICK: The most significant analysis of UFOs I've seen recently was written by L. M. Chassin, a French Air Force general who had been a high-ranking NATO officer. He argues that by any legal rules of evidence, there is now sufficient sighting data amassed from reputable sources—astronomers, pilots, radar operators and the like—to initiate a serious and thorough worldwide investigation of UFO phenomena. Actually, if you examine even a fraction of the extant testimony you will find that people have been sent to the gas chamber on far less substantial evidence. Of course, it's possible that all the governments in the world really *do* take UFOs seriously and perhaps are already engaging in secret study projects to determine their origin, nature and intentions. If so, they may not be disclosing their findings for fear that the public would be alarmed—the danger of cultural shock deriving from confrontation with the unknown which we discussed earlier, and which is an element of *2001,* when news of the monolith's discovery on the Moon is suppressed. But I think even the two percent of sightings that the Air Force's Project Blue Book admits is unexplainable by conventional means should dictate a serious, searching probe. From all indications, the current Government-authorized investigation at the University of Colorado is neither serious nor searching.

One hopeful sign that this subject may at last be accorded the serious discussion it deserves, however, is the belated but exemplary conversion of Dr. J. Allen Hynek, since 1948 the Air Force's consultant on UFOs and currently chairman of the astronomy department at Northwestern University. Hynek, who in his official capacity pooh-poohed UFO sightings, now believes that UFOs deserve top-priority attention and even concedes that the existing evidence may indicate a possible connection with extraterrestrial life. He predicts: "I will be surprised if an intensive study yields nothing. To the contrary, I think that mankind may be in for the greatest adventure since dawning human intelligence turned outward to contemplate the universe." I agree with him.

PLAYBOY: If flying saucers are real, who or what do you think they might be?

KUBRICK: I don't know. The evidence proves they're up there, but it gives us very little clue as to what they are. Some science-fiction writers theorize half-seriously that they could be time shuttles flicking back and forth between eons to a future age when man has mastered temporal travel; and I understand that biologist Ivan Sanderson has even advanced a theory that they may be some kind of living space animal inhabiting the upper stratosphere—though I can't give much credence to that suggestion. It's also possible that they are perfectly natural phenomena, perhaps chain lightning, as one American science writer has suggested; although this, again, does not explain some of the photographs taken by reputable sources, such as the Argentine navy, which clearly show spherical metallic objects hovering in the sky. As you've probably deduced, I'm really fascinated by UFOs and I only regret that this field of investigation has to a considerable extent been pre-empted by a crackpot fringe that claims to have soared to Mars on flying saucers piloted by three-foot-tall green humanoids with pointy heads. That kind of kook approach makes it very easy to dismiss the whole phenomenon, which we do at our own risk.

I think another problem here—and one of the reasons that, despite the overwhelming evidence, there has been remarkably little public interest—is that most people don't really *want* to think about extraterrestrial beings patrolling our skies and perhaps observing us like bugs on a slide. The thought is too disturbing; it upsets our tidy, soothing, sanitized suburban *Weltanschauung;* the cosmos is more than light-years away from Scarsdale. This could be a survival mechanism, but it could also blind us to what may be the most dramatic and important moment in man's history—contact with another civilization.

PLAYBOY: Among the reasons adduced by those who doubt the interstellar origin of UFOs is Einstein's special theory of relativity, which states that the speed of light is absolute and that nothing can exceed it. A journey from even the nearest star to Earth would consequently take thousands of years. They claim this virtually rules out interstellar travel—at least for sentient beings with life spans as short as the longest known to man. Do you find this argument valid?

KUBRICK: I find it difficult to believe that we have penetrated to the ultimate depths of knowledge about the physical laws of the universe. It seems rather presumptuous to believe that in the space of a few hundred years, we've figured out most of what there is to know. So

I don't think it's right to declaim with unshakable certitude that light is the absolute speed limit of the universe. I'm suspicious of dogmatic scientific rules; they tend to have a rather short life span. The most eminent European scientists of the early nineteenth century scoffed at meteorites, on the grounds that "stones can't fall from the sky"; and just a year before Sputnik, one of the world's leading astrophysicists stated flatly that "space flight is bunk." Actually, there are already some extremely interesting theoretical studies under way—one by Dr. Gerald Feinberg at Columbia University—which indicate that short cuts could be found that would enable some things under certain conditions to exceed the speed of light.

In addition, there's always the possibility that the speed-of-light limitation, even if it's rigid, could be circumvented via a space-time warp, as Arthur Clarke has proposed. But let's take another, slightly more conservative, means of evading the speed of light's restrictions: If radio contact is developed between ourselves and another civilization, within two hundred years we will have reached a stage in genetic engineering where the other race could transmit its genetic code to us by radio and we could then re-create their DNA pattern and artificially duplicate one of their species in our laboratories—and vice versa. This sounds fantastic only to those who haven't followed the tremendous breakthroughs being made in genetic engineering.

But actual interstellar travel wouldn't be impossible even if light speed *can't* be achieved. Whenever we dismiss space flight beyond our solar system on the grounds that it would take thousands of years, we are thinking of beings with life spans similar to ours. Fruit flies, I understand, live out their entire existence—birth, reproduction and death—within twenty-four hours; well, man may be to other creatures in the universe as the fruit fly is to man. There may be countless races in the universe with life spans of hundreds of thousands or even millions of years, to whom a ten-thousand-year journey to Earth would be about as intimidating as an afternoon outing in the park. But even in terms of our own time scale, within a few years it should be possible to freeze astronauts or induce a hibernatory suspension of life functions for the duration of an interstellar journey. They could spend three hundred or one thousand years in space and be awakened automatically, feeling no different than if they had had a hearty eight hours' sleep.

The speed-of-light theory, too, could work in favor of long journeys; the peculiar "time dilation" factor in Einstein's relativity theory means that as an object accelerates toward the speed of light, time slows down. Everything would appear normal to those on board; but if they had been away from Earth for, say, fifty-six years, upon their return they would be merely twenty years older than when they departed. So, taking all these factors into consideration, I'm not unduly impressed by the claims of some scientists that the speed-of-light limitation renders interstellar travel impossible.

PLAYBOY: You mentioned freezing astronauts for lengthy space journeys, as in the "hibernacula" of *2001.* As you know, physicist Robert Ettinger and others have proposed freezing *dead* bodies in liquid nitrogen until a future time when they can be revived. What do you think of this proposal?

KUBRICK: I've been interested in it for many years, and I consider it eminently feasible. Within ten years, in fact, I believe that freezing of the dead will be a major industry in the United States and throughout the world; I would recommend it as a field of investment for imaginative speculators. Dr. Ettinger's thesis is quite simple: If a body is frozen cryogenically in liquid nitrogen at a temperature near absolute zero—minus 459.6 degrees Fahrenheit—and stored in adequate facilities, it may very well be possible at some as-yet-indeterminate date in the future to thaw and revive the corpse and then cure the disease or repair the physical damage that was the original cause of death. This would, of course, entail a considerable gamble; we have no way of knowing that future science will be sufficiently advanced to cure, say, terminal cancer, or even successfully revive a frozen body. In addition, the dead body undergoes damage in the course of the freezing process itself; ice crystallizes within the blood stream. And unless a body is frozen at the precise moment of death, progressive brain-cell deterioration also occurs. But what do we have to lose? Nothing—and we have immortality to gain. Let me read you what Dr. Ettinger has written: "It used to be thought that the distinction between life and death was simple and obvious. A living man breathes, sweats and makes stupid remarks; a dead one just lies there, pays no attention, and after a while gets putrid. But nowadays nothing is that simple."

Actually, when you really examine the concept of freezing the dead, it's nowhere nearly as fantastic—though every bit as revolutionary—as it appears at first. After all, countless thousands of patients "die" on the operating table and are revived by artificial stimulation of the heart after a few seconds or even a few minutes—and there is really little substantive difference between bringing a patient back to life after three minutes of clinical death or after an "intermezzo" stage of three hundred years. Fortunately, the freezing concept is now gaining an increasing amount of attention within the scientific community. France's Dr. Jean Rostand, an internationally respected biologist, has proposed that every nation begin a freezer program immediately, funded by government money and utilizing the top scientific minds in each country. "For every day that we delay," he says, "untold thousands are going to an unnecessary grave."

PLAYBOY: Are you interested in being frozen yourself?

KUBRICK: I would be if there were adequate facilities available at the present time—which, unfortunately, there are not. A number of organizations are attempting to disseminate information and raise funds to implement an effective freezing program—the Life Extension Society of Washington, the Cryonics Society of New York, et cetera—but we are still in the infancy of cryobiology. Right now, all existing freezer facilities—and there are only a handful—aren't sufficiently sophisticated to offer any realistic hope. But that could and probably will change far more rapidly than we imagine.

A key point to remember, particularly by those ready to dismiss this whole concept as preposterous, is that science has made fantastic strides in just the past forty years; within this brief period of time, a wide range of killer diseases that once were the scourge of mankind, from smallpox to diphtheria, have been virtually eliminated through vaccines and antibiotics; while others, such as diabetes, have been brought under control—though not yet completely eliminated—by drugs such as insulin. Already, heart transplants are almost a viable proposition, and organ banks are being prepared to stock supplies of spleens, kidneys, lungs and hearts for future transplant surgery.

Dr. Ettinger predicts that a "freezee" who died after a severe accident or massive internal damage would emerge resuscitated from a hospital of the future a "crazy quilt of patchwork." His internal organs—heart, lungs, liver, kidneys, stomach and the rest—may be grafts, implanted after being grown in the laboratory from someone's donor cells. His arms and legs may be "bloodless artifacts of fabric, metal and plastic, directed by tiny motors." His brain cells, writes Ettinger, "may be mostly new, regenerated from the few which would be saved, and some of his memories and personality traits may have had to be imprinted onto the new cells by micro-techniques of chemistry and physics." The main challenge to the scientist of the future will not be revival but eliminating the original cause of death; and in this area, we have every reason for optimism as a result of recent experience. So before anyone dismisses the idea of freezing, he should take a searching look at what we have accomplished in a few decades—and ponder what we're capable of accomplishing over the next few centuries.

PLAYBOY: If such a program does succeed, the person who is frozen will have no way of knowing, of course, if he will ever be successfully revived. Do you think future scientists will be willing, even if they're able, to bring their ancestors back to life?

KUBRICK: Well, twentieth-century man may not be quite the cup of tea for a more advanced civilization of even one hundred years in the future; but unless the future culture has achieved immortality—which is scientifically quite possible—they themselves would be frozen at death, and every generation would have a vested interest in the preservation of the preceding frozen generation in order to be, in turn, preserved by its own descendants. Of course, it would be something of a letdown if, three hundred years from now, somebody just pulled the plug on us all, wouldn't it?

Another problem here, quite obviously, is the population explosion; what will be the demographic effect on the Earth of billions of frozen bodies suddenly revived and taking their places in society? But by the time future scientists have mastered the techniques to revive their frozen ancestors, space flight will doubtless be a reality and other planets will be open for colonization. In addition, vast freezer facilities could possibly be constructed on the dark side of the Moon to store millions of bodies. The problems are legion, of course, but so are the potentialities.

PLAYBOY: Opponents of cryogenic freezing argue that death is the natural and inevitable culmination of life and that we shouldn't tamper with it—even if we're able to do so. How would you answer them?

KUBRICK: Death is no more natural or inevitable than smallpox or diphtheria. Death is a disease and as susceptible to cure as any other disease. Over the eons, man's powerlessness to prevent death has led him to force it from the forefront of his mind, for his own psychological health, and to accept it unquestioningly as the unavoidable termination. But with the advance of science, this is no longer necessary—or desirable. Freezing is only one possible means of conquering death, and it certainly would not be binding on everyone; those who desire a "natural" death can go ahead and die, just as those in the nineteenth century who desired "God-ordained" suffering resisted anesthesia. As Dr. Ettinger has written, "To each his own, and to those who choose not to be frozen, all I can say is—rot in good health."

PLAYBOY: Freezing and resuscitation of the dead is just one revolutionary scientific technique that could transform our society. Looking ahead to the year of your film, 2001, what major social and scientific changes do you foresee?

KUBRICK: Perhaps the greatest breakthrough we may have made by 2001 is the possibility that man may be able to eliminate old age. We've just discussed the steady scientific conquest of disease; even when this is accomplished, however, the scourge of old age will remain. But too many people view senile decay, like death itself, as inevitable. It's nothing of the sort. The highly respected Russian scientist V. F. Kuprevich has written, "I am sure we can find means for switching off the mechanisms which make cells age." Dr. Bernard Strehler, an eminent gerontology expert, contends that there is no inherent contradiction, no inherent property of cells or of Metazoa that precludes their organization into perpetually functioning and self-replenishing individuals.

One encouraging indication that we may already be on this road is the work of Dr. Hans Selye, who in his book *Calciphylaxis* presents an intriguing and well-buttressed argument that old age is caused by the transfer of calcium within the body—a transfer that can be arrested by circulating throughout the system specific iron compounds that flush out the calcium, absorb it and prevent it from permeating the tissue. Dr. Selye predicts that we may soon be able to prevent the man of sixty from progressing to the condition of the man of ninety. This is something of an understatement; Selye could have added that the man of sixty could *stay* sixty for hundreds or even thousands of years if all other diseases have been eradicated. Even accidents would not necessarily impair his relative immortality; even if a man is run over by a steam-roller, his mind and body will be completely re-creatable from the tiniest fragment of his tissue, if genetic engineering continues its rapid progress.

PLAYBOY: What impact do you think such dramatic scientific break-throughs will have on the life style of society at the turn of the century?

KUBRICK: That's almost impossible to say. Who could have pre-dicted in 1900 what life in 1968 would be like? Technology is, in many ways, more predictable than human behavior. Politics and world affairs change so quickly that it's difficult to predict the future of social insti-tutions for even ten years with a modicum of accuracy. By 2001, we could be living in a Gandhiesque paradise where all men are brothers, or in a neofascist dictatorship, or just be muddling along about the way we are today. As technology evolves, however, there's little doubt that the whole concept of leisure will be both quantitatively and qualita-tively improved.

PLAYBOY: What about the field of entertainment?

KUBRICK: I'm sure we'll have sophisticated three-D holographic television and films, and it's possible that completely new forms of en-tertainment and education will be devised. You might have a machine that taps the brain and ushers you into a vivid dream experience in which you are the protagonist in a romance or an adventure. On a more serious level, a similar machine could directly program you with knowledge; in this way, you might, for example, easily be able to learn fluent German in twenty minutes. Currently, the learning processes are so laborious and time-consuming that a breakthrough is really needed.

On the other hand, there are some risks in this kind of thing; I un-derstand that at Yale they've been engaging in experiments in which the pleasure center of a mouse's brain has been localized and stimu-lated by electrodes; the result is that the mouse undergoes an eight-hour orgasm. If pleasure that intense were readily available to all of us, we might well become a race of sensually stultified zombies plugged into pleasure stimulators while machines do our work and our bodies and minds atrophy. We could also have this same problem with psychedelic drugs; they offer great promise of unleashing perceptions, but they also hold commensurate dangers of causing withdrawal and disengagement from life into a totally inner-directed kind of Soma world. At the present time, there are no ideal drugs; but I believe by 2001 we will have devised chemicals with no adverse physical, mental or genetic results that can give wings to the mind and enlarge percep-tion beyond its present evolutionary capacities.

Actually, up to now, perception on the deepest level has really, from an evolutionary point of view, been detrimental to survival; if primitive man had been content to sit on a ledge by his cave absorbed in a beautiful sunset or a complex cloud configuration, he might never have exterminated his rival species—but neither would he have achieved mastery of the planet. Now, however, man is faced with the unprecedented situation of potentially unlimited material and technological resources at his disposal and a tremendous amount of leisure time. At last, he has the opportunity to look both within and beyond himself with a new perspective—without endangering or impeding the progress of the species. Drugs, intelligently used, can be a valuable guide to this new expansion of our consciousness. But if employed just for kicks, or to dull rather than to expand perception, they can be a highly negative influence. There should be fascinating drugs available by 2001; what *use* we make of them will be the crucial question.

PLAYBOY: Have you ever used LSD or other so-called consciousness-expanding drugs?

KUBRICK: No. I believe that drugs are basically of more use to the audience than to the artist. I think that the illusion of oneness with the universe, and absorption with the significance of every object in your environment, and the pervasive aura of peace and contentment is not the ideal state for an artist. It tranquilizes the creative personality, which thrives on conflict and on the clash and ferment of ideas. The artist's transcendence must be within his own work; he should not impose any artificial barriers between himself and the mainspring of his subconscious. One of the things that's turned me against LSD is that all the people I know who use it have a peculiar inability to distinguish between things that are really interesting and stimulating and things that *appear* so in the state of universal bliss the drug induces on a "good" trip. They seem to completely lose their critical faculties and disengage themselves from some of the most stimulating areas of life. Perhaps when *everything* is beautiful, nothing is beautiful.

PLAYBOY: What stage do you believe today's sexual revolution will have reached by 2001?

KUBRICK: Here again, it's pure speculation. Perhaps there will have been a reaction against present trends, and the pendulum will swing back to a kind of neo-puritanism. But it's more likely that the so-called sexual revolution, midwifed by the pill, will be extended.

Through drugs, or perhaps via the sharpening or even mechanical amplification of latent ESP functions, it may be possible for each partner to simultaneously experience the sensations of the other; or we may eventually emerge into polymorphous sexual beings, with the male and female components blurring, merging and interchanging. The potentialities for exploring new areas of sexual experience are virtually boundless.

PLAYBOY: In view of these trends, do you think romantic love may have become unfashionable by 2001?

KUBRICK: Obviously, people are finding it increasingly easy to have intimate and fulfilling relationships outside the concept of romantic love—which, in its present form, is a relatively recent acquisition, developed at the court of Eleanor of Aquitaine in the twelfth century—but the basic love relationship, even at its most obsessional, is too deeply ingrained in man's psyche not to endure in one form or another. It's not going to be easy to circumvent our primitive emotional programming. Man still has essentially the same set of pair-bonding instincts—love, jealousy, possessiveness—imprinted for individual and tribal survival millions of years ago, and these still lie quite close to the surface, even in these allegedly enlightened and liberated times.

PLAYBOY: Do you think that by 2001 the institution of the family, which some social scientists have characterized as moribund, may have evolved into something quite different from what it is today?

KUBRICK: One can offer all kinds of impressive intellectual arguments against the family as an institution—its inherent authoritarianism, et cetera; but when you get right down to it, the family is the most primitive and visceral and vital unit in society. You may stand outside your wife's hospital room during childbirth muttering, "My God, what a responsibility! Is it right to take on this terrible obligation? What am I really doing here?"; and then you go in and look down at the face of your child and—zap!—that ancient programming takes over and your response is one of wonder and joy and pride. It's a classic case of genetically imprinted social patterns. There are very few things in this world that have an unquestionable importance in and of themselves and are not susceptible to debate or rational argument, but the family is one of them. Perhaps man has been too "liberated" by science and evolutionary social trends. He has been turned loose from religion and has hailed the death of his gods; the imperative loyalties of the old nation-state are dissolving and all the old social and ethical values, however reactionary and narrow they often were, are disappearing. Man in the twentieth century has been cut adrift in a rudderless boat on an uncharted sea; if he is going to stay sane throughout the voyage, he must have someone to care about, something that is more important than himself.

PLAYBOY: Some critics have detected not only a deep pessimism but also a kind of misanthropy in much of your work. In *Dr. Strangelove*, for example, one reviewer commented that your directorial attitude, despite the film's antiwar message, seemed curiously aloof and detached and unmoved by the annihilation of mankind, almost as if the Earth were being cleansed of an infection. Is there any truth to that?

KUBRICK: Good God, no. You don't stop being concerned with man because you recognize his essential absurdities and frailties and pretensions. To me, the only real immorality is that which endangers the species; and the only absolute evil, that which threatens its annihilation. In the deepest sense, I believe in man's potential and in his capacity for progress. In *Strangelove*, I was dealing with the inherent irrationality in man that threatens to destroy him; that irrationality is with us as strongly today, and must be conquered. But a recognition of insanity doesn't imply a celebration of it—nor a sense of despair and futility about the possibility of curing it.

PLAYBOY: In the five years since *Dr. Strangelove* was released, the two major nuclear powers, the U.S. and the U.S.S.R., have reached substantial accommodation with each other. Do you think this has reduced the danger of nuclear war?

KUBRICK: No. If anything, the overconfident Soviet-American *détente increases* the threat of accidental war through carelessness; this has always been the greatest menace and the one most difficult to cope with. The danger that nuclear weapons may be used—perhaps by a secondary power—is as great if not greater than it has ever been, and it is really quite amazing that the world has been able to adjust to it psychologically with so little apparent dislocation.

Particularly acute is the possibility of war breaking out as the result of a sudden unanticipated flare-up in some part of the world, triggering a panic reaction and catapulting confused and frightened men into decisions they are incapable of making rationally. In addition, the serious threat remains that a psychotic figure somewhere in the modern command structure could start a war, or at the very least a limited exchange of nuclear weapons that could devastate wide areas and cause innumerable casualties. This, of course, was the theme of *Dr. Strangelove;* and I'm not entirely assured that somewhere in the Pentagon or the Red army upper echelons there does not exist the real-life prototype of General Jack D. Ripper.

PLAYBOY: Fail-safe strategists have suggested that one way to obviate the danger that a screwball might spark a war would be to administer psychological-fitness tests to all key personnel in the nuclear command structure. Would that be an effective safeguard?

KUBRICK: No, because any seriously disturbed individual who rose high within the system would have to possess considerable self-discipline and be able to effectively mask his fixations. Such tests already do exist to a limited degree, but you'd really have to be pretty far gone to betray yourself in them, and the type of individual we're discussing would have to be a highly controlled psychopathic personality not to have given himself away long ago. But beyond those tests, how are you going to objectively assess the sanity of the President, in whom, as Commander-in-Chief, the ultimate responsibility for the use of nuclear weapons resides? It's improbable but not impossible that we could someday have a psychopathic President, or a President who suffers a nervous breakdown, or an alcoholic President who, in the course of some stupefying binge, starts a war. You could say that such a man would be detected and restrained by his aides—but with the powers of the Presidency what they are today, who really knows? Less farfetched and even more terrifying is the possibility that a psychopathic individual could work his way into the lower echelons of the White House staff. Can you imagine what might have happened at the height of the Cuban Missile Crisis if some deranged waiter had slipped LSD into Kennedy's coffee—or, on the other side of the fence, into Khrushchev's vodka? The possibilities are chilling.

PLAYBOY: Do you share the belief of some psychiatrists that our continued reliance on the balance of nuclear power, with all its attendant risks of global catastrophe, could reflect a kind of collective death wish?

KUBRICK: No, but I think the *fear* of death helps explain why people accept this Damoclean sword over their heads with such bland equanimity. Man is the only creature aware of his own mortality and is at the same time generally incapable of coming to grips with this awareness and all its implications. Millions of people thus, to a greater or lesser degree, experience emotional anxieties, tensions and unresolved conflicts that frequently express themselves in the form of neuroses and a general joylessness that permeates their lives with frustration and bitterness and increases as they grow older and see the grave yawning before them. As fewer and fewer people find solace in religion as a buffer between themselves and the terminal moment, I actually believe that they unconsciously derive a kind of perverse solace from the idea that in the event of nuclear war, the world dies with them. God is dead, but the bomb endures; thus, they are no longer alone in the terrible vulnerability of their mortality. Sartre once wrote that if there was one thing you could tell a man about to be executed that would make him happy, it was that a comet would strike the earth the next day and destroy every living human being. This is not so much a collective death wish or self-destructive urge as a reflection of the awesome and agonizing loneliness of death. This is extremely pernicious, of course, because it aborts the kind of fury and indignation that should galvanize the world into defusing a situation where a few political leaders on both sides are seriously prepared to incinerate millions of people out of some misguided sense of national interest.

PLAYBOY: Are you a pacifist?

KUBRICK: I'm not sure what pacifism really means. Would it have been an act of superior morality to have submitted to Hitler in order to avoid war? I don't think so. But there have also been tragically senseless wars such as World War One and the current mess in Vietnam and the plethora of religious wars that pockmark history. What makes today's situation so radically different from anything that has gone before, however, is that, for the first time in history, man has the means to destroy the entire species—and possibly the planet as well. The problem of dramatizing this to the public is that it all seems so abstract and unreal; it's rather like saying, "The sun is going to die in a billion years." What is required as a minimal first corrective step is a concrete alternative to the present balance of terror—one that people can understand and support.

PLAYBOY: Do you believe that some form of all-powerful world government, or some radically new social, political and economic system, could deal intelligently and farsightedly with such problems as nuclear war?

KUBRICK: Well, none of the present systems has worked very well, but I don't know what we'd replace them with. The idea of a group of philosopher kings running everything with benign and omniscient paternalism is always attractive, but where do we find the philosopher kings? And if we do find them, how do we provide for their successors? No, it has to be conceded that democratic society, with all its inherent strains and contradictions, is unquestionably the best system anyone ever worked out. I believe it was Churchill who once remarked that democracy is the worst social system in the world, except for all the others.

PLAYBOY: You've been accused of revealing, in your films, a strong hostility to the modern industrialized society of the democratic West, and a particular antagonism—ambivalently laced with a kind of morbid fascination—toward automation. Your critics claim this was especially evident in *2001,* where the archvillain of the film, the computer HAL 9000, was in a sense the only human being. Do you believe that machines are becoming more like men and men more like machines—and do you detect an eventual struggle for dominance between the two?

KUBRICK: First of all, I'm not hostile toward machines at all; just the opposite, in fact. There's no doubt that we're entering a mechanarchy, however, and that our already complex relationship with our machinery will become even more complex as the machines become more and more intelligent. Eventually, we will have to share this planet with machines whose intelligence and abilities far surpass our own. But the interrelationship—if intelligently managed by man—could have an immeasurably enriching effect on society.

Looking into the distant future, I suppose it's not inconceivable that a semisentient robot-computer subculture could evolve that might one day decide it no longer needed man. You've probably heard the story about the ultimate computer of the future: For months scientists think of the first question to pose to it, and finally they hit on the right one: "Is there a God?" After a moment of whirring and flashing lights, a card comes out, punched with the words: THERE IS NOW. But this problem is a distant one and I'm not staying up nights worrying about it; I'm convinced that our toasters and TVs are fully domesticated, though I'm not so sure about integrated telephone circuits, which sometimes strike me as possessing a malevolent life all their own.

PLAYBOY: Speaking of futuristic electronics and mechanics, *2001*'s incredibly elaborate gadgetry and scenes of space flight have been hailed—even by hostile critics—as a major cinematic breakthrough. How were you able to achieve such remarkable special effects?

KUBRICK: I can't answer that question technically in the time we have available, but I can say that it was necessary to conceive, design and engineer completely new techniques in order to produce the special effects. This took eighteen months and $6.5 million out of a $10.5 million budget. I think an extraordinary amount of credit must go to Robert H. O'Brien, the president of M-G-M, who had sufficient faith to allow me to persevere at what must have at times appeared to be a task without end. But I felt it was necessary to make this film in such a way that every special-effects shot in it would be completely convincing—something that had never before been accomplished in a motion picture.

PLAYBOY: Thanks to those special effects, *2001* is undoubtedly the most graphic depiction of space flight in the history of films—and yet you have admitted that you yourself refuse to fly, even in a commercial jet liner. Why?

KUBRICK: I suppose it comes down to a rather awesome awareness of mortality. Our ability, unlike the other animals, to conceptualize our own end creates tremendous psychic strains within us; whether we like to admit it or not, in each man's chest a tiny ferret of fear at this ultimate knowledge gnaws away at his ego and his sense of purpose. We're fortunate, in a way, that our body, and the fulfillment of its needs and functions, plays such an imperative role in our lives; this physical shell creates a buffer between us and the mind-paralyzing realization that only a few years of existence separate birth from death. If man really sat back and thought about his impending termination, and his terrifying insignificance and aloneness in the cosmos, he would surely go mad, or succumb to a numbing sense of futility. Why, he might ask himself, should he bother to write a great symphony, or strive to make a living, or even to love another, when he is no more than a momentary microbe on a dust mote whirling through the unimaginable immensity of space?

Those of us who are forced by their own sensibilities to view their lives in this perspective—who recognize that there is no purpose they can comprehend and that amidst a countless myriad of stars their existence goes unknown and unchronicled—can fall prey all too easily to the ultimate *anomie*. I can well understand how life became for Matthew Arnold "a darkling plain... where ignorant armies clash by night... and there is neither love nor hope nor certitude nor faith nor surcease from pain." But even for those who lack the sensitivity to more than vaguely comprehend their transience and their triviality, this inchoate awareness robs life of meaning and purpose; it's why "the mass of men lead lives of quiet desperation," why so many of us find our lives as absent of meaning as our deaths.

The world's religions, for all their parochialism, did supply a kind of consolation for this great ache; but as clergymen now pronounce the death of God and, to quote Arnold again, "the sea of faith" recedes around the world with a "melancholy, long, withdrawing roar," man has no crutch left on which to lean—and no hope, however irrational, to give purpose to his existence. This shattering recognition of our mortality is at the root of far more mental illness than I suspect even psychiatrists are aware.

PLAYBOY: If life is so purposeless, do you feel that it's worth living?

KUBRICK: Yes, for those of us who manage somehow to cope with our mortality. The very meaninglessness of life forces man to create his own meaning. Children, of course, begin life with an untarnished sense of wonder, a capacity to experience total joy at something as simple as the greenness of a leaf; but as they grow older, the awareness of death and decay begins to impinge on their consciousness and subtly erode their *joie de vivre*, their idealism—and their assumption of immortality. As a child matures, he sees death and pain everywhere about him, and begins to lose faith in faith and in the ultimate goodness of man. But if he's reasonably strong—and lucky—he can emerge from this twilight of the soul into a rebirth of life's *élan*. Both because of and in spite of his awareness of the meaninglessness of life, he can forge a fresh sense of purpose and affirmation. He may not recapture the same pure sense of wonder he was born with, but he can shape something far more enduring and sustaining. The most terrifying fact about the universe is not that it is hostile but that it is indifferent; but if we can come to terms with this indifference and accept the challenges of life within the boundaries of death—however mutable man may be able to make them—our existence as a species can have genuine meaning and fulfillment. However vast the darkness, we must supply our own light.

PLAYBOY: Will we be able to find any deep meaning or fulfillment, either as individuals or as a species, as long as we continue to live with the knowledge that all human life could be snuffed out at any moment in a nuclear catastrophe?

KUBRICK: We *must*, for in the final analysis, there may be no sound way to eliminate the threat of self-extinction without changing human nature; even if you managed to get every country disarmed down to the bow and arrow, you would still be unable to lobotomize either the knowledge of how to build nuclear warheads or the perversity that allows us to rationalize their use. Given these two categorical imperatives in a disarmed world, the first country to amass even a few weapons would have a great incentive to use them quickly. So an argument might be made that there is a greater chance for *some* use of nuclear weapons in a totally disarmed world, though less chance of global extinction; while in a world armed to the teeth, you have less chance for *some* use—but a great chance of extinction if they're used.

If you try to remove yourself from an Earthly perspective and look at this tragic paradox with the detachment of an extraterrestrial, the whole thing is totally irrational. Man now has the power in one mad, incandescent moment, as you point out, to exterminate the entire species; our own generation could be the last on Earth. One miscalculation and all the achievements of history could vanish in a mushroom cloud; one misstep and all of man's aspirations and strivings over the millennia could be terminated. One short circuit in a computer, one lunatic in a command structure and we could negate the heritage of the billions who have died since the dawn of man and abort the promise of the billions yet unborn—the ultimate genocide. What an irony that the discovery of nuclear power, with its potential for annihilation, also constitutes the first tottering step into the universe that must be taken by all intelligent worlds. Unhappily, the infant-mortality rate among emerging civilizations in the cosmos may be very high. Not that it will matter except to us; the destruction of this planet would have no significance on a cosmic scale; to an observer in the Andromeda nebulae, the sign of our extinction would be no more than a match flaring for a second in the heavens; and if that match does blaze in the darkness, there will be none to mourn a race that used a power that could have lit a beacon in the stars to light its funeral pyre. The choice is ours.

Appendix:
Stanley Kubrick Filmography

1951

Day of the Fight

RKO-Pathé, Inc., Presents *This Is America. Producer:* Jay Bonafield. *Director:* Stanley Kubrick. *Script:* Robert Rein. *Editor:* Julian Bergman. *Music:* Gerald Fried. *Narrator:* Douglas Edwards. *Running time:* 16 minutes. Black and white. *Note:* Kubrick states he photographed, edited, and did the sound editing on the film.

Flying Padre

RKO-Pathé, Inc., Presents An RKO-Pathé Screenliner. *Producer:* Burton Benjamin. *Director:* Stanley Kubrick. *Editor:* Isaac Kleinerman. *Music:* Nathaniel Shilkret. *Narrator:* Bob Hite. *Sound:* Harold R. Vivian. *Running time:* 8 minutes 30 seconds. Black and white. *Note:* Kubrick states he photographed, edited, and did the sound editing on the film.

1953

The Seafarers

Presented by the Seafarers International Union, Atlantic and Gulf Coast District, AFL. *Producer:* Lester Cooper. *Directed and photographed by* Stanley Kubrick. *Written by* Will Chasan. Technical assistance by the staff of the *Seafarers Log. Narrator:* Don Hollenbeck. *Running time:* 30 minutes. Color.

Fear and Desire

Distributed by Joseph Burstyn, Inc. *Produced, photographed, and edited by* Stanley Kubrick. *Associate producer:* Martin Perveler. *Screenplay:* Howard O. Sackler. *Music:* Gerald Fried. *Unit manager:* Bob Dierks. *Assistant director:* Steve Hahn. *Makeup:* Chet Fabian. *Art director:* Herbert Lebowitz. *Title design:* Barney Ettengoff. *Dialogue director:* Toba Kubrick. *Cast:* Frank Silvera (Mac), Kenneth Harp (Corby/General), Paul Mazursky (Sidney), Steve Coit (Fletcher/aide), Virginia Leith (The Girl), David Allen (Narrator). *Running time:* 68 minutes. Black and white.

1955

Killer's Kiss

Released through United Artists. A Minotaur Production. *Producers:* Stanley Kubrick, Morris Bousel. *Edited, photographed, and directed by* Stanley Kubrick. *Story:* Stanley Kubrick. *Music composed and conducted by* Gerald Fried. *Production manager:* Ira Marvin. *Camera operators:* Jesse Paley, Max Glenn. *Chief electrician:* Dave Golden. *Sound recordists:* Walter Ruckersberg, Clifford van Praag. *Assistant editors:* Pat Jaffe, Anthony Bezich. *Assistant director:* Ernest Nukanen. *Sound by* Titra Sound Studio. Love theme from the song "Once" by Norman Gimbel and Arden Clar. Ballet sequence danced by Ruth Sobotka. *Choreography:* David Vaughan. *Cast:* Frank Silvera (Vincent Rapallo), Jamie Smith (Davey Gordon), Irene Kane (Gloria Price), Jerry Jarret (Albert), Mike Dana, Felice Orlandi, Ralph Roberts, Phil Stevenson (gangsters), Skippy Adelman (owner of mannequin factory), David Vaughan, Alec Rubin (conventioneers), Ruth Sobotka (Iris), Shaun O'Brien, Barbara Brand, Arthur Feldman, Bill Funaro. *Running time:* 67 minutes. Black and white. *Note:* Howard O. Sackler worked on the screenplay uncredited.

1956

The Killing

A Harris-Kubrick presentation. Released through United Artists. *Producer:* James B. Harris. *Associate producer:* Alexander Singer. *Director:*

Stanley Kubrick. *Screenplay:* Stanley Kubrick. *Dialogue:* Jim Thompson. Based on the novel *Clean Break* by Lionel White. *Director of photography:* Lucien Ballard, A.S.C. *Art director:* Ruth Sobotka. *Film editor:* Betty Steinberg. *Music composed and conducted by* Gerald Fried. *Wardrobe:* Jack Masters. *Special effects:* Dave Koehler. *Camera operator:* Dick Tower. *Gaffer:* Bobby Jones. *Head grip:* Carl Gibson. *Script supervisor:* Mary Gibsone. *Sound:* Earl Snyder. *Best boy:* Lou Cortese. *Second assistant cameraman:* Robert Hosler. *Construction supervisor:* Bud Pine. *Chief carpenter:* Christopher Ebsen. *Chief painter:* Robert L. Stephen. *Makeup:* Robert Littlefield. *Set decorator:* Harry Reif. *Assistant set decorator:* Carl Brainard. *Music editor:* Gilbert Marchant. *Sound effects editor:* Rex Lipton, M.P.S.E. *Assistant director:* Milton Carter. *Second assistant directors:* Paul Feiner, Howard Joslin. *Production assistant:* Marguerite Olson. *Propman:* Ray Zambel. *Transportation:* Dave Lesser. *Women's wardrobe:* Rudy Harrington. *Hairdresser:* Lillian Shore. *Process cameraman:* Paul Eagler. *Director's assistant:* Joyce Hartman. *Marie Windsor's costumes:* Beaumelle. *Photographic effects:* Jack Rabin, Louis DeWitt. *Sound:* RCA Sound System. *Cast:* Sterling Hayden (Johnny Clay), Coleen Gray (Fay), Vince Edwards (Val Cannon), Jay C. Flippen (Marvin Unger), Ted DeCorsia (Randy Kennan), Marie Windsor (Sherry Peatty), Elisha Cook, Jr. (George Peatty), Joe Sawyer (Mike O'Reilly), Timothy Carey (Nikki Arane), Kola Kwariani (Maurice Oboukhoff), Jay Adler (Leo), Joseph Turkel (Tiny), James Edwards (parking lot attendant), Tito Vuolo, Dorothy Adams, Herbert Ellis, James Griffith, Cecil Elliot, Steve Mitchell, Mary Carroll, William Benedict, Charles R. Cane, Robert B. Williams. *Running time:* 83 minutes. Black and white.

1957

Paths of Glory

Released through United Artists. A Bryna Productions presentation. *Producer:* James B. Harris. *Director:* Stanley Kubrick. *Screenplay:* Stanley Kubrick, Calder Willingham, and Jim Thompson. Based on the novel *Paths of Glory* by Humphrey Cobb. *Photographed by* George Krause. *Art director:* Ludwig Reiber. *Film editor:* Eva Kroll. *Music:* Gerald Fried. *Costume designer:* Ilse Dubois. *Special effects:* Erwin Lange. *Unit manager:* Helmut Ringelmann. *Assistant directors:* H. Stumpf, D. Sensburg, F. Spieker. *Script clerk:* Trudy von Trotha. *Sound:* Martin Muller. *Military adviser:*

Baron V. Waldenfels. *Assistant editor:* Helene Fischer. *Camera grip:* Hans Elsinger. *Makeup:* Arthur Schramm. Produced at Bavaria Filmkunst Studios—Munich. *Camera operator:* Hannes Staudinger. *American production manager:* John Pommer. *German production manager:* George von Block. *Cast:* Kirk Douglas (Colonel Dax), Ralph Meeker (Corporal Paris), Adolphe Menjou (General Broulard), George Macready (General Mireau), Wayne Morris (Lieutenant Roget), Richard Anderson (Major Saint-Auban), Joseph Turkel (Arnaud), Timothy Carey (Ferol), Peter Capell (Judge), Susanne Christian (young German girl), Bert Freed (Sergeant Boulanger), Emile Meyer (priest), Ken Dibbs (Lejeune), Jerry Hausner (Meyer), Fred Bell (wounded soldier), Harold Benedict (Sergeant Nichols), John Stein (Captain Rousseau). *Running time:* 86 minutes. Black and white.

1960

Spartacus

Released through Universal International. A Bryna Productions, Inc., presentation. *Producer:* Edward Lewis. *Executive producer:* Kirk Douglas. *Directed by* Stanley Kubrick. *Screenplay:* Dalton Trumbo. Based on the novel by Howard Fast. *Director of photography:* Russell Metty, A.S.C. Technicolor. Filmed in Super Technirama-70. Lenses by Panavision. *Production designer:* Alexander Golitzen. *Art director:* Eric Orbom. *Set decorations:* Russell A. Gausman, Julia Heron. *Film editor:* Robert Lawrence. *Music composed and conducted by* Alex North. *Costumes:* Valles. *Assistant director:* Marshall Green. *Main titles and design consultant:* Saul Bass. *Sound:* Waldon O. Watson, Joe Lapis, Murray Spivack, Ronald Pierce. *Historical and technical advisor:* Vittorio Nino Novarese. *Unit production manager* Norman Deming. *Additional scenes photographed by* Clifford Stine, A.S.C. *Production aide:* Stan Margulies. *Wardrobe:* Peruzzi. *Miss Simmons's costumes:* Bill Thomas. *Assistants to the film editor:* Robert Schulte, Fred Chulack. *Score co-conducted by* Joseph Gershenson. *Music editor:* Arnold Schwarzwald. *Makeup:* Bud Westmore. *Hair stylist:* Larry Germain. *Cast:* Kirk Douglas (Spartacus), Laurence Olivier (Marcus Crassus), Jean Simmons (Varinia), Charles Laughton (Gracchus), Peter Ustinov (Lentulus Batiatus), John Gavin (Julius Caesar), Nina Foch (Helena), John Ireland (Crixus), Herbert Lom (Tigranes), John Dall (Glabrus), Charles McGraw (Marcellus), Joanna Barnes (Claudia), Harold J. Stone (David), Woody Strode (Draba), Peter Brocco (Ramon), Paul Lambert (Gannicus), Robert J. Wilke (captain of the guard), Nicholas Dennis (Dionysius), John Hoyt (Roman officer), Frederic Worlock (Laelius), Tony Curtis (Antoninus), Dayton Lummis (Symmachus), Jill Jarmyn, Jo Summers. *Running time:* 184 minutes. Color; *restored version (1992):* 196 minutes.

1962

Lolita

A Metro-Goldwyn-Mayer presentation in association with Seven Arts Productions. An Anya Production S.A.—Transworld Pictures S.A. Production. James B. Harris and Stanley Kubrick's Lolita. *Producer:* James B. Harris. *Director:* Stanley Kubrick. *Screenplay:* Vladimir Nabokov based on his novel *Lolita*. *Director of photography:* Oswald Morris, B.S.C. *Art director:* Bill Andrews. *Editor:* Anthony Harvey. *Music composed and conducted by* Nelson Riddle. "Lolita" theme by Bob Harris. *Orchestrations:* Gil Grau. *Production supervisor:* Raymond Anzarut. *Wardrobe supervisor:* Elsa Fennell. *Miss Winters's costumes by* Gene Coffin. *Assistant art director:* Sidney Cain. *Production manager:* Robert Sterne. *Assistant director:* Rene Dupont. *Camera operator:* Denys N. Coop. *Continuity:* Pamela Davies. *Dubbing editor:* Winston Ryder. *Sound recordists:* Len Shilton, H. L. Bird. *Casting director:* James Liggat. *Makeup:* George Partleton. *Hairdresser:* Betty Galsow. *Second-unit director:* Dennis Stock. *Assistant editor:* Lois Gray. *Titles by* Chambers and Partners. Produced at Associated British Studios, Elstree, England. *Production secretary:* Joan Purcell. *Producer's secretary:* Josephine Baker. *Production accountant:* Jack Smith. *Assistant accountant:* Doreen Wood. *Secretaries:* Jack Smith, Jennifer Halford. *Second assistant director:* Ray Millichip. *Third assistant director:* Joan Sanischewsky. *Director's secretary:* Stella Magee. *Special writer:* David Sylvester. *Assistant continuity:* Joyce Herlihy. *Focus puller:* Jimmy Turrell. *Clapper loader:* Michael Rutter. *Camera grip:* A. Osborne, W. Thompson. *Second assistant editor:* W. W. Armor. *Chief draughtsman:* Frank Wilson. *Draughtsmen:* John Siddal, Roy Dorman. *Scenic artist:* A. Van Montagu. *Set decorator:* Andrew Low. *Set dresser:* Peter James. *Construction manager:* Harry Phipps. *Wardrobe mistress:* Barbara Gillett. *Wardrobe assistant:* Wyn Keeley. *Assistant makeup:* Stella Morris. *Production buyer:* Terry Parr. *Unit publicist:* Enid Jones. *Assistant boom operators:*

Peter Carnody, T. Staples. *Sound maintenance:* L. Grimmel, Jack Lovelace. *Boom operator:* Dan Wortham. *Stills:* Joe Pearce. *Publicity secretary.* Amy Allen. *Cast:* James Mason (Humbert Humbert), Shelley Winters (Charlotte Haze), Sue Lyon (Lolita), Peter Sellers (Clare Quilty), Gary Cockrell (Dick), Diana Decker (Jean Farlow), Jerry Stovin (John Farlow), Suzanne Gibbs (Mona Farlow), Lois Maxwell (Nurse Mary Lore), Bill Greene (George Swine), Shirley Douglas (Mrs. Starch), Marianne Stone (Vivian Darkbloom), Marion Mathie (Miss Lebone), James Dyrenforth (Beale), Maxine Holden (hospital receptionist), John Harrison (Tom), Colin Maitland (Charlie), C. Denier Warren (Potts), Roland Brand (Bill), Roberta Shore (Lorna), Cec Linder (doctor), Isobel Lucas (Louise), Eric Lane (Roy), Irvin Allen (hospital intern), Craig Sams (Rex), Terence Kilburn. *Running time:* 152 minutes. Black and white.

1964

Dr. Strangelove or: How I Learned to Stop Worrying and Love the Bomb. A Columbia Pictures Corporation presentation. A Stanley Kubrick production. *Producer:* Stanley Kubrick. *Associate producer:* Victor Lyndon. *Director:* Stanley Kubrick. *Screenplay:* Stanley Kubrick, Terry Southern and Peter George. Based on the book *Red Alert* by Peter George. *Director of photography:* Gilbert Taylor, B.S.C. *Production designer:* Ken Adam. *Art director:* Peter Murton. *Film editor:* Anthony Harvey. *Music:* Laurie Johnson. *Wardrobe:* Bridget Sellers. *Special effects:* Wally Veevers. *Camera operator:* Kelvin Pike. *Camera assistant:* Bernard Ford. *Production manager:* Clifton Brandon. *Assistant director:* Eric Rattray. *Continuity:* Pamela Carlton. *Dubbing mixer:* John Aldred. *Makeup:* Stewart Freeborn. *Traveling Matte:* Vic Margutti. *Sound editor:* Leslie Hodgson. *Hairdresser:* Barbara Ritchie. *Recordist:* Richard Bird. *Assistant editor:* Ray Lovejoy. *Aviation adviser:* Captain John Crewdson. *Sound supervisor:* John Cox. *Assembly editor:* Geoffrey Fry. *Main titles:* Pablo D. Ferro. Made at Shepperton Studios, England, by Hawk Films, Ltd. A Hawk Film. *Cast:* Peter Sellers (Group Capt. Lionel Mandrake/President Muffley/Dr. Strangelove), George C. Scott (General "Buck" Turgidson), Sterling Hayden (General Jack D. Ripper), Keenan Wynn (Colonel "Bat" Guano), Slim Pickens (Major T. J. "King" Kong), Peter

Bull (Ambassador de Sadesky), James Earl Jones (Lieutenant Lothar Zogg), Tracy Reed (Miss Scott), Jack Creley (Mr. Staines), Frank Berry (Lieutenant H. R. Dietrich), Robert O'Neil (Admiral Randolf), Roy Stephens (Frank), Glen Beck (Lieutenant W. D. Kival), Shane Rimmer (Captain G. A. "Ace" Owens), Paul Tamarin (Lieutenant B. Goldberg), Gordon Tanner (General Faceman), John McCarthy, Laurence Herder, Hal Galili (members of Burpelson Defense Team). *Running time:* 93 minutes. Black and white.

1968

2001: A Space Odyssey

Metro-Goldwyn-Mayer presents A Stanley Kubrick Production. *Producer:* Stanley Kubrick. *Director:* Stanley Kubrick. *Screenplay:* Stanley Kubrick and Arthur C. Clarke. *Director of photography:* Geoffrey Unsworth, B.S.C. *Additional photography.* John Alcott. *Production designers:* Tony Masters, Harry Lange, Ernest Archer. *Film editor:* Ray Lovejoy. *Music:* Aram Khatchaturian, *Gayane* ballet performed by the Leningrad Philharmonic Orchestra conducted by Gennadi Rozhdestvensky, courtesy Deutsche Grammophon. Gyorgy Ligeti, *Atmosphères,* performed by the Southwest German Radio Orchestra conducted by Ernest Bour; *Lux Aeterna,* performed by the Stuttgart State Orchestra conducted by Clytus Gottwald; *Requiem,* performed by the Bavarian Radio Orchestra conducted by Francis Travis. Johann Strauss, The "Blue Danube," performed by the Berlin Philharmonic Orchestra conducted by Herbert Von Karajan, Courtesy Deutsche Grammophon. Richard Strauss, *Also Sprach Zarathustra,* performed by the Berlin Philharmonic Orchestra conducted by Karl Bohm. *Special photographic effects* designed and directed by Stanley Kubrick. *Special photographic effects supervisors:* Wally Veevers, Douglas Trumbull, Con Pederson, Tom Howard. *Wardrobe:* Hardy Amies. *First assistant director:* Derek Cracknell. *Special photographic effects unit:* Colin J. Cantwell, Bruck Logan, Bryan Loftus, David Osborne, Frederick Martin, John Jack Malick. Technicolor. Metrocolor. *Camera operator:* Kelvin Pike. *Art director:* John Hoesli. *Sound editor:* Winston Ryder. *Makeup:* Stuart Freeborn. *Editorial assistant:* David De Wilde. *Sound supervisor:* A. W. Watkins. *Sound mixer:* H. L. Bird. *Chief dubbing mixer:* J. B. Smith. *Scientific consultant·* Frederick

I. Ordway III. Filmed in Super Panavision. Made at MGM British Studios, Ltd., Boreham Wood, England. In Cinerama. Distributed by MGM. *Cast:* Keir Dullea (David Bowman), Gary Lockwood (Frank Poole), William Sylvester (Dr. Heywood Floyd), Daniel Richter (Moon-Watcher), Leonard Rossiter (Smyslov), Margaret Tyzack (Elena), Robert Beatty (Halvorsen), Sean Sullivan (Michaels), Douglas Rain (voice of HAL 9000), Frank Miller (Mission Controller), Vivian Kubrick (Dr. Floyd's daughter), Alan Gifford (Poole's father), Penny Brahms (stewardess), Bill Weston, Edward Bishop, Glenn Beck, Ann Gillis, Edwina Carroll, Heather Downham, Mike Lovell, John Ashley, Peter Delmar, David Hines, Darryl Paes, Jimmy Bell, Terry Duggan, Tony Jackson, Joe Refalo, David Charkham, David Fleetwood, John Jordan, Andy Wallace, Simon Davis, Danny Grover, Scott Mackee, Bob Wilyman, Jonathan Daw, Brian Hawley, Laurence Marchant, Richard Wood. *Running time:* 139 minutes. Color.

1971

A Clockwork Orange

Warner Bros. presents A Stanley Kubrick Production. *Producer:* Stanley Kubrick. *Executive Producers:* Max L. Raab, Si Litvinoff. *Associate Producer:* Bernard Williams. *Assistant to the producer:* Jan Harlan. *Director:* Stanley Kubrick. *Screenplay:* Stanley Kubrick. Based on the novel by Anthony Burgess. *Lighting cameraman:* John Alcott. *Production designer:* John Barry. *Editor:* Bill Butler. *Electronic music composed and realized by* Walter Carlos. Symphony No. 9 in D Minor, Opus 125, by Ludwig van Beethoven; Overtures to *The Thieving Magpie* and *William Tell* by Gioacchino Rossini; recorded by Deutsche Grammophon Gesellschaft. *Pomp and Circumstance* Marches No. 1 and 4 by Edward Elgar, conducted by Marcus Dods. "Singin' in the Rain" by Arthur Freed and Nacio Herb Brown, from the MGM picture, performed by Gene Kelly. "Overture to the Sun," composed by Terry Tucker. Song: "I Want to Marry a Lighthouse Keeper," composed and performed by Erika Eigen. *Costume designer:* Milena Canonero. *Consultant on hair and coloring:* Leonard of London. *Sound editor:* Brian Blamey. *Sound recordist:* John Jordan. *Dubbing mixers:* Bill Rowe, Eddie Haben. *Art directors:* Russell Hagg, Peter Shields. *Wardrobe supervisor:* Ron Beck. *Stunt arranger:*

Roy Scammell. *Special paintings and sculpture:* Herman Makkink, Cornelius Makkink, Liz Moore, Christiane Kubrick. *Casting:* Jimmy Liggat. *Location manager:* Terence Clegg. *Supervising electrician:* Frank Wardale. *Assistant directors:* Derek Cracknell, Dusty Symonds. *Construction manager:* Bill Welch. *Prop master:* Frank Bruton. *Assistant editors:* Gary Shepherd, Peter Burgess, David Beesley. *Camera operators:* Ernie Day, Mike Molloy. *Focus puller:* Ron Drinkwater. *Camera assistants:* Laurie Frost, David Lenham. *Boom operator:* Peter Glossop. *Grips:* Don Budge, Tony Cridlin. *Electricians:* Louis Bogue, Derek Gatrell. *Prop men:* Peter Hancock, Tommy Ibbetson, John Oliver. *Promotion coordinator:* Mike Kaplan. *Production accountant:* Len Barnard. *Continuity:* June Randall. *Hairdresser:* Olga Angelinetta. *Makeup:* Fred Williamson, George Partleton, Barbara Daly. *Production secretary:* Loretta Ordewer. *Director's secretary:* Kay Johnson. *Production assistant:* Andros Epaminondas. *Location liaison:* Arthur Morgan. *Technical adviser:* John Marshall. *With special acknowledgment to:* Braun AG Frankfurt, Dolby Laboratories, Inc., Kontakt Werkstaetten, Ryman Conran Limited, Steinheimer Leuchtenindustrie, Temde AG. Made at Pinewood Studios, London, England, at EMI-MGM Studios, Boreham Wood, Herts., England, and on location in England by Hawk Films, Limited. Distributed by Warner Bros. A Warner Communications Company. *Cast:* Malcolm McDowell (Alex), Patrick Magee (Mr. Alexander), Michael Bates (chief guard), Warren Clarke (Dim), John Clive (stage actor), Adrienne Corri (Mrs. Alexander), Carl Duering (Dr. Brodsky), Paul Farrell (tramp), Clive Francis (lodger), Michael Gover (prison governor), Miriam Karlin (Cat Lady), James Marcus (Georgie), Aubrey Morris (Deltoid), Godfrey Quigley (prison chaplain), Sheila Raynor (Mum), Madge Ryan (Dr. Branom), John Savident (conspirator), Anthony Sharp (minister), Philip Stone (Dad), Pauline Taylor (psychiatrist), Margaret Tyzack (conspirator), Steven Berkoff (constable), Lindsay Campbell (inspector), Michael Tarn (Pete), David Prowse (Julian), Jan Adair, Vivienne Chandler, Prudence Drage (handmaidens), Richard Connaught (Billyboy), John J. Carney (C.I.D. man), Carol Drinkwater (Nurse Feeley), Virginia Wetherell (actress), Gillian Hills (Sonietta), Katya Wyeth (girl), Barbara Scott (Marty), Barrie Cookson, Gaye Brown, Peter Burton, Lee Fox, Shirley Jaffe, Neil Wilson, Craig Hunter, Cheryl Grunwald. *Running time:* 137 minutes. Color.

1975

Barry Lyndon

Warner Bros. presents A Film by Stanley Kubrick. *Producer:* Stanley Kubrick. *Executive producer:* Jan Harlan. *Associate producer:* Bernard Williams. *Director:* Stanley Kubrick. *Written for the screen by* Stanley Kubrick. Based on the novel by William Makepeace Thackeray. *Photographed by* John Alcott. *Production designer:* Ken Adam. *Editor:* Tony Lawson. *Music adapted and conducted by* Leonard Rosenman. From works by Johann Sebastian Bach, Frederick the Great, George Friedrich Handel, Wolfgang Amadeus Mozart, Giovanni Paisiello, Franz Schubert, Antonio Vivaldi. Irish traditional music by The Chieftains. Schubert Piano Trio in E-flat, Op. 100, performed by Ralph Holmes, violin, Moray Welsh, cello, Anthony Goldstone, piano. Vivaldi Cello Concerto in E minor, Pierre Fournier, cello, recorded on Deutsche Grammophon. *Hairstyles and wigs:* Leonard. *Costumes designed by* Ulla-Britt Soderlund, Milena Canonero. *Art director:* Roy Walker. *Assistant to the producer:* Andros Epaminondas. *Assistant director:* Brian Cook. *Sound editor:* Rodney Holland. *Sound recordist:* Robin Gregory. *Dubbing mixer:* Bill Rowe. *Assistant editor:* Peter Krook. *Sound editor's assistant:* George Akers. *Second unit cameraman:* Paddy Carey. *Camera operators:* Mike Molloy, Ronnie Taylor. *Focus puller:* Douglas Milsome. *Color grading:* Dave Dowler. *Camera assistants:* Laurie Frost, Dodo Humphreys. *Camera grips:* Tony Cridlin, Luke Quigley. *Gaffer:* Lou Bogue. *Chief electrician:* Larry Smith. *Production managers:* Douglas Twiddy, Terence Clegg. *Assistant directors:* David Tomblin, Michael Stevenson. *Unit managers:* Malcolm Christopher, Don Geraghty. *Cast:* Ryan O'Neal (Barry Lyndon—Redmond Barry), Marisa Berenson (Lady Lyndon), Patrick Magee (Chevalier de Balibari), Hardy Kruger (Captain Potzdorf), Steven Berkoff (Lord Ludd), Gay Hamilton (Nora Brady), Marie Kean (Mrs. Barry), Diana Koerner (young German woman), Murray Melvin (Reverend Samuel Runt), Frank Middlemass (Sir Charles Lyndon), André Morell (Lord Wendover), Arthur O'Sullivan (highwayman), Godfrey Quigley (Captain Grogan), Leonard Rossiter (Captain Quin), Philip Stone (Graham), Leon Vitali (Lord Bullingdon), Dominic Savage (young Bullingdon), David Morley (little Bryan), John Bindon, Roger Booth (George III), Norman Mitchell (Brock), Billy Boyle, Jonathan Cecil, Peter Cellier, Geoffrey Chater,

Anthony Dawes, Patrick Dawson, Bernard Hepton, Anthony Herrick, Barry Jackson, Wolf Kahler, Patrick Laffan, Hans Meyer, Ferdy Mayne, Liam Redmond, Pat Roach (Toole), Frederick Schiller, George Sewell, Anthony Sharp (Lord Harlan), John Sharp, Roy Spencer, John Sullivan, Harry Towb, Michael Hordern (narrator). *Running time:* 187 minutes. Color.

1980

The Shining

Warner Bros. presents A Stanley Kubrick Film. *Executive producer:* Jan Harlan. *Producer:* Stanley Kubrick. *Director:* Stanley Kubrick. Based on the novel by Stephen King. Produced in association with The Producers Circle Company, Robert Fryer, Martin Richards, Mary John. *Screenplay:* Stanley Kubrick and Diane Johnson. *Photographed by* John Alcott. *Production designer:* Roy Walker. *Film editor:* Ray Lovejoy. *Music:* Béla Bartók, *Music for Strings, Percussion and Celesta,* conducted by Herbert Von Karajan, recorded by Deutsche Grammophon; Krzysztof Penderecki; Wendy Carlos and Rachel Elkind; Gyorgy Ligeti. *Costumes designed by* Milena Canonero. *Production manager:* Douglas Twiddy. *Assistant director:* Brian Cook. *Steadicam operator:* Garrett Brown. *Helicopter photography:* Macgillivray Freeman Films. *Personal assistant to the director:* Leon Vitali. *Assistant to the producer:* Andros Epaminondas. *Art director:* Les Tomkins. *Makeup:* Tom Smith. *Hairstyles:* Leonard. *Camera operators:* Kelvin Pike, James Dewis. *Second-unit photography:* Douglas Milsome, Macgillivray Freeman Films. *Focus assistants:* Douglas Milsome, Maurice Arnold. *Camera assistants:* Peter Robinson, Martin Kenzie, Danny Shelmerone. *Grip:* Dennis Lewis. *Gaffers:* Lou Bogue, Larry Smith. *Sound editors:* Wyn Ryder, Dino Di Campo, Jack Knight. *Sound recorders:* Ivan Sharrock, Richard Daniel. *Dubbing mixer:* Bill Rowe. *Assistant editors:* Gill Smith, Gordon Stainforth. *1920s music advisers:* Brian Rust, John Wadley. *Assistant directors:* Terry Needham, Michael Stevenson. *Makeup artist:* Barbara Daly. *Continuity:* June Randall. *Production accountant:* Jo Gregory. *Set dresser:* Tessa Davies. *Construction manager:* Len Fury. *Titles:* Chapman Beauvais and National Screen Service. *Property master:* Peter Hancock. *Decor artist:* Robert Walker. *Second assistant editors:* Adam Unger, Steve Pickard. *Color grading:* Eddie Gordon. *Hotel consultant:* Tad Michel. *Casting:* James Liggat. *Location research:* Jan

Schlubach, Katharina Kubrick, Murray Close. *Production secretaries:* Pat Pennelegion, Marlene Butland. *Producer's secretary:* Margaret Adams. *Production assistant:* Emilio Dalessandro. *Engineering by* Norank of Elstree. *Wardrobe supervisors:* Ken Lawton, Ron Beck. *Draughtsmen:* John Fenner, Michael Lamont, Michael Boone. *Property buyers:* Edward Rodrigo, Karen Brookes. *Video operator:* Dan Grimmel. *Boom operators:* Ken Weston, Michael Charman. *Drapes:* Barry Wilson. *Master plasterer:* Tom Tarry. *Head rigger:* Jim Kelly. *Head carpenter:* Fred Gunning. *Head painter:* Del Smith. *Property men:* Barry Arnold, Philip McDonald, Peter Spencer. With special acknowledgment to Timberline Lodge, Mount Hood National Forest, Oregon. Continental Airlines. State of Colorado Motion Picture Commission. KBTV Channel D. Denver, WPLG Channel 10 Miami, KHOW Radio Denver, Harrods of London, American Motor Company, Carl Zeiss of West Germany, National Vendors, Music Hire Group LTD., Cherry Leisure (U.K.) Ltd. Filmed with Arreiflex cameras. A Peregrine film. Distributed by Warner Bros. A Warner Communications Company. Made by Hawk Films, Ltd., at EMI Elstree Studios, Ltd., England. *Cast:* Jack Nicholson (Jack Torrance), Shelley Duvall (Wendy Torrance), Danny Lloyd (Danny), Scatman Crothers (Halloran), Barry Nelson (Ullman), Philip Stone (Grady), Joe Turkel (Lloyd), Anne Jackson (doctor), Tony Burton (Durkin), Lia Beldam (young woman in bath), Billie Gibson (old woman in bath), Barry Dennen (Watson), David Baxt (forest ranger 1), Manning Redwood (forest ranger 2), Lisa Burns (Grady daughter), Louise Burns (Grady daughter), Allison Coleridge (secretary), Burnell Tucker (policeman), Jana Sheldon (stewardess), Kate Phelps (receptionist), Norman Gay (injured guest). *Running time:* 142 minutes. Color.

1987

Full Metal Jacket

Warner Bros. presents A Stanley Kubrick Film. *Executive producer:* Jan Harlan. *Producer:* Stanley Kubrick. *Co-producer:* Philip Hobbs. *Associate producer:* Michael Herr. *Director:* Stanley Kubrick. *Screenplay:* Stanley Kubrick, Michael Herr, Gustav Hasford. Based on the novel *The Short-Timers* by Gustaf Hasford. *Lighting cameraman:* Douglas Milsome. *Production designer.* Anton Furst. *Editor:* Martin Hunter. *Original music:*

Abigail Mead. *Costume designer:* Keith Denny. *Special effects senior technicians:* Peter Dawson, Jeff Clifford, Alan Barnard. *Assistant to the director:* Leon Vitali. *Sound recording:* Edward Tise. *Boom operator:* Martin Trevis. *Sound editors:* Nigel Galt, Edward Tise. *Dubbing mixers:* Andy Nelson, Mike Dowson. *Re-recording:* Delta Sound, Shepperton. *Special effects supervisor:* John Evans. *Casting:* Leon Vitali. *Additional casting:* Mike Fenton and Jane Feinberg, C.S., Marion Dougherty. *Additional Vietnamese casting:* Dan Tran, Nguyen Thi My Chau. *First assistant director:* Terry Needham. *Second assistant director:* Christopher Thomson. *Production manager:* Phil Kohler. *Unit production manager:* Bill Shepherd. *Production coordinator:* Margaret Adams. *Wardrobe master:* John Birkenshaw. *Wardrobe assistant:* Helen Gill. *Co-makeup artists:* Jennifer Boost, Christine Allsop. *Dialogue editor:* Joe Illing. *Assistant sound editors:* Paul Conway, Peter Culverwell. *Montage editing engineer:* Adam Watkins. *Video operator:* Manuel Harlan. *Camera trainees:* Vaughn Matthews, Michaela Mason. *Editing trainee:* Rona Buchanan. *Hair by* Leonard. *Art directors:* Rod Stratford, Les Tomkins, Keith Pain. *Set dresser:* Stephen Simmonds. *Assistant art directors:* Nigel Phelps, Andrew Rothschild. *Technical adviser:* Lee Ermey. *Art department research:* Anthony Frewin. *Armourers:* Hills Small Arms, Ltd., Robert Hills, John Oxlade. *Modeler:* Eddie Butler. *Prop master:* Brian Wells. *Construction manager:* George Crawford. *Assistant construction manager:* Joe Martin. *Prop buyer:* Jane Cooke. *Color:* Rank Film Laboratories, Denham. *Steadicam operators:* John Ward, Jean-Marc Bringuier. *Follow focus:* Jonathan Taylor, Maurice Arnold, James Ainslie, Brian Rose. *Grip:* Mark Ellis. *Camera assistant:* Jason Wrenn. *Chief electrician:* Seamus O'Kane. *Helicopter pilot:* Bob Warren. *Continuity:* Julie Robinson. *Production accountant:* Paul Cadiou. *Assistants to the producer:* Emilio D'Alessandro, Anthony Frewin. *Producer's secretary:* Wendy Shorter. *Production assistant:* Steve Millson. *Assistant accountant:* Rita Dean. *Accounts computer operator:* Alan Steele. *Production runners:* Michael Shevloff, Matthew Coles. *Nurses:* Linda Glatzel, Carmel Fitzgerald. *Special computer editing programs:* Julian Harcourt. *Unit drivers:* Steve Coulridge, Bill Wright, James Black, Paul Karamadza. *Helicopter:* Sykes Group. *Laboratory contact:* Chester Eyre. *Louma crane technician:* Adam Samuelson. *Louma crane and montage video editing system:* Samuelsons, London. *Aerial photography:* Ken Arlidge, Samuelsons Australia. *Optical sound:* Kay-Metrocolor Sound Studios. *Sound transfers:* Roger Cherrill. *Titles:* Chapman Beauvais. *Catering:* The

Location Caterers, Ltd. *Transport:* D&D International, Daven Croucher, Ron Digweed, Chalky White. *Facilities:* Willies Wheels, Ron Lowe. *Unit transport:* Focus Cars. *Action vehicle engineer:* Nick Johns. *Chargehand prop:* Paul Turner. *Standby props:* Danny Hunter, Steven Allett, Terry Wells. *Propmen:* R. Dave Favell Clarke, Frank Billington-Marks. *Dressing props:* Marc Dillon, Michael Wheeler, Winston Depper. *Supervising painter:* John Chapple. *Painters:* Leonard Chubb, Tom Roberts, Leslie Evans Pearce. *Riggers:* Peter Wilkinson, Les Pipps. *Carpenters:* Mark Wilkinson, A. R. Carter, T. R. Carter. *Plasterers:* Dominic Farrugia, Michael Quinn. *Stagehands:* David Gruer, Michael Martin, Stephen Martin, Ronald Boyd. *Standby construction:* George Reynolds, Brian Morris, Jim Cowan, Colin McDonagh, John Marsella. *Cast:* Matthew Modine (Private Joker), Adam Baldwin (Animal Mother), Vincent D'Onofrio (Private Pyle), Lee Ermey (Gunnery Sergeant Hartman), Dorian Harewood (Eightball), Arliss Howard (Private Cowboy), Kevyn Major Howard (Rafterman), Ed O'Ross (Lieutenant Touchdown), John Terry (Lieutenant Lockhart), Kieron Jecchinis (Crazy Earl), Bruce Boa (Poge Colonel), Kirk Taylor (Payback), John Stafford (Doc Jay), Tim Colceri (Doorgunner), Ian Tyler (Lieutenant Cleves), Gary Lanon (Donlon), Sal Lopez (T.H.E. Rock), Papillon Soo Soo (Da Nang hooker), Ngoc Le (VC sniper), Peter Edmund (Snowball), Tan Hung Francione (ARVN Pimp), Leanne Hong (motorbike hooker), Marcus D'Amico (hand job), Costas Dino Chimona (Chili), Gil Kopel (Stork), Keith Hodiak (Daddy Da), Peter Merrill (TV journalist), Herbert Norville (Daytona Dave), Nguyen Hue Phong (camera thief), Duc Hu Ta (dead N.V.A.). Parris Island recruits and Vietnam platoon: Martin Adams, Kevin Aldridge, Del Anderson, Philip Bailey, Louis Barlotti, John Beddows, Patrick Benn, Steve Boucher, Adrian Bush, Tony Carey, Gary Cheeseman, Wayne Clark, Chris Cornibert, Danny Cornibert, John Curtis, Harry Davies, John Davis, Kevin Day, Gordon Duncan, Phil Elmer, Colin Elvis, Hadrian Follett, Sean Frank, David George, Laurie Gomes, Brian Goodwin, Nigel Goulding, Tony Hague, Steve Hands, Chris Harris, Bob Hart, Derek Hart, Barry Hayes, Tony Hayes, Kenneth Head, Robin Hedgeland, Duncan Henry, Liam Hogan, Trevor Hogan, Luke Hogdal, Tony Howard, Steve Hudson, Sean Lamming, Dan Landin, Tony Leete, Nigel Lough, Terry Lowe, Frank McCardle, Gary Meyer, Brett Middleton, David Milner, Sean Minmagh, Tony Minmagh, John

Morrison, Russell Mott, John Ness, Robert Nichols, David Perry, Peter Rommely, Pat Sands, Chris Schmidt-Maybach, Al Simpson, Russell Slater, Gary Smith, Roger Smith, Tony Smith, Anthony Styliano, Bill Thompson, Mike Turyansky, Dan Weldon, Dennis Wells, Michael Williams, John Wilson, John Wonderling. *Music:* "Hello Vietnam," performed by Johnny Wright, courtesy of MCA Records, written by Tom T. Hall, Unichappell Music, Inc., Morris Music, Inc.; "The Marines Hymn" performed by The Goldman Band, courtesy of MCA Records; "These Boots Are Made for Walking," performed by Nancy Sinatra, courtesy of Boots Enterprises, Inc., written by Lee Hazelwood, Criterion Music Corp.; "Chapel of Love," performed by The Dixie Cups by arrangement with Shelby Singleton Enterprises c/o Original Sound Entertainment, written by Jeff Barry, Ellie Greenwich, and Phil Spector, Trio Music Co., Inc., Mother Bertha Music, Inc.; "Wooly Bully" performed by Sam the Sham and the Pharaohs, courtesy of PolyGram, a Division of PolyGram Records, Inc., written by Domingo Samudio, Beckle Publishing Co., Inc.; "Paint It Black," written by Mick Jagger and Keith Richards, performed by the Rolling Stones, produced by Andrew Loog Oldham, courtesy of ABKCO Music and Records, Inc. Cameras by Arri Munich. Fairlight Digital Audio-Post Music System. Lexicon: Time Compression/Expander. With grateful acknowledgment to: Depot Queens Division Bassingbourn, PSA Bassingbourn Barracks, British Gas PLC North Thames, The Vietnamese Community, National Trust Norfolk. A Natant Film. Filmed on location and at Pinewood Studios, Iver, Bucks. Distributed by Warner Bros. A Warner Communications Company. *Running time:* 116 minutes. Color.

1999

Eyes Wide Shut

Producer and director: Stanley Kubrick. *Screenplay by:* Stanley Kubrick and Frederic Raphael. *Inspired by "Traumnovelle" by* Arthur Schnitzler. *Executive producer:* Jan Harlan. *Co-producer:* Brian W. Cook. *Assistant to the director* Leon Vitali. *Lighting cameraman* Larry Smith. *Production designers:* Les Tomkins, Roy Walker. *Editor:* Nigel Galt. *Original music by:* Jocelyn Pook; *also featuring* Gyorgy Ligeti: Musica Ricercata II (Dominic Harlan, piano); Dmitri Shostakovich: from *Jazz Suite, Waltz 2* (Royal Concertgebouw Orchestra, conducted by Riccardo Chailly); Chris Isaak:

"Baby Did a Bad Bad Thing." *Costume designer:* Marit Allen. *Costume supervisor:* Nancy Thompson. *Wardrobe mistress:* Jacqueline Durran. *Hair:* Kerry Warn. *Makeup:* Robert McCann. *Sound recordist:* Edward Tise. *Supervising sound editor:* Paul Conway. *Sound maintenence:* Tony Bell, Graham V. Hartstone, A.M.P.S. *Re-recording mixers:* Michael A. Carter, Nigel Galt, Anthony Cleal. *Production manager:* Margaret Adams. *Script supervisor:* Ann Simpson. *Assistant to Stanley Kubrick:* Anthony Frewin. *Casting:* Denise Chamian, Leon Vitali. *First assistant director:* Brian W. Cook. *Second assistant director:* Adrian Toynton. *Third assistant directors:* Becky Hunt, Rhun Francis. *Location managers:* Simon McNair Scott, Angus More Gordon. *Location research:* Manuel Harlan. *Location assistant:* Tobin Hughes. *Supervising art director:* Kevin Phipps. *Art director:* John Fenner. *Draughtsperson:* Stephen Dobric. *Assistant draughtsperson:* Pippa Rawlinson. *Art department assistants:* Samantha Jones, Kira-Anne Pelican. *Original paintings:* Christiane Kubrick, Katharina Hobbs. *Venetian masks research:* Barbara Del Greco. *Production accountant:* John Trehy. *Assistant accountant:* Lara Sargent. *Account assistants:* Matthew Dalton, Stella Wycherley. *Set decorators:* Terry Wells, Lisa Leone. *Production buyers:* Michael King, Jeanne Vertigan, Sophie Batsford. *First assistant editor:* Melanie Viner Cuneo. *Avid assistant editor:* Claus Wehlisch. *Assistant editor:* Claire Ferguson. *Foley editor:* Becki Ponting. *Assistant sound editor:* Iain Eyre. *Steadicam operators:* Elizabeth Ziegler, Peter Cavaciutti. *Camera operator:* Martin Hume. *Focus pullers:* Rawdon Hayne, Nick Penn, Jason Wrenn. *Clapper loaders:* Craig Bloor, Keith Roberts. *Camera grips:* William Geddes, Andy Hopkins. *Back projection supervisor:* Charles Staffell. *Camera technical advisor:* Joe Dunton. *Translights:* Stilled Movie LTD. *Translight photography:* Gerard Maguire. *Stills photography:* Manuel Harlan. *Video co-ordinator:* Andrew Haddock. *Video assistant:* Martin Ward. *Gaffers:* Ronnie Phillips, Paul Toomey. *Best boy:* Michael White. *Electricians:* Ron Emery, Joe Allen, Shawn White. *Production associate:* Michael Doven. *Choreographer:* Yolande Smith. *Dialect coach to Ms. Kidman:* Elizabeth Himelstein. *Assistants to Ms. Kidman:* Andrea Doven, Kerry David. *Assistant to Mr. Kubrick:* Emelio D'Allessandro. *Chargehand standby propman:* Jake Wells. *Standby propman:* John O'Connell. *Property master:* Terry Wells. *Property storeman:* Ken Bacon. *Dressing propmen:* Todd Quattromini, Gerald O'Connor. *Production co-ordinator:* Kate Garbett. *Unit nurse:* Claire Litchfield. *Catering:* Location Caterers LTD. *Security:* Alan Reid. *Extras casting:* 20-20 Productions

LTD. *Medical advisor:* Dr. C. J. Scheiner MD, PhD. *Journalistic advisor:* Larry Celona. *Secretary:* Rachel Hunt. *Computer assistant:* Nick Frewin. *Production assistant:* Tracey Crawley. *Construction manager:* John Maher. *Standby carpenter:* Roy Hansford. *Standby stagehand:* Desmond O'Boy. *Standby painter:* Steve Clark. *Standby rigger:* Anthony Richards. *Action vehicle mechanic:* Tom Watson. *Action vehicle co-ordinator:* Martin Ward. *Facility vehicles:* Location Facilities LTD. *Equipment vehicles:* Lays International LTD. *Facilities supervisor:* David Jones. *Action vehicles:* Dream Cars. *Fire cover:* First Unit Fire and Safety LTD. SECOND UNIT: *Production manager:* Lisa Leone, Patrick Turley. *Cinematography:* Malik Sayeed, Arthur Jaffa. *Steadicam operator:* Jim C. McConkey. *Grip:* Donovan C. Lambert. *Camera assistants:* Carlos Omar Guerra, Jonas Steadman. *Production assistant:* Nelson Pena. *Cast:* Tom Cruise (Dr. Bill Harford), Nicole Kidman (Alice Harford), Madison Eginton (Helena Harford), Marie Richardson (Marion Nathanson), Jackie Sawris (Roz), Rade Serbedzija (Milich), Sydney Pollack (Victor Ziegler), Leslie Lowe (Illona), Peter Benson (Bandleader), Vinessa Shaw (Domino), Alan Cumming (Hotel Desk Clerk), Todd Field (Nick Nightingale), Michael Doven (Ziegler's Secretary), Sky Dumont (Sandor Szavost), Louise J. Taylor (Gayle), Stewart Thorndike (Nuala), Randall Paul (Harris), Julienne Davis (Amanda "Mandy" Curran), Lisa Leone (Lisa, receptionist), Kevin Connealy (Lou Nathanson), Thomas Gibson (Carl), Mariana Hewett (Rosa), Leelee Sobieski (Milich's daughter), Fay Masterson (Sally). *Running time:* 159 minutes. Color.

ABOUT THE SERIES EDITOR

Born in 1942 in New York City, MARTIN SCORSESE grew up in the tough downtown neighborhood of Little Italy, which later proved the inspiration for several of his films. He suffered from severe asthma as a child and could not play outside, so his parents took him to the movies. Fascinated by the images on the screen, he often drew his own movies at home. Scorsese received a B.S. and M.S. from New York University.

At NYU he made several award-winning student films and wrote the script for his first feature film, *Who's That Knocking at My Door?*, released theatrically in 1969. Since then, Scorsese has directed over twenty feature and documentary films, including *Mean Streets, Taxi Driver, Raging Bull, GoodFellas, The Age of Innocence, Kundun,* and, most recently, *Bringing Out the Dead.* Among the numerous awards he has received are the American Film Institute Life Achievement Award (1997) and the Lifetime Career Award from the Film Society of Lincoln Center (1998). He has been a tireless fighter for film preservation and artists' rights. Scorsese is currently working on his next film, set in 1850, entitled *Gangs of New York,* and a documentary about Italian cinema.

A Note on the Type

The principal text of this Modern Library edition
was set in a digitized version of Janson, a typeface
that dates from about 1690 and was cut by Nicholas Kis,
a Hungarian working in Amsterdam. The original matrices have
survived and are held by the Stempel foundry in Germany.
Hermann Zapf redesigned some of the weights and sizes for
Stempel, basing his revisions on the original design.

CPSIA information can be obtained
at www.ICGtesting.com
Printed in the USA
LVOW08s1632120418
573254LV00001B/271/P